3 6059 00129 2402

W9-BMV-200

SEQUOIA & KINGS CANYON CAMPING & HIKING

TOM STIENSTRA • ANN MARIE BROWN

How to Use This Book

ABOUT THE CAMPGROUND PROFILES

The campgrounds are listed in a consistent, easy-to-read format to help you choose the ideal camping spot. If you already know the name of the specific campground you want to visit, or the name of the surrounding geological area or nearby feature (town, national or state park, forest, mountain, lake, river, etc.), look it up in the index and turn to the corresponding page. Here is a sample profile:

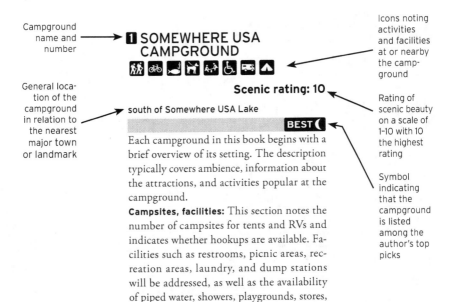

Campground name and number →

General location of the campground in relation to the nearest major town or landmark →

1 SOMEWHERE USA CAMPGROUND

Icons noting activities and facilities at or nearby the campground

Scenic rating: 10

south of Somewhere USA Lake

Rating of scenic beauty on a scale of 1-10 with 10 the highest rating

BEST

Symbol indicating that the campground is listed among the author's top picks

Each campground in this book begins with a brief overview of its setting. The description typically covers ambience, information about the attractions, and activities popular at the campground.

Campsites, facilities: This section notes the number of campsites for tents and RVs and indicates whether hookups are available. Facilities such as restrooms, picnic areas, recreation areas, laundry, and dump stations will be addressed, as well as the availability of piped water, showers, playgrounds, stores, and other amenities. The campground's pet policy and wheelchair accessibility is also mentioned here.

Reservations, fees: This section notes whether reservations are accepted, and provides rates for tent sites and RV sites. If there are additional fees for parking or pets, or discounted weekly or seasonal rates, they will also be noted here.

Directions: This section provides mile-by-mile driving directions to the campground from the nearest major town or highway.

Contact: This section provides an address, phone number, and website, if available, for the campground.

ABOUT THE ICONS

The icons in this book are designed to provide at-a-glance information on activities, facilities, and services available on-site or within walking distance of each campground.

- 👣 Hiking trails
- 🚲 Biking trails
- 🏊 Swimming
- 🎣 Fishing
- 🚤 Boating
- 🛶 Canoeing and/or kayaking

- ❄️ Winter sports
- 🐾 Pets permitted
- 🛝 Playground
- ♿ Wheelchair accessible
- 🚐 RV sites
- ⛺ Tent sites

ABOUT THE SCENIC RATING

Each campground profile employs a scenic rating on a scale of 1 to 10, with 1 being the least scenic and 10 being the most scenic. A scenic rating measures only the overall beauty of the campground and environs; it does not take into account noise level, facilities, maintenance, recreation options, or campground management. The setting of a campground with a lower scenic rating may simply not be as picturesque that of as a higher rated campground, however other factors that can influence a trip, such as noise or recreation access, can still affect or enhance your camping trip. Consider both the scenic rating and the profile description before deciding which campground is perfect for you.

How to Use This Book

ABOUT THE TRAIL PROFILES

Each hike in this book is listed in a consistent, easy-to-read format to help you choose the ideal hike. From a general overview of the setting to detailed driving directions, the profile will provide all the information you need. Here is a sample profile:

Map number and hike number →

Round-trip mileage → (unless otherwise noted) and the approximate amount of time needed to complete the hike (actual times can vary widely, especially on longer hikes)

1 SOMEWHERE USA HIKE

9.0 mi/5.0 hrs   🏃3 ⛰8 ← Difficulty and quality ratings

at the mouth of the Somewhere River ← General location of the trail, named by its proximity to the nearest major town or landmark

BEST (← Symbol indicating that the hike is listed among the author's top picks

Each hike in this book begins with a brief overview of its setting. The description typically covers what kind of terrain to expect, what might be seen, and any conditions that may make the hike difficult to navigate. Side trips, such as to waterfalls or panoramic vistas, in addition to ways to combine the trail with others nearby for a longer outing, are also noted here. In many cases, mile-by-mile trail directions are included.

User Groups: This section notes the types of users that are permitted on the trail, including hikers, mountain bikers, horseback riders, and dogs. Wheelchair access is also noted here.

Permits: This section notes whether a permit is required for hiking, or, if the hike spans more than one day, whether one is required for camping. Any fees, such as for parking, day use, or entrance, are also noted here.

Maps: This section provides information on how to obtain detailed trail maps of the hike and its environs. Whenever applicable, names of U.S. Geologic Survey (USGS) topographic maps and national forest maps are also included.

Directions: This section provides mile-by-mile driving directions to the trail head from the nearest major town.

Contact: This section provides an address and phone number for each hike. The contact is usually the agency maintaining the trail but may also be a trail club or other organization.

ABOUT THE ICONS

The icons in this book are designed to provide at-a-glance information on the difficulty and quality of each hike.

[icon] The difficulty rating (rated **1-5** with **1** being the lowest and **5** the highest) is based on the steepness of the trail and how difficult it is to traverse

[icon] The quality rating (rated **1-10** with **1** being the lowest and **10** the highest) is based largely on scenic beauty, but also takes into account how crowded the trail is and whether noise of nearby civilization is audible

ABOUT THE DIFFICULTY RATINGS

Trails rated 1 are very easy and suitable for hikers of all abilities, including young children.

Trails rated 2 are easy-to-moderate and suitable for most hikers, including families with active children 6 and older.

Trails rated 3 are moderately challenging and suitable for reasonably fit adults and older children who are very active.

Trails rated 4 are very challenging and suitable for physically fit hikers who are seeking a workout.

Trails rated 5 are extremely challenging and suitable only for experienced hikers who are in top physical condition.

MAP SYMBOLS

Expressway		Interstate Freeway		Airfield
Primary Road		U.S. Highway		Airport
Secondary Road		State Highway		City/Town
Unpaved Road		County Highway		Mountain
Ferry		Lake		Park
National Border		Dry Lake		Pass
State Border		Seasonal Lake		State Capital

ABOUT THE MAPS

This book is divided into chapters based on major regions in the state; an overview map of these regions precedes the table of contents. Each chapter begins with a map of the region, which is further broken down into detail maps. Sites are noted on the detail maps by number.

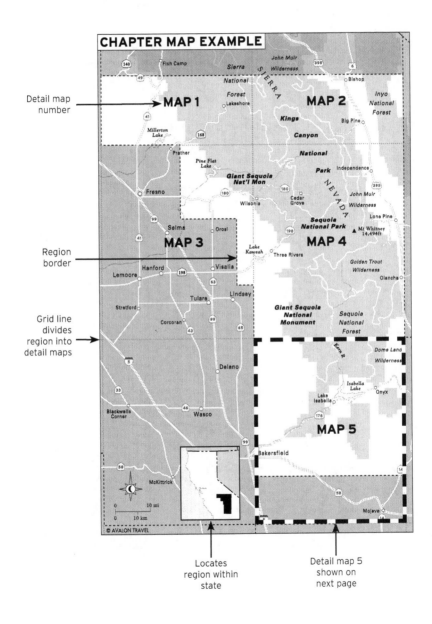

CHAPTER MAP EXAMPLE

Detail map number

MAP 1

MAP 2

MAP 3

MAP 4

MAP 5

Region border

Grid line divides region into detail maps

© AVALON TRAVEL

Locates region within state

Detail map 5 shown on next page

Locates detail
map within
region

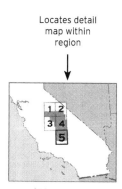

Map
number ➤ **Map 5**

Sites shown
on detail map ➤ **Sites 106-119**

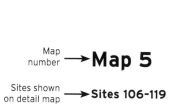

Site number ➤

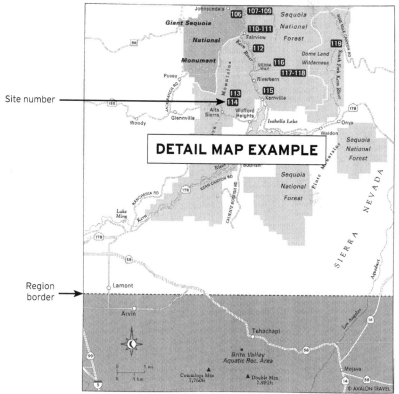

DETAIL MAP EXAMPLE

Region
border ➤

SEQUOIA AND KINGS CANYON CAMPING

© US FOREST SERVICE, INYO NATIONAL FOREST

BEST CAMPGROUNDS

There is no place on earth like the high Sierra,

from Mount Whitney north through Sequoia and Kings Canyon National Parks. This is a paradise filled with deep canyons, high peaks, and fantastic natural beauty, and sprinkled with groves of the largest living things in the history of the earth – giant sequoias.

Though the area is primarily known for the national parks, the campgrounds available span a great variety of settings. The most popular spots, though, are in the vicinity of Sequoia and Kings Canyon National Parks, or on the parks' access roads.

Sooner or later, everyone will want to see the biggest tree of them all – the General Sherman Tree, estimated to be 2,300-2,700 years old and with a circumference of 102.6 feet. It is in the Giant Forest at Sequoia National Park. To stand in front of it is to know true awe. That said, I find the Grant Grove and the Muir Grove even more enchanting.

These are among the highlights of a driving tour through both parks. A must for most is taking in the view from Moro Rock – parking and then making the 300-foot walk up a succession of stairs to reach the 6,725-foot summit. Here you can scan a series of mountain rims and granite peaks, highlighted by the Great Western Divide.

The drive out of Sequoia and into Kings Canyon features rim-of-the-world-type views as you first enter the Kings River canyon. You then descend to the bottom of the canyon, right along the Kings River, gaze up at the high glacial-carved canyon walls, and drive all the way out to Cedar Grove, the end of the road. The canyon rises 8,000 feet from the river to Spanish Peak, making it the deepest canyon in the continental United States.

Crystal Cave is another point of fascination. Among the formations are adjoined crystal columns that look like the sound pipes in the giant organ at the Mormon Tabernacle. Lights are placed strategically for perfect viewing.

This is only a start. Bears, marmots, and deer are abundant and are commonly seen in Sequoia, especially at Dorst Creek Campground. If you drive up to Mineral King and take a hike, it can seem like the marmot capital of the world.

But this region also harbors many wonderful secrets having nothing to do with the national parks. One of them, for instance, is the Muir Trail Ranch near Florence Lake. The ranch is set in the John Muir Wilderness and requires a trip by foot, boat, or horse to reach it. Other unique launching points for trips into the wilderness lie nearby.

On the western slopes of the Sierra, pretty lakes with good trout fishing include Edison, Florence, and Hume Lakes. Hidden spots in Sierra National Forest provide continual fortune hunts, especially up the Dinkey Creek drainage above Courtright Reservoir. On the eastern slopes, a series of small streams offers good vehicle access; here, too, you'll encounter the beautiful Rock Creek Lake, Sabrina and South Lakes (west of Bishop), and great wilderness trailheads at the end of almost every road.

The remote Golden Trout Wilderness on the southwest flank of Mount Whitney is one of the most pristine areas in California. Yet it is lost in the shadow of giant Whitney, elevation 14,497.6 feet, the highest point in the continental United States, where hiking has become so popular that reservations are required at each trailhead for overnight use, and quotas are enforced to ensure an undisturbed experience for each visitor.

In the Kernville area, there are campgrounds along the Kern River. Most choose this canyon for one reason: the outstanding white-water rafting and kayaking.

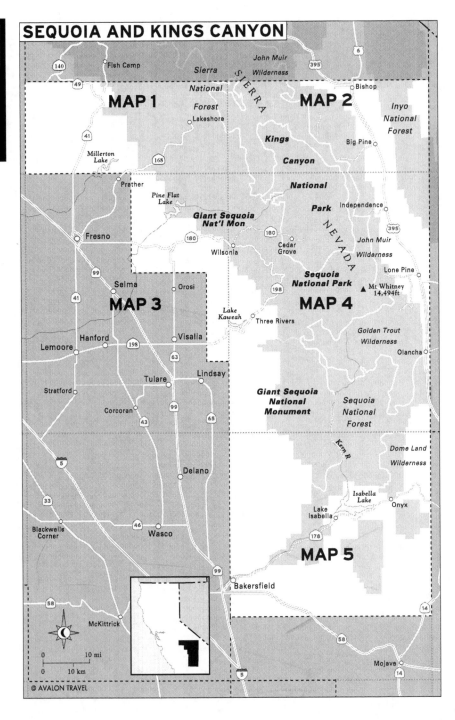

Map 1

Sites 1-40

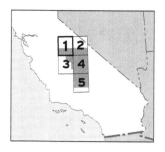

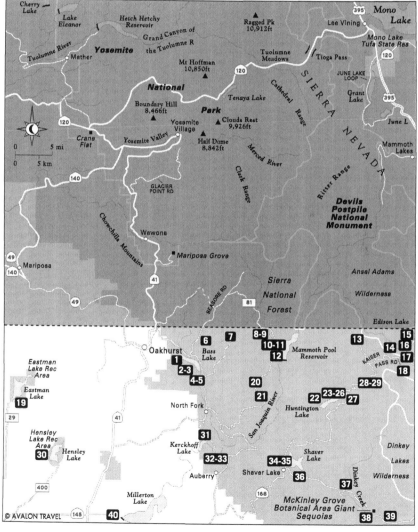

Map 2

Sites 41-70

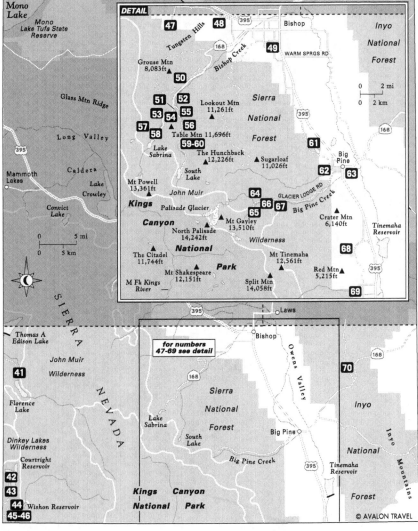

DETAIL

Mono Lake

Mono Lake Tufa State Reserve

Bishop

Inyo National Forest

Tungsten Hills

Grouse Mtn 8,083ft

Bishop Creek

WARM SPRGS RD

Glass Mtn Ridge

Lookout Mtn 11,261ft

Sierra National Forest

Long Valley

Table Mtn 11,696ft

Lake Sabrina

The Hunchback 12,226ft

Sugarloaf 11,026ft

Big Pine

Mammoth Lakes

Caldera

Lake Crowley

South Lake

Mt Powell 13,361ft

John Muir

GLACIER LODGE RD

Big Pine Creek

Convict Lake

Kings

Palisade Glacier

Crater Mtn 6,140ft

Tinemaha Reservoir

Canyon

North Palisade 14,242ft

Mt Gayley 13,510ft

Wilderness

0   5 mi
0   5 km

The Citadel 11,744ft

National Park

Mt Tinemaha 12,561ft

Red Mtn 5,215ft

SIERRA

Mt Shakespeare 12,151ft

M Fk Kings River

Split Mtn 14,058ft

Laws

0   2 mi
0   2 km

Thomas A Edison Lake

Bishop

John Muir Wilderness

for numbers 47-69 see detail

Owens Valley

Florence Lake

Sierra

NEVADA

National

Dinkey Lakes Wilderness

Lake Sabrina

Forest

Big Pine

Inyo

Courtright Reservoir

South Lake

Big Pine Creek

National

Inyo Mountains

Wishon Reservoir

Kings   Canyon
National   Park

Tinemaha Reservoir

Forest

© AVALON TRAVEL

Map 3

Sites 71-79

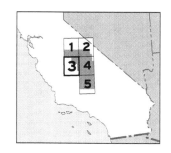

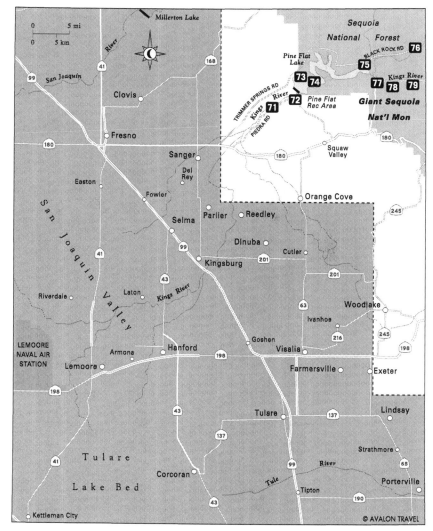

CAMPING

Map 4

Sites 80-133

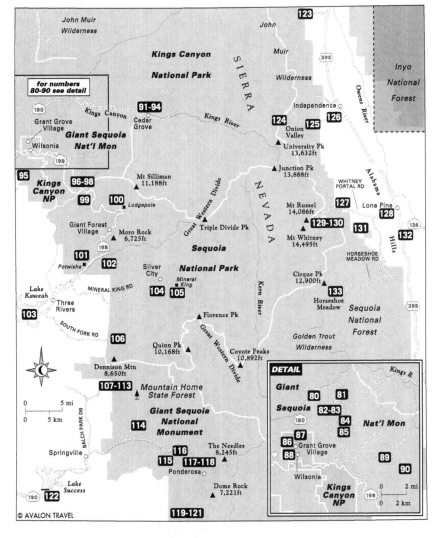

John Muir
Wilderness

Kings Canyon

National Park

SIERRA

John

Muir

Wilderness

395

Inyo

National

Forest

Owens River

for numbers
80-90 see detail

123

180

Grant Grove
Village

Kings Canyon

Cedar
Grove

91-94

Kings River

Independence

124   125   126

Giant Sequoia
Nat'l Mon

Wilsonia

198

95

Kings
Canyon
NP

96-98

99   100

Mt Silliman
11,188ft

Lodgepole

Onion
Valley

University Pk
13,632ft

Junction Pk
13,888ft

NEVADA

WHITNEY
PORTAL RD

Alabama

Mt Russel
14,086ft

Lone Pine

127   128

136

Giant Forest
Village

Moro Rock
6,725ft

Great Western Divide

Triple Divide Pk

Sequoia

129-130   131

132

Hills

198

101   102

Potwisha

Silver
City

Mineral
King

National Park

Mt Whitney
14,495ft

HORSESHOE
MEADOW RD

Kern River

Cirque Pk
12,900ft   133

Lake
Kaweah

MINERAL KING RD

104   105

Horseshoe
Meadow

Sequoia

395

Three
Rivers

103

SOUTH FORK RD

106

Florence Pk

Great Western Divide

Golden Trout

National

Forest

Wilderness

Quinn Pk
10,168ft

Coyote Peaks
10,892ft

Dennison Mtn
8,650ft

107-113   Mountain Home
State Forest

DETAIL

Kings R

0   5 mi

0   5 km

BALCH PARK DR

Giant Sequoia
National
Monument

114

Springville

115   116

117-118

Ponderosa

Giant

Sequoia

80   81

82-83

180   84

85

87

86   Grant Grove
Village

88

Nat'l Mon

89

The Needles
8,245ft

Wilsonia

90

190   122

Lake
Success

Dome Rock
7,221ft

119-121

Kings
Canyon
NP

198

0   2 mi

0   2 km

© AVALON TRAVEL

Map 5

Sites 134-172

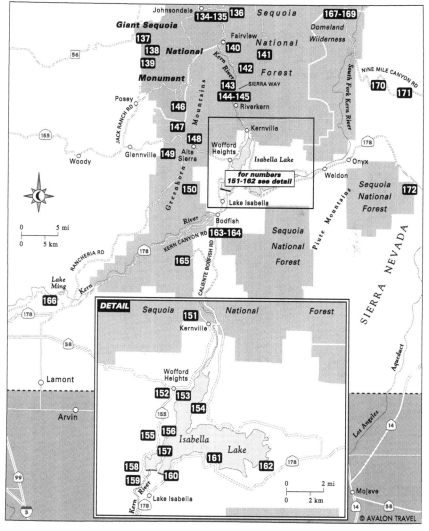

CAMPING

◼ LUPINE-CEDAR BLUFF
🏕 🏊 🛶 🚤 🎣 ♿ 🚐 ⛺

Scenic rating: 8

on Bass Lake in Sierra National Forest

Bass Lake is a popular vacation spot, a pretty lake, long and narrow, covering 1,200 acres when full and surrounded by national forest. The elevation is 3,500 feet. This is camping headquarters, with the only year-round individual sites at the lake. Though these camps are adjoining, the concessionaire treats them as separate camps, with Cedar Bluff reserved for RV camping only. Most of the campgrounds are filled on weekends and three-day holidays. Fishing is best in the spring for rainbow trout and largemouth bass, and by mid-June waterskiers have usually taken over. Boats must be registered at the Bass Lake observation tower after launching.

Campsites, facilities: There are 113 sites for tents or RVs up to 40 feet (no hookups); 50 sites are at Lupine and 62 sites are at Cedar Bluff. Picnic tables and fire grills are provided. Drinking water, flush toilets, and a camp host are available. Groceries, coin showers, and boat ramp are within two miles. Some facilities are wheelchair-accessible. Leashed pets are permitted.

Reservations, fees: Reservations are accepted at 877/444-6777 or www.recreation.gov ($9 reservation fee). Single sites are $22 per night, $44 per night for double sites, $88 for quadruple sites, $5 per night for each additional vehicle. Fees increase on holiday weekends. Open year-round.

Directions: From Fresno, drive north on Highway 41 to Oakhurst and continue 2.5 miles to Yosemite Forks and Bass Lake Road/County Road 222. Turn right at Bass Lake Road and drive eight miles (staying right at two forks) to the campground (on the south shore of Bass Lake).

Contact: Sierra National Forest, Bass Lake Ranger District, 559/877-2218, www.fs.fed.us; California Land Management, 559/642-3212.

◼ RECREATION POINT GROUP AND CRANE VALLEY GROUP
🏕 🏊 🛶 🚤 🎣 🐕 🚐 ⛺

Scenic rating: 8

on Bass Lake in Sierra National Forest

Bass Lake is a long, narrow, mountain lake set in the Sierra foothills at 3,400 feet elevation. It's especially popular in the summer for waterskiing, personal watercraft riding, and swimming. There are two separate group camps at Bass Lake: Recreation Point and Crane Valley. There are no individual sites. Crane Valley is the better of the two because it has drinking water and flush toilets.

Campsites, facilities: At Recreation Point, there are 14 group sites for tents only that can accommodate 30–50 people. Drinking water and flush toilets are available. At Crane Valley, there are seven group sites for tents or RVs up to 40 feet (no hookups) that can accommodate 45 people each. Vault toilets are available, but there is no drinking water. Picnic tables and fire grills are provided at both camps. A store is nearby. Leashed pets are permitted.

Reservations, fees: Reservations are required at 877/444-6777 or www.recreation.gov ($9 reservation fee). Sites are $130–220 per night at Recreation Point; sites are $35–95 per night at Crane Valley. All vehicles pay a $3–5 parking fee. Open year-round.

Directions: From Fresno, drive north on Highway 41 to Oakhurst and continue 2.5 miles to Yosemite Forks and Bass Lake Road/County Road 222. Turn right at Bass Lake Road and drive four miles to the campground.

Contact: Sierra National Forest, Bass Lake Ranger District, 559/877-2218, www.fs.fed.us; California Land Management, 559/642-3212.

3 FORKS

Scenic rating: 8

on Bass Lake in Sierra National Forest

Bass Lake is set in a canyon. It's a long, narrow, deep lake that is popular for fishing in the spring and waterskiing in the summer. It's a pretty spot, set at 3,500 feet elevation in the Sierra National Forest. This is one of several camps at the lake. Boats must be registered at the Bass Lake observation tower after launching.

Campsites, facilities: There are 31 sites for tents or RVs up to 40 feet (no hookups). Picnic tables and fire grills are provided. Drinking water, flush toilets, and a camp host are available. A store, dump station, and coin laundry are nearby. Some facilities are wheelchair-accessible. Leashed pets are permitted.

Reservations, fees: Reservations are accepted at 877/444-6777 or www.recreation.gov ($9 reservation fee). Single sites are $22 per night, double sites are $44 per night, $5 per night for each additional vehicle. Fees increase on holiday weekends. Open May through September.

Directions: From Fresno, drive north on Highway 41 to Oakhurst and continue 2.5 miles to Yosemite Forks and Bass Lake Road/County Road 222. Turn right at Bass Lake Road and drive six miles (staying right at two forks) to the campground (on the south shore of Bass Lake). Note: The road is narrow and curvy.

Contact: Sierra National Forest, Bass Lake Ranger District, 559/877-2218, www.fs.fed.us; California Land Management, 559/642-3212.

4 SPRING COVE

Scenic rating: 8

on Bass Lake in Sierra National Forest

This is one of several camps beside Bass Lake, a long, narrow reservoir in the Sierra foothill country. A bonus here is that the shoreline is quite sandy nearly all around the lake. That makes for good swimming and sunbathing. Expect hot weather in the summer. Boats must be registered at the Bass Lake observation tower after launching. The elevation is 3,400 feet.

Campsites, facilities: There are 63 sites for tents or RVs up to 35 feet (no hookups). Picnic tables and fire grills are provided. Drinking water, flush toilets, and camp host are available. Groceries and a boat ramp are nearby. Some facilities are wheelchair-accessible. Leashed pets are permitted.

Reservations, fees: Reservations are accepted at 877/444-6777 or www.recreation.gov ($9 reservation fee). Single sites are $22 per night, double sites are $44 per night, $5 per night for each additional vehicle. Fees increase on holiday weekends. Open May through August.

Directions: From Fresno, drive north on Highway 41 to Oakhurst and continue 2.5 miles to Yosemite Forks and Bass Lake Road/County Road 222. Turn right at Bass Lake Road and drive 8.5 miles (staying right at two forks) to the campground (on the south shore of Bass Lake).

Contact: Sierra National Forest, Bass Lake Ranger District, 559/877-2218, www.fs.fed.us; California Land Management, 559/642-3212.

5 WISHON POINT

Scenic rating: 9

on Bass Lake in Sierra National Forest

This camp on Wishon Point is the smallest, and many say the prettiest, of the camps at Bass Lake. The elevation is 3,400 feet.

Campsites, facilities: There are 47 sites for tents or RVs up to 30 feet (no hookups). Some sites are pull-through. Picnic tables and fire grills are provided. Drinking water and flush toilets are available. Groceries and a boat ramp are nearby. Some facilities are wheelchair-accessible. Leashed pets are permitted.

Reservations, fees: Reservations are accepted at 877/444-6777 or www.recreation.gov ($9 reservation fee). Single sites are $22 per night, double sites are $44, $5 per night for additional vehicle. Fees increase on holiday weekends. Open June through September.

Directions: From Fresno, drive north on Highway 41 to Oakhurst and continue 2.5 miles to Yosemite Forks and Bass Lake Road/ County Road 222. Turn right at Bass Lake Road and drive nine miles (staying right at two forks) to the campground (on the south shore of Bass Lake).

Contact: Sierra National Forest, Bass Lake Ranger District, 559/877-2218, www.fs.fed.us; California Land Management, 559/642-3212.

6 CHILKOOT

Scenic rating: 7

near Bass Lake in Sierra National Forest

A lot of people have heard of Bass Lake, but only the faithful know about Chilcoot Creek. That's where this camp is, but it's just two miles from Bass Lake. It provides a primitive option to use either as an overflow area for Bass Lake or for folks who don't want to get jammed into one of the Bass Lake campgrounds on a popular weekend. The elevation is 4,600 feet.

Campsites, facilities: There are 14 sites for tents or RVs up to 20 feet (no hookups). Picnic tables and fire grills are provided. Vault toilets are available. No drinking water is available. Groceries and a coin laundry are available at Bass Lake. Leashed pets are permitted.

Reservations, fees: Reservations are accepted at 877/444-6777 or www.recreation.gov ($9 reservation fee). Single sites are $17 per night, double sites are $34, $5 per night for each

additional vehicle. Open early May through early September.

Directions: From Fresno, drive north on Highway 41 to Oakhurst and continue 2.5 miles to Yosemite Forks and Bass Lake Road/County Road 222. Turn right at Bass Lake Road and drive six miles to the town of Bass Lake and Beasore Road. Turn left at Beasore Road and drive 4.5 miles to the campground.

Contact: Sierra National Forest, Bass Lake Ranger District, 559/877-2218, www.fs.fed.us.

7 GAGGS CAMP

Scenic rating: 7

in Sierra National Forest

The masses are not exactly beating a hot trail to this camp. It's a small, remote, and primitive spot, set along a little creek at 5,700 feet elevation, deep in the interior of Sierra National Forest. A Forest Service map is advisable. With that in hand, you can make the three-mile drive to Little Shuteye Pass, where the road is often gated in the winter (the gate is open when the look-out station is staffed); from here it is a three-mile trip to Shuteye Peak, at 8,351 feet, where there is a drop-dead gorgeous view of the surrounding landscape.

Campsites, facilities: There are 11 sites for tents or RVs up to 16 feet (no hookups). Picnic tables and fire grills are provided. Vault toilets are available. No drinking water is available. Garbage bins are located at campground entrance. Leashed pets are permitted.

Reservations, fees: Reservations are not accepted. Single sites are $17 per night, double sites are $34 per night, $5 per night for each additional vehicle. Open June through October, weather permitting.

Directions: From Fresno, drive north on Highway 41 for about 25 miles to North Fork Road/County Road 200. Turn right and drive northeast for 17.5 miles to Auberry Road/County Road 222. Turn left (north) and

CAMPING

drive one mile to the town of North Fork and Mammoth Pool Road. Turn right and drive 0.5 mile to Malum Ridge Road/County Road 274. Turn left (north) and drive 4.5 miles to Central Camp Road/Forest Road 6S42. Turn right and drive 11.5 miles (narrow, dirt road) to the campground on the right.

Contact: Sierra National Forest, Bass Lake Ranger District, 559/877-2218, www.fs.fed.us.

8 SODA SPRINGS
🚶 🏊 🚤 🚣 🏕 🐕 🚐 ⛺

Scenic rating: 7

on the West Fork of Chiquito Creek in Sierra National Forest

Soda Springs is set at 4,400 feet elevation on West Fork Chiquito Creek, about five miles from Mammoth Pool Reservoir. It is used primarily as an overflow area if the more developed camps with drinking water have filled up. As long as you remember that the camp is primitive, it is a good overflow option.

Campsites, facilities: There are 18 sites for tents or RVs up to 20 feet (no hookups). Picnic tables and fire grills are provided. Vault toilets are available. No drinking water is available. A store and boat ramp are nearby. Leashed pets are permitted.

Reservations, fees: Reservations are not accepted. Single sites are $17 per night, $34 per night for double sites, $5 per night for each additional vehicle. Open May through September, weather permitting.

Directions: From Fresno, drive north on Highway 41 for about 25 miles to North Fork Road/County Road 200. Turn right and drive northeast for 17.5 miles to Auberry Road/ County Road 222. Turn left (north) and drive one mile to the town of North Fork and Mammoth Pool Road. Turn right and drive 1.5 miles to County Road 225 (still Mammoth Pool Road). Turn right and drive 35 miles (the road becomes Minarets Road/Forest Road 81) to the campground.

Contact: Sierra National Forest, Bass Lake Ranger District, 559/877-2218, www.fs.fed.us.

9 LOWER CHIQUITO
🐕 🚐 ⛺

Scenic rating: 7

on Chiquito Creek in Sierra National Forest

Lower Chiquito is a primitive, little-known, pretty camp in Sierra National Forest, about eight miles from Mammoth Pool Reservoir. Mosquitoes can be abundant in summer. The elevation is 4,900 feet, with a very warm climate in summer. Note that Lower Chiquito is a long distance (a twisting, 30- to 40-minute drive) from Upper Chiquito, despite the similarity in names and streamside settings along the same creek.

Campsites, facilities: There are seven sites for tents or RVs up to 25 feet (no hookups). Picnic tables and fire grills are provided. Vault toilets are available. No drinking water is available. Leashed pets are permitted.

Reservations, fees: Reservations are not accepted. Single sites are $17 per night, $34 per night for double sites, $5 per night for each additional vehicle. Open June through September, weather permitting.

Directions: From the town of North Fork (south of Bass Lake), drive east on Mammoth Pool Road/County Road 225 (it becomes Minarets Road/Forest Road 4S81). Bear left (north, still Minarets Road/Forest Road 4S81) and drive to Forest Road 6S71. Turn left on Forest Road 6S71 and drive three miles to the campground. (The distance is about 40 miles from North Fork.)

Contact: Sierra National Forest, Bass Lake Ranger District, 559/877-2218, www.fs.fed.us.

10 PLACER

Scenic rating: 7

near Mammoth Pool Reservoir on
Chiquito Creek in Sierra National Forest

This little camp is just three miles from Mammoth Pool Reservoir. With Forest Road access and a pretty setting along Chiquito Creek, it is one of the better campgrounds used as an overflow area for Mammoth Pool visitors. The elevation is 4,100 feet. (For more information, see the Mammoth Pool listing in this chapter.)

Campsites, facilities: There are eight sites for tents or RVs up to 28 feet. Picnic tables and fire grills are provided. Vault toilets are available. No drinking water is available. Leashed pets are permitted.

Reservations, fees: Reservations are not accepted. Single sites are $17 per night, $34 per night for double sites, $5 per night for each additional vehicle. Open May through September.

Directions: From Fresno, drive north on Highway 41 for about 25 miles to North Fork Road/County Road 200. Turn right and drive northeast for 17.5 miles to Auberry Road/County Road 222. Turn left (north) and drive one mile to the town of North Fork and Mammoth Pool Road. Turn right and drive 1.5 miles to County Road 225 (still Mammoth Pool Road). Turn right and drive about 37 miles (the road becomes Minarets Road/Forest Road 81) to a junction. Bear right (still Mammoth Pool Road) and drive one mile to the campground on the right. The drive from North Fork takes 1.5–2 hours.

Contact: Sierra National Forest, Bass Lake Ranger District, 559/877-2218, www.fs.fed.us.

11 SWEETWATER

Scenic rating: 6

near Mammoth Pool Reservoir on
Chiquito Creek in Sierra National Forest

Sweetwater is small and primitive, but if the camp at Mammoth Pool Reservoir is filled up, this spot provides an alternative. It is set on Chiquito Creek, just a mile from the lake. The elevation is 3,800 feet. (See the Mammoth Pool listing in this chapter for more information.)

Campsites, facilities: There are seven sites for tents or RVs up to 20 feet (no hookups). Picnic tables and fire grills are provided. Vault toilets are available. No drinking water is available. A store and boat ramp are within 1.5 miles. Leashed pets are permitted.

Reservations, fees: Reservations are accepted at 877/444-6777 or www.recreation.gov ($9 reservation fee). Single sites are $17 per night, double sites are $34 per night, $5 per night per additional vehicle. Open mid-May through mid-September.

Directions: From Fresno, drive north on Highway 41 for about 25 miles to North Fork Road/County Road 200. Turn right and drive northeast for 17.5 miles to Auberry Road/County Road 222. Turn left (north) and drive one mile to the town of North Fork and Mammoth Pool Road. Turn right and drive 1.5 miles to County Road 225 (still Mammoth Pool Road). Turn right and drive about 37 miles (the road becomes Minarets Road/Forest Road 81) to a junction. Bear right (still Mammoth Pool Road) and drive 1.5 miles to the campground on the right. The drive from North Fork takes 1.5–2 hours.

Contact: Sierra National Forest, Bass Lake Ranger District, 559/877-2218, www.fs.fed.us; California Land Management, 559/642-3212.

12 MAMMOTH POOL

🏊 🛶 ⛴ 🏕 🚐 ⛺

Scenic rating: 7

near Mammoth Pool Reservoir in
Sierra National Forest

Mammoth Pool was created by a dam in the
San Joaquin River gorge, a steep canyon,
resulting in a long, narrow lake with steep,
high walls. The lake seems much higher than
its official elevation of 3,330 feet, but that is
because of the high ridges. This is the only
drive-in camp at the lake, though there is
a boat-in camp, China Camp, on the lake's
upper reaches. Trout fishing can be good in
the spring and early summer, with waterskiing
dominant during warm weather. All water
sports are allowed during part of the season,
but get this: Water sports are restricted from
May 1 to June 15 because of deer migrating
across the lake—that's right, swimming—but
the campgrounds here are still open. Note that
the water level can drop significantly by late
summer.

Campsites, facilities: There are 47 sites for
tents or RVs up to 30 feet (no hookups). Picnic
tables and fire grills are provided. Drinking
water and vault toilets are available. A store
and boat ramp are within a mile. Leashed pets
are permitted.

Reservations, fees: Reservations are accepted
at 877/444-6777 or www.recreation.gov ($9
reservation fee). Single sites are $18 per night,
double sites are $36 per night, $5 per night
per additional vehicle. Open June through
October.

Directions: From Fresno, drive north on High-
way 41 for about 25 miles to North Fork Road/
County Road 200. Turn right and drive north-
east for 17.5 miles to Auberry Road/County
Road 222. Turn left (north) and drive one mile
to the town of North Fork and Mammoth
Pool Road. Turn right and drive 1.5 miles to
County Road 225 (still Mammoth Pool Road).
Turn right and drive about 37 miles (the road
becomes Minarets Road/Forest Road 81) to
a junction. Bear right (still Mammoth Pool
Road) and drive three miles to Mammoth
Pool Reservoir and the campground. The drive
from North Fork takes 1.5–2 hours.

Contact: Sierra National Forest, Bass Lake
Ranger District, 559/877-2218, www.fs.fed.us;
California Land Management, 559/642-3212.

13 SAMPLE MEADOW

🚶 🏕 🚐 ⛺

Scenic rating: 7

on Kaiser Creek in Sierra National Forest

This is a pretty, secluded spot set at 7,800
feet elevation along Kaiser Creek, with nearby
trailheads available for backpackers. While
there is a trail out of camp, most hikers drive
a mile down Forest Road 80 to the Rattlesnake Parking Area. From here, one trail is
routed three miles southwest to Kaiser Ridge
and Upper and Lower Twin Lakes in the Kaiser Wilderness, a great hike. Another trail is
routed north for three miles to Rattlesnake
Creek, and then enters the western slopes of
the Ansel Adams Wilderness, with this section
featuring a series of canyons, streams, and very
few people. Horse camping is permitted.

Campsites, facilities: There are 16 sites for
tents or RVs up to 16 feet (no hookups). Picnic
tables and fire grills are provided. Vault toilets
are available. No drinking water is available.
Garbage must be packed out. Leashed pets
are permitted.

Reservations, fees: Reservations are not accepted. There is no fee for camping. Open
June through October, weather permitting.

Directions: From Fresno, drive east on Highway 168 to Shaver Lake, and then continue
21 miles to Huntington Lake and Kaiser Pass
Road/Forest Road 80. Bear right on Forest
Road 80 and drive eight miles to a fork with
Forest Road 7505. Turn left on Forest Road
7505 and drive 3.5 miles to a fork with the
campground entrance road. Bear left at the
campground entrance road and drive 0.25

mile to the campground. The road is narrow and curvy, with blind turns.

Contact: Sierra National Forest, High Sierra Ranger District, 559/855-5355, www.fs.fed.us.

14 PORTAL FOREBAY

Scenic rating: 8

on Forebay Lake in Sierra National Forest

This small, primitive camp is set along the shore of little Forebay Lake at 7,200 feet elevation. The camp is pretty and provides a good hiking option, with a trailhead near the camp that is routed up Camp 61 Creek and then to Mono Creek, with a ford of Mono Creek required about two miles in. Another side trip is visiting Mono Hot Springs about five miles to the east, just off the road to Lake Edison.

Campsites, facilities: There are 11 sites for tents or RVs up to 16 feet (no hookups). Picnic tables and fire grills are provided. Vault toilets are available. No drinking water is available. Groceries are available nearby at Mono Hot Springs. Leashed pets are permitted.

Reservations, fees: Reservations are not accepted. Single sites are $16 per night, double sites are $32 per night, $5 per night per each additional vehicle. Open June through October.

Directions: From Fresno, drive east on Highway 168 to Shaver Lake, and then continue 21 miles to Huntington Lake and Kaiser Pass Road/Forest Road 80. Bear right on Forest Road 80 and drive eight miles to a fork with Forest Road 5. Stay right at the fork on Forest Road 80 and continue five miles to the campground entrance on the left. The road is narrow and curvy, with blind turns.

Contact: Sierra National Forest, High Sierra Ranger District, 559/855-5355, www.fs.fed.us; California Land Management, 559/893-2111.

15 VERMILLION

Scenic rating: 8

on Lake Edison in Sierra National Forest

If you don't mind the drive, Lake Edison is a premium vacation destination. It is a large, high-mountain camp set just a few miles from the border of the John Muir Wilderness. The elevation is 7,700 feet. A 15-mph speed limit on the lake guarantees quiet water, and trout fishing is often quite good in early summer, with occasionally huge brown trout hooked. Swimming is allowed. A day-trip option is to hike the trail from the camp out along the north shore of Lake Edison for five miles to Quail Meadows, where it intersects with the Pacific Crest Trail in the John Muir Wilderness. A lodge at the lake provides meals and supplies, with a hikers boat shuttle available to the head of the lake. Hang out here for long and you are bound to see John Muir Trail hikers taking a break. Note that the drive in is long and extremely twisty on a narrow road. Also note that the lake level can drop dramatically here by late summer.

Campsites, facilities: There are 31 sites for tents or RVs up to 25 feet (no hookups). Picnic tables, fire grills, and food lockers are provided. Drinking water and vault toilets are available. A boat ramp, boat rentals, bait and tackle, horseback-riding facilities, convenience store, and restaurant are nearby. Leashed pets are permitted.

Reservations, fees: Reservations are accepted at 877/444-6777 or www.recreation.gov ($9 reservation fee). Single sites are $18 per night, double sites are $36 per night, $5 per night for each additional vehicle. Open June through October.

Directions: From the town of Shaver Lake, drive east on Highway 168 for 21 miles to Kaiser Pass Road. Bear northeast on Kaiser Pass Road/Forest Road 80 (slow and curvy) to Mono Hot Springs (the road becomes Edison Lake Road). Continue on Kaiser Pass/Edison

Lake Road for five miles to the campground. It is about 0.25 mile from the west shore of Lake Edison. Be warned that the access road is narrow with many blind turns and may be difficult for RVs.

Contact: Sierra National Forest, High Sierra Ranger District, 559/855-5355, www.fs.fed.us; California Land Management, 559/893-2111.

16 MONO HOT SPRINGS

Scenic rating: 8

on the San Joaquin River in
Sierra National Forest

The campground is set in the Sierra at 7,400 feet elevation along the San Joaquin River directly adjacent to the Mono Hot Springs Resort. The hot springs are typically 104°F, with public pools (everybody wears swimming suits) available just above the river on one side, and the private resort (rock cabins available) with its private baths on the other. A small convenience store and excellent restaurant are available at the lodge. Many find the hot springs perfect, but for some the water is too hot. No problem; the best swimming lake in the Sierra Nevada, Dorris Lake, is a 15-minute walk past the lodge. Dorris is clear, clean, and not too cold since it too is fed by hot springs. There are walls on one side for fun jumps into deep water. The one downer: The drive in to the campground is long, slow, and hellacious, with many blind corners in narrow sections.

Campsites, facilities: There are 31 sites for tents or RVs up to 25 feet (no hookups). Picnic tables and fire grills are provided. Vault toilets are available. Drinking water is not available. You can buy supplies in Mono Hot Springs. Leashed pets are permitted.

Reservations, fees: Reservations are accepted at 877/444-6777 or www.recreation.gov ($9 reservation fee). Single sites are $18 per night, $36 per night for double sites, $5 per night for additional vehicle. Open June through mid-September, weather permitting.

Directions: From the town of Shaver Lake, drive east on Highway 168 for 21 miles to Kaiser Pass Road. Bear northeast on Kaiser Pass Road/Forest Road 80 (slow and curvy) to Mono Hot Springs Campground Road (signed). Turn left and drive a short distance to the campground. Be warned that the access road is narrow with many blind turns and may be difficult for RVs.

Contact: Sierra National Forest, High Sierra Ranger District, 559/855-5355, www.fs.fed.us; California Land Management, 559/893-2111.

17 MONO CREEK

Scenic rating: 6

near Lake Edison in Sierra National Forest

Here's a beautiful spot in the forest near Mono Creek that makes for an overflow campground when the camps at Mono Hot Springs and Lake Edison are filled, or when you want a quieter, more remote spot. The camp is set at 7,400 feet elevation about three miles from Lake Edison, via a twisty and bumpy road. Edison has good evening trout fishing and a small restaurant. For side trips, the Mono Hot Springs Resort is three miles away (slow, curvy, and bumpy driving), and there are numerous trails nearby into the backcountry. A camp host is on-site.

Campsites, facilities: There are 14 sites for tents or RVs up to 25 feet (no hookups). Picnic tables, fire grills, and food lockers are provided. Vault toilets are available. Drinking water is not available. Limited supplies and small restaurants are at Lake Edison and Mono Hot Springs. Leashed pets are permitted.

Reservations, fees: Reservations are accepted at 877/444-6777 or www.recreation.gov ($9 reservation fee). Single sites are $18 per night, $36 per night for double site, $5 per night for

CAMPING

each additional vehicle. Open June through October, weather permitting.

Directions: From the town of Shaver Lake, drive east on Highway 168 for 21 miles to Kaiser Pass Road. Bear northeast on Kaiser Pass Road/Forest Road 80 (slow and curvy) to Mono Hot Springs (the road becomes Edison Lake Road). Continue on Kaiser Pass/Edison Lake Road for three miles to the campground on the left.

Contact: Sierra National Forest, High Sierra Ranger District, 559/855-5355, www.fs.fed.us; California Land Management, 559/893-2111.

18 BOLSILLO

Scenic rating: 4

on Bolsillo Creek in Sierra National Forest

This tiny camp has many first-class bonuses. It is set at 7,400 feet elevation along Bolsillo Creek, just three miles by car to Mono Hot Springs and seven miles to Lake Edison. A trailhead out of camp provides the chance for a three-mile hike south, climbing along Bolsillo Creek and up to small, pretty Corbett Lake on the flank of nearby Mount Givens, at 10,648 feet.

Campsites, facilities: There are three tent sites. Picnic tables and fire grills are provided. Drinking water and vault toilets are available. Garbage must be packed out. You can buy supplies in Mono Hot Springs. Leashed pets are permitted.

Reservations, fees: Reservations are not accepted. There is no fee for camping. Open June through October, weather permitting.

Directions: From Fresno, drive east on Highway 168 to Shaver Lake, then continue 21 miles to Huntington Lake and Kaiser Pass Road/Forest Road 80. Bear right on Forest Road 80 and drive eight miles to a fork with Forest Road 5. Stay right on Forest Road 80 and drive seven miles (two miles past Portal Forebay) to the campground entrance on the right. The road is narrow and curvy

with blind turns, and RVs and trailers are not recommended.

Contact: Sierra National Forest, High Sierra Ranger District, 559/855-5355, www.fs.fed.us.

19 CODORNIZ RECREATION AREA

Scenic rating: 6

on Eastman Lake

Eastman Lake provides relief on your typical 90- and 100-degree summer day out here. It is tucked in the foothills of the San Joaquin Valley at an elevation of 650 feet and covers 1,800 surface acres. Shade shelters have been added at 12 of the more exposed campsites, a big plus. The warm water in summer makes it a good spot for a dip, thus it is a favorite for waterskiing, swimming, and, in the spring, fishing. Swimming is best at the large beach on the west side. The Department of Fish and Game has established a trophy bass program here, and fishing can be good in the appropriate season for rainbow trout, catfish, bluegill, and redear sunfish. Check fishing regulations, posted on all bulletin boards. The lake is also a designated "Watchable Wildlife" site; it is home to 163 species of birds and a nesting pair of bald eagles. A small area near the upper end of the lake is closed to boating to protect a bald eagle nest site. Some may remember the problem that Eastman Lake had with hydrilla, an invasive weed. The problem has been largely solved, and a buoy line has been placed at the mouth. No water activities are allowed upstream of this line. Mild winter temperatures are a tremendous plus at this lake.

Campsites, facilities: There are 62 sites for tents or RVs of any length (some have full hookups/50 amps and one is pull-through), three group sites for 40–160 people, three equestrian sites, and one group equestrian site. Picnic tables and fire grills are provided. Drinking water, flush toilets with showers, dump station, playground, horseshoe pits, volleyball court, Frisbee golf course, and two boat ramps are available. An equestrian staging area is available for overnight use, and there are seven miles of hiking, biking, and equestrian trails. Some facilities are wheelchair accessible. Leashed pets are permitted.

Reservations, fees: Reservations are accepted at 877/444-6777 or www.recreation.gov ($9 reservation fee). Sites are $16–24 per night, $55–80 per night for group sites, and $10–25 per night for equestrian sites. Open year-round.

Directions: Drive on Highway 99 to Chowchilla and the Avenue 26 exit. Take that exit and drive east for 17 miles to County Road 29. Turn left (north) on County Road 29 and drive eight miles to the lake.

Contact: U.S. Army Corps of Engineers, Sacramento District, Eastman Lake, 559/689-3255.

20 ROCK CREEK

Scenic rating: 6

in Sierra National Forest

Drinking water is the big bonus here. It's easier to live with than the no-water situation at Fish Creek, the other camp in the immediate area. It is also why this camp tends to fill up on weekends. A side trip is the primitive road that heads southeast out of camp. It has a series of sharp turns as it heads east and drops down the canyon near where pretty Aspen Creek feeds into Rock Creek. The elevation at camp is 4,300 feet. (For the best camp in the immediate region, see the Mammoth Pool listing in this chapter.)

Campsites, facilities: There are 18 sites for tents or RVs up to 30 feet (no hookups). Picnic tables and fire grills are provided. Drinking water and vault toilets are available. A camp host is on-site. Leashed pets are permitted.

Reservations, fees: Reservations are accepted at 877/444-6777 or www.recreation.gov ($9 reservation fee). Single sites are $18 per night,

$36 per night for a double site, $5 per night per each additional vehicle. Open mid-May through mid-September, weather permitting.

Directions: From Fresno, drive north on Highway 41 for about 25 miles to North Fork Road/County Road 200. Turn right and drive northeast for 17.5 miles to Auberry Road/County Road 222. Turn left (north) and drive one mile to the town of North Fork and Mammoth Pool Road. Turn right and drive 1.5 miles to County Road 225 (still Mammoth Pool Road). Turn right and drive about 25 miles (the road becomes Minarets Road/Forest Road 81) to the campground on the right.

Contact: Sierra National Forest, Bass Lake Ranger District, 559/877-2218, www.fs.fed.us; California Land Management, 559/642-3212.

21 FISH CREEK

Scenic rating: 6

in Sierra National Forest

This is a small, primitive camp set along Fish Creek at 4,600 feet elevation in the Sierra National Forest. It's a nearby option to Rock Creek, both set on the access road to Mammoth Pool Reservoir.

Campsites, facilities: There are seven sites for tents or RVs up to 20 feet (no hookups). Picnic tables and fire grills are provided. Vault toilets are available. No drinking water is available. Leashed pets are permitted.

Reservations, fees: Reservations are accepted at 877/444-6777 or www.recreation.gov ($9 reservation fee). Sites are $17–34 per night, $5 per night per each additional vehicle. Open June through November, weather permitting.

Directions: From Fresno, drive north on Highway 41 for about 25 miles to North Fork Road/County Road 200. Turn right and drive northeast for 17.5 miles to Auberry Road/County Road 222. Turn left (north) and drive one mile to the town of North Fork and Mammoth Pool Road. Turn right and drive 1.5 miles to

County Road 225 (still Mammoth Pool Road). Turn right and drive about 21 miles (the road becomes Minarets Road/Forest Road 81) to the campground on the right.

Contact: Sierra National Forest, Bass Lake Ranger District, 559/877-2218, www.fs.fed.us; California Land Management, 559/642-3212.

22 UPPER AND LOWER BILLY CREEK

Scenic rating: 8

on Huntington Lake in Sierra National Forest

Huntington Lake is at an elevation of 7,000 feet in the Sierra Nevada. These camps are at the west end of the lake along the north shore, where Billy Creek feeds the lake. Of these two adjacent campgrounds, Lower Billy Creek is smaller than Upper Billy and has lakeside sites available. The lake is four miles long and 0.5 mile wide, with 14 miles of shoreline, several resorts, boat rentals, and a trailhead for hiking into the Kaiser Wilderness.

Campsites, facilities: Upper Billy has 44 sites for tents or RVs up to 30 feet. Lower Billy has 15 sites for tents or RVs up to 30 feet. No hookups. Picnic tables and fire grills are provided. Drinking water and vault toilets are available at both camps; Upper Billy also has flush toilets available. A camp host is on-site. Campfire programs are often available. A small store is nearby. Leashed pets are permitted.

Reservations, fees: Reservations are accepted at 877/444-6777 or www.recreation.gov ($9 reservation fee). Single sites are $20–22 per night, double sites are $40–42, $5 per night for each additional vehicle. Open June through October, weather permitting.

Directions: From Fresno, drive east on Highway 168 to Shaver Lake, then continue 21 miles to Huntington Lake and Huntington Lake Road. Turn left on Huntington Lake Road and drive about five miles to the campgrounds on the left.

Contact: Sierra National Forest, High Sierra Ranger District, 559/855-5355, www.fs.fed.us; California Land Management, 559/893-2111.

23 CATAVEE

Scenic rating: 7

on Huntington Lake in Sierra National Forest

Catavee is one of three camps in the immediate vicinity, set on the north shore at the eastern end of Huntington Lake. The camp sits near where Bear Creek enters the lake. Huntington Lake is a scenic, High Sierra Ranger District lake at 7,000 feet elevation, where visitors can enjoy fishing, hiking, and sailing. Sailboat regattas take place here regularly during the summer. All water sports are allowed. Nearby resorts offer boat rentals and guest docks, and a boat ramp is nearby. Tackle rentals and bait are also available. A trailhead near camp offers access to the Kaiser Wilderness.

Campsites, facilities: There are 23 sites for tents or RVs up to 30 feet (no hookups). Picnic tables and fire grills are provided. Drinking water and flush toilets are available. A camp host is on-site. Horseback-riding facilities and a small store are nearby. Some facilities are wheelchair-accessible. Leashed pets are permitted.

Reservations, fees: Reservations are accepted at 877/444-6777 or www.recreation.gov ($9 reservation fee). Single sites are $22–23 per night, double sites are $44–46, $5 per night for each additional vehicle. Open June through October, weather permitting.

Directions: From Fresno, drive east on Highway 168 to Shaver Lake, then continue 21 miles to Huntington Lake and Huntington Lake Road. Turn left on Huntington Lake Road and drive one mile (just past Kinnikinnick) to the campground on the right.

Contact: Sierra National Forest, High Sierra Ranger District, 559/855-5355, www.fs.fed.us; California Land Management, 559/893-2111.

24 KINNIKINNICK

Scenic rating: 7

on Huntington Lake in Sierra National Forest

Flip a coin; there are three camps in the immediate vicinity on the north shore of the east end of Huntington Lake and, with a boat ramp nearby, they are all favorites. Kinnikinnick is set between Catavee and Deer Creek Campgrounds. The elevation is 7,000 feet.

Campsites, facilities: There are 27 sites for tents or RVs up to 40 feet (no hookups). Picnic tables and fire grills are provided. Drinking water and flush toilets are available. Horseback-riding facilities and a store are nearby. Some facilities are wheelchair-accessible. Leashed pets are permitted.

Reservations, fees: Reservations are accepted at 877/444-6777 or www.recreation.gov ($9 reservation fee). Sites are $22–44 per night, $5 per night for each additional vehicle. Open June through October, weather permitting.

Directions: From Fresno, drive east on Highway 168 to Shaver Lake, then continue 21 miles to Huntington Lake and Huntington Lake Road. Turn left on Huntington Lake Road and drive one mile to the campground on the right.

Contact: Sierra National Forest, High Sierra Ranger District, 559/855-5355, www.fs.fed.us; California Land Management, 559/893-2111.

25 DEER CREEK

Scenic rating: 8

on Huntington Lake in Sierra National Forest

This is one of the best camps at Huntington Lake, set near lakeside at Bear Cove with a boat ramp nearby. It is on the north shore of the lake's eastern end. Huntington Lake is four miles long and 0.5 mile wide, with 14 miles of shoreline, several resorts, boat rentals, and a trailhead for hiking into the Kaiser Wilderness. Two other campgrounds are nearby.

Campsites, facilities: There are 28 sites for tents or RVs up to 40 feet (no hookups). Picnic tables and fire grills are provided. Drinking water and flush toilets are available. A store and propane gas are nearby. Some facilities are wheelchair-accessible. Leashed pets are permitted.

Reservations, fees: Reservations are accepted at 877/444-6777 or www.recreation.gov ($9 reservation fee). Sites are $22–44 per night, $5 per night for each additional vehicle. Open June through October, weather permitting.

Directions: From Fresno, drive east on Highway 168 to Shaver Lake, then continue 21 miles to Huntington Lake and Huntington Lake Road. Turn left on Huntington Lake Road and drive one mile to the campground entrance road on the left.

Contact: Sierra National Forest, High Sierra Ranger District, 559/855-5355, www.fs.fed.us; California Land Management, 559/893-2111.

26 COLLEGE

Scenic rating: 7

on Huntington Lake in Sierra National Forest

College is a beautiful site along the shore of the northeastern end of Huntington Lake, at 7,000 feet elevation. This camp is close to a small store in the town of Huntington Lake.

Campsites, facilities: There are 11 sites for tents or RVs up to 30 feet (no hookups). Picnic tables and fire grills are provided. Vault and flush toilets, drinking water and a camp host are available. Interpretive programs are offered. Horseback-riding facilities, store, and propane gas are nearby. Leashed pets are permitted.

Reservations, fees: Reservations are accepted at 877/444-6777 or www.recreation.gov ($9 reservation fee). Single sites are $20–22 per night, double sites are $40–44 per night, $5 per night for each additional vehicle. Open June through October, weather permitting.

Directions: From Fresno, drive east on Highway 168 to Shaver Lake, then continue 21 miles to Huntington Lake and Huntington Lake Road. Turn left on Huntington Lake Road and drive 0.5 mile to the campground.

Contact: Sierra National Forest, High Sierra Ranger District, 559/855-5355, www.fs.fed.us; California Land Management, 559/893-2111.

27 RANCHERIA

🏃 🏊 ⛵ 🚣 🐕 🚐 ⛺

Scenic rating: 8

on Huntington Lake in Sierra National Forest

This is the granddaddy of the camps at Huntington Lake, and also the easiest to reach. It is along the shore of the lake's eastern end. A bonus here is nearby Rancheria Falls National Recreation Trail, which provides access to beautiful Rancheria Falls. Another side trip is the 15-minute drive to Bear Butte (the access road is across from the campground entrance) at 8,598 feet elevation, providing a sweeping view of the lake below. The elevation at camp is 7,000 feet.

Campsites, facilities: There are 149 sites for tents or RVs up to 40 feet (no hookups). Picnic tables and fire grills are provided. Drinking water and flush and vault toilets are available. A camp host is on-site. Interpretive programs are offered. A store and propane gas are nearby. Leashed pets are permitted.

Reservations, fees: Reservations are accepted at 877/444-6777 or www.recreation.gov ($9 reservation fee). Single sites are $20–22 per night, double sites are $40–44 per night, $5 per night for each additional vehicle. Open June through October, weather permitting.

Directions: From Fresno, drive east on Highway 168 to Shaver Lake, then continue 20 miles to Huntington Lake and the campground on the left.

Contact: Sierra National Forest, High Sierra

Ranger District, 559/855-5355, www.fs.fed.us; California Land Management, 559/893-2111.

28 BADGER FLAT

🏃 🐕 🚐 ⛺

Scenic rating: 7

on Rancheria Creek in Sierra National Forest

This camp is a good launching pad for backpackers. It is set at 8,200 feet elevation along Rancheria Creek. The trail leading out of the camp is routed into the Kaiser Wilderness to the north and Dinkey Lakes Wilderness to the south.

Campsites, facilities: There are 15 sites for tents or RVs up to 25 feet (no hookups). Fire grills and picnic tables are provided. Vault toilets and horseback-riding facilities are available. No drinking water is available. Leashed pets are permitted.

Reservations, fees: Reservations are not accepted. Sites are $18 per night, $5 per night for each additional vehicle. Open June through October, weather permitting.

Directions: From Fresno, drive east on Highway 168 to Shaver Lake, then continue 21 miles to Huntington Lake and Kaiser Pass Road/Forest Road 80. Turn right and drive four miles to the campground.

Contact: Sierra National Forest, High Sierra Ranger District, 559/855-5355, www.fs.fed.us; California Land Management, 559/893-2111.

29 BADGER FLAT GROUP AND HORSE CAMP

🏃 🐕 🚐 ⛺

Scenic rating: 7

on Rancheria Creek in Sierra National Forest

Badger Flat is a primitive site along Rancheria Creek at 8,200 feet elevation, about five miles east of Huntington Lake. It is a popular horse camp and a good jump-off spot for wilderness

CAMPING

trekkers. A trail that passes through camp provides two options: Head south for three miles to enter the Dinkey Lakes Wilderness, or head north for two miles to enter the Kaiser Wilderness.

Campsites, facilities: There is one group site for tents or RVs up to 35 feet (no hookups) that can accommodate up to 100 people. Picnic tables, fire grills, and food lockers are provided. Vault toilets and horse facilities are available. No drinking water is available. A store is nearby. Leashed pets are permitted.

Reservations, fees: Reservations are required at 877/444-6777 or www.recreation.gov ($9 reservation fee). Sites are $120 per night. Open June through October, weather permitting.

Directions: From Fresno, drive east on Highway 168 to Shaver Lake, then continue 21 miles to Huntington Lake and Kaiser Pass Road/Forest Road 80. Turn right and drive five miles to the campground on the right.

Contact: Sierra National Forest, High Sierra Ranger District, 559/855-5355, www.fs.fed.us; California Land Management, 559/893-2111.

30 HIDDEN VIEW

Scenic rating: 5

north of Fresno on Hensley Lake

Hensley Lake is popular with water-skiers and personal watercraft users in spring and summer, and it has good prospects for bass fishing as well. Hensley covers 1,500 surface acres with 24 miles of shoreline and, as long as water levels are maintained, makes for a wonderful water playland. Swimming is good, with the best spot at Buck Ridge on the east side of the lake, where there are picnic tables and trees for shade. The reservoir was created by a dam on the Fresno River. A nature trail is also here. The elevation is 540 feet.

Campsites, facilities: There are 55 sites for tents or RVs of any length, some with electric hookups (30 amps), and two group sites for

25–100 people. Picnic tables and fire grills are provided. Restrooms with flush toilets and showers, drinking water, dump station, playground, and boat ramp are available. Some facilities are wheelchair accessible. Leashed pets are permitted.

Reservations, fees: Reservations are accepted at 877/444-6777 or www.recreation.gov ($9 reservation fee). Sites are $14–22 per night, $65 per night for group sites. Boat launching is free for campers. Open year-round.

Directions: From Madera, drive northeast on Highway 145 for about six miles to County Road 400. Bear left on County Road 400 and drive to County Road 603 below the dam. Turn left and drive about two miles on County Road 603 to County Road 407. Turn right on County Road 407 and drive 0.5 mile to the campground.

Contact: U.S. Army Corps of Engineers, Sacramento District, Hensley Lake, 559/673-5151.

31 SMALLEY COVE

Scenic rating: 7

on Kerckhoff Reservoir near Madera

Kerckhoff Reservoir can get so hot that it might seem you could fry an egg on the rocks. Campers should be certain to have some kind of tarp they can set up as a sun screen. The lake is small and remote, and the use of boat motors more than five horsepower is prohibited. Most campers bring rafts or canoes, and there is a good swimming beach near the picnic area and campground. Fishing is not so good here. The elevation is 1,000 feet.

Campsites, facilities: There are five sites for tents or RVs up to 30 feet (no hookups). Picnic tables and fire grills are provided. Drinking water and vault toilets are available. Five group picnic sites are available. You can buy supplies in Auberry. Some facilities are wheelchair-accessible. Leashed pets are permitted.

Reservations, fees: Reservations are not

accepted. Sites are $14 per night, $3 per night for each additional vehicle, $7 per night for additional RV, $1 per pet per night. Open year-round.

Directions: From Fresno, take Highway 41 north for three miles to the exit for Highway 168 east. Take that exit and drive east on Highway 168 for about 22 miles to Auberry Road. Turn left (north) and drive 2.8 miles to Powerhouse Road. Turn left and drive 8.5 miles to the campground.

Contact: PG&E Land Services, 916/386-5164, www.pge.com/recreation.

32 YEH-GUB-WEH-TUH CAMPGROUND
🏃 ⛵ 🐕 ♿ ⛺

Scenic rating: 8

on the San Joaquin River

Not many folks know about this spot. It's a primitive setting, but it has some bonuses. For one thing, there's access to the San Joaquin River if you drive to the fishing access trailhead at the end of the road. From there, you get great views of the San Joaquin River Gorge. The camp is a trailhead for two excellent hiking and equestrian trails. Note that the terrain is steep and can be difficult to traverse. Also, this area has poison oak and rattlesnakes. And one more thing: It can get very hot here in summer. Are we having fun yet? The setting is primarily oaks, gray pine, and chaparral. Beautiful wildflower displays are highlights in the late winter and spring.

Campsites, facilities: There are six walk-in sites for tents only, including two double sites and one triple site for up to 24 people. Drinking water and vault toilets are available. Bring your own firewood. Supplies are available in Auberry. Some facilities are wheelchair-accessible. Leashed pets are permitted.

Reservations, fees: Reservations are not accepted. There is no fee for camping, but donations are accepted. Open year-round.

Directions: From Fresno, take Highway 41 north for three miles to the exit for Highway 168 east. Take that exit and drive east on Highway 168 for about 22 miles to Auberry Road. Turn left and drive 2.8 miles to Powerhouse Road. Turn left and drive two miles to Smalley Road (signed "Smalley Road and San Joaquin River Gorge Management Area"). Turn left and drive four miles to the campground on the right.

Contact: San Joaquin River Gorge Management Area, 559/855-3492; Bureau of Land Management, Bakersfield Field Office, 661/391-6000, www.blm.gov/ca.

33 AHOLUL GROUP CAMPGROUND
🏃 ⛵ 🐕 ♿ ⛺

Scenic rating: 8

on the San Joaquin River

Aholul is located near Yeh-gub-weh-tuh Campground, and is the group site option. We have no idea how you pronounce Aholul or Yeh-gub-weh-tuh, and the kind fellow at BLM refused to try. Heh, heh.

Campsites, facilities: There is one group site for tents only that can accommodate up to 250 people. A large paved parking lot can accommodate RVs and large trailers. Stock water and vault toilets are available. Bring your own drinking water and firewood. Horse corrals are available and are very popular; call 559/855-3492 for availability. Supplies are available in Auberry. Some facilities are wheelchair-accessible. Leashed pets are permitted.

Reservations, fees: Reservations are required at 661/391-6120. There is no fee for camping, but donations are accepted. Open year-round.

Directions: From Fresno, take Highway 41 north for three miles to the exit for Highway 168 east. Take that exit and drive east on Highway 168 for about 22 miles to Auberry Road. Turn left and drive 2.8 miles to

Powerhouse Road. Turn left and drive two miles to Smalley Road (signed "Smalley Road and San Joaquin River Gorge Management Area"). Turn left and drive four miles to the campground on the right.

Contact: San Joaquin River Gorge Management Area, 559/855-3492; Bureau of Land Management, Bakersfield Field Office, 661/391-6000, www.blm.gov/ca, www.blm.gov/ca.

34 CAMP EDISON

Scenic rating: 8

on Shaver Lake

Camp Edison is the best camp at Shaver Lake, set on a peninsula along the lake's western shore, with a boat ramp and marina. The lake is at an elevation of 5,370 feet in the Sierra, a pretty area that has become popular for its calm, warm days and cool water. Boat rentals and bait and tackle are available at the marina. Newcomers with youngsters will discover that the best area for swimming and playing in the water is on the east side of the lake. Though more distant, this part of the lake offers sandy beaches rather than rocky drop-offs.

Campsites, facilities: There are 252 sites for RVs or tents; some sites have full or partial hookups (20, 30, and 50 amps). During the summer season, six tent trailers also are available. Picnic tables, fire rings, and barbecues are provided. Restrooms with flush toilets and pay showers, drinking water, cable TV, Wi-Fi, general store, dump station, coin laundry, marina, boat ramp, and horseback-riding facilities are available. Some facilities are wheelchair-accessible. Leashed pets are permitted.

Reservations, fees: Reservations are required and must be made by fax or mail. Standard sites are $25 per night, preferred sites are $32 per night, paved sites are $33 per night, RV sites with full hookups are $38 per night, lakeside sites are $39 per night, premium front sites are $60 per night, $7.50–18 per night for each additional vehicle, $4 per person per night for more than two people, $6 per day for boat launching, $5 per pet per night. Tent trailers are $75 per night. Group rates are available. Open year-round with limited winter services.

Directions: From Fresno, take the exit for Highway 41 north and drive north on Highway 41 to the exit for Highway 180 east. Take that exit and drive east on Highway 180 to Highway 168 east. Take that exit and drive east on Highway 168 to the town of Shaver Lake. Continue one mile on Highway 168 to the campground entrance road on the right. Turn right and drive to the campground on the west shore of Shaver Lake.

Contact: Camp Edison, P.O. Box 600, 42696 Tollhouse Road, Shaver Lake, CA 93664; Southern California Edison, 559/841-3134, www.sce.com/campedison.

35 DORABELLE

Scenic rating: 7

on Shaver Lake in Sierra National Forest

This is one of the few Forest Service camps in the state that is set up more for RVers than for tenters. The camp is along a long cove at the southwest corner of the lake, well protected from winds out of the northwest. Several hiking trails are available here. Shaver Lake is a popular lake for vacationers, and waterskiing and wakeboarding are extremely popular. It is well stocked with trout and kokanee salmon. Boat rentals and bait and tackle are available at the nearby marina. The elevation is 5,400 feet.

Campsites, facilities: There are 68 sites for tents or RVs up to 40 feet (no hookups). Picnic tables and fire grills are provided. Drinking water and vault toilets are available. A store is nearby. Leashed pets are permitted.

Reservations, fees: Reservations are accepted

CAMPING

at 877/444-6777 or www.recreation.gov ($9 reservation fee). Sites are $20 per night, $5 per night for each additional vehicle. Open May through September, weather permitting.

Directions: From Fresno, drive east on Highway 168 to Dorabelle Road (on the right just as you enter the town of Shaver Lake). Turn right on Dorabelle Road and drive one mile to the campground at the southwest end of Shaver Lake.

Contact: Sierra National Forest, High Sierra Ranger District, 559/855-5355, www.fs.fed. us; California Land Management, 559/893-2111.

36 SWANSON MEADOW

Scenic rating: 4

near Shaver Lake in Sierra National Forest

This is the smallest and most primitive of the camps near Shaver Lake; it is used primarily as an overflow area if lakeside camps are full. It is about two miles south of Shaver Lake at an elevation of 5,600 feet.

Campsites, facilities: There are eight sites for tents or RVs up to 25 feet (no hookups). Picnic tables and fire grills are provided. Vault toilets are available. No drinking water is available. A store is nearby. Leashed pets are permitted.

Reservations, fees: Reservations are not accepted. Single sites are $16 per night, double sites are $32 per night, $5 per night for each additional vehicle. Open May through October, weather permitting.

Directions: From Fresno, drive east on Highway 168 to Dinkey Creek Road (on the right just as you enter the town of Shaver Lake). Turn right and drive three miles to the campground entrance road on the left. Turn left and drive a short distance to the campground.

Contact: Sierra National Forest, High Sierra Ranger District, 559/855-5355, www.fs.fed.us; California Land Management, 559/893-2111.

37 DINKEY CREEK AND GROUP CAMP

Scenic rating: 7

in Sierra National Forest

This is a huge Forest Service camp set along Dinkey Creek at 5,700 feet elevation, well in the interior of Sierra National Forest. It is a popular camp for anglers who take the trail and hike upstream along the creek for small-trout fishing in a pristine setting. Backpackers occasionally lay over here before driving on to the Dinkey Lakes Parking Area, for hikes to Mystery Lake, Swede Lake, South Lake, and others in the nearby Dinkey Lakes Wilderness.

Campsites, facilities: There are 128 sites for tents or RVs up to 35 feet (no hookups), and one group site for up to 50 people. Picnic tables and fire grills are provided. Drinking water, flush and vault toilets, interpretive programs and a camp host are available. Horseback-riding facilities are nearby. You can buy supplies in Dinkey Creek. Some facilities are wheelchair-accessible. Leashed pets are permitted.

Reservations, fees: Reservations are required at 877/444-6777 or www.recreation.gov ($9 reservation fee). Sites are $23 per night, $5 per night for each additional vehicle, $165 per night for the group site. Open May through September, weather permitting.

Directions: From Fresno, drive east on Highway 168 to Dinkey Creek Road (on the right just as you enter the town of Shaver Lake). Turn right and drive 13 miles to the campground. A map of Sierra National Forest is advised.

Contact: Sierra National Forest, High Sierra Ranger District, 559/855-5355, www.fs.fed.us; California Land Management, 559/893-2111.

38 GIGANTEA

Scenic rating: 7

on Dinkey Creek in Sierra National Forest

This primitive campground is set along Dinkey Creek adjacent to the McKinley Grove Botanical Area, which features a little-known grove of giant sequoias. The campground is set on a short loop spur road, and day visitors are better off stopping at the McKinley Grove Picnic Area. The elevation is 6,400 feet.

Campsites, facilities: There are 10 sites for tents or RVs up to 35 feet (no hookups). Picnic tables and fire grills are provided. Vault toilets are available. No drinking water is available. You can buy supplies in Dinkey Creek. Leashed pets are permitted.

Reservations, fees: Reservations are not accepted. Sites are $16 per night, $5 per night for each additional vehicle. Open May through October, weather permitting.

Directions: From Fresno, drive east on Highway 168 to Dinkey Creek Road (on the right just as you enter the town of Shaver Lake). Turn right and drive 13 miles to McKinley Grove Road/Forest Road 40. Turn right and drive 6.5 miles to the campground.

Contact: Sierra National Forest, High Sierra Ranger District, 559/855-5355, www.fs.fed.us; California Land Management, 559/893-2111.

39 BUCK MEADOW

Scenic rating: 7

on Deer Creek in Sierra National Forest

This is one of the three little-known, primitive camps in the area. It's set at 6,800 feet elevation along Deer Creek, about seven miles from Wishon Reservoir, a more popular destination.

Campsites, facilities: There are 10 sites for tents or RVs up to 35 feet (no hookups). Picnic tables and fire grills are provided. Vault toilets are available. No drinking water is available. Garbage must be packed out. Some facilities are wheelchair-accessible. Leashed pets are permitted.

Reservations, fees: Reservations are not accepted. Sites are $16 per night, $5 per night for each additional vehicle. Open May through October, weather permitting.

Directions: From Fresno, drive east on Highway 168 to Dinkey Creek Road (on the right just as you enter the town of Shaver Lake). Turn right and drive 13 miles to McKinley Grove Road (Forest Road 40). Turn right and drive eight miles to the campground.

Contact: Sierra National Forest, High Sierra Ranger District, 559/855-5355, www.fs.fed.us; California Land Management, 559/893-2111.

40 MILLERTON LAKE STATE RECREATION AREA

Scenic rating: 6

near Madera

As the temperature gauge goes up in the summer, the value of Millerton Lake increases at the same rate. The lake is set at 578 feet in the foothills of the San Joaquin Valley, and the water is like gold here. The campground and recreation area are set on a peninsula along the north shore of the lake; there are sandy beach areas on both sides of the lake with boat ramps available near the campgrounds. It's a big lake, with 43 miles of shoreline, from a narrow lake inlet extending to an expansive main lake body. The irony at Millerton is that when the lake is filled to the brim, the beaches are covered, so ideal conditions are actually when the lake level is down a bit, typically from early summer on. Fishing for bass can be good here in spring. Catfish are popular for shoreliners on summer evenings. Waterskiing is very popular in summer, of course. Anglers head upstream, water-skiers downstream. The lake's south side has a huge day-use area. During winter, boat tours are available to view bald eagles. A note of history: The original Millerton County Courthouse, built in 1867, is in the park.

Campsites, facilities: There are 148 sites, 26 with full hookups, for tents or RVs up to 36 feet, three boat-in sites, and two group sites for 45–75 people. Picnic tables and fire grills are provided. Drinking water, restrooms with flush toilets and coin showers, dump station, picnic areas, full-service marina, snack bar, boat rentals, and boat ramps are available. You can buy supplies in Friant. Some facilities are wheelchair-accessible. Leashed pets are permitted.

Reservations, fees: Reservations are accepted at 800/444-7275 or www.reserveamerica.com ($8 reservation fee). Drive-in sites are $30 per night, RV sites (hookups) are $40 per night, $8 per night for each additional vehicle, $11 for boat-in sites, $150–200 per night for group sites. Boat launching is $7 per day. Open year-round.

Directions: Drive on Highway 99 to Madera at the exit for Highway 145 East. Take that exit east and drive on Highway 145 for 22 miles (six miles past the intersection with Highway 41) to the park entrance on the right.

Contact: Millerton Lake State Recreation Area, 559/822-2332, www.parks.ca.gov.

41 JACKASS MEADOW

Scenic rating: 7

on Florence Lake in Sierra National Forest

Jackass Meadow is a pretty spot adjacent to Florence Lake, near the Upper San Joaquin River. There are good canoeing, rafting, and float-tubing possibilities, all high-Sierra style, and swimming is allowed. The boat speed limit is 15 mph. The elevation is 7,200 feet. The lake is remote and can be reached only after a long, circuitous drive on a narrow road with many blind turns. A trailhead at the lake offers access to the wilderness and the John Muir Trail. A hikers water taxi is available.

Campsites, facilities: There are 44 sites for tents or RVs up to 25 feet (no hookups). Picnic tables and fire grills are provided. Vault toilets are available, but there is no drinking water. A boat launch, fishing boat rentals, and wheelchair-accessible fishing pier are available nearby. Leashed pets are permitted.

Reservations, fees: Reservations are accepted at 877/444-6777 or www.recreation.gov ($9 reservation fee). Single sites are $18 per night, $36 per night for a double site, $5 per night for each additional vehicle. Open June through October, weather permitting.

Directions: From the town of Shaver Lake, drive east on Highway 168 for 21 miles to Kaiser Pass Road. Bear northeast on Kaiser Pass Road/Forest Road 80 (slow and curvy) to a junction (left goes to Mono Hot Springs and Lake Edison) with Florence Lake Road. Bear right at the junction and drive seven miles to the campground.

Contact: Sierra National Forest, High Sierra Ranger District, 559/855-5355, www.fs.fed.us; California Land Management, 559/893-2111.

42 TRAPPER SPRINGS

Scenic rating: 8

on Courtright Reservoir in Sierra National Forest

Trapper Springs is on the west shore of Courtright Reservoir, set at 8,200 feet elevation on the west slope of the Sierra. Courtright is a great destination, with excellent camping, boating, fishing, and hiking into the nearby John Muir Wilderness. A 15-mph speed limit makes the lake ideal for fishing, canoeing, and rafting. Swimming is allowed, but the water is very cold. The lake level can drop dramatically by late summer. A trailhead a mile north of camp by car heads around the north end of the lake to a fork; to the left it is routed into the Dinkey Lakes Wilderness, and to the right it is routed to the head of the lake, then follows Dusy Creek in a long climb into spectacular country in the John Muir Wilderness. There are two driving routes to this lake, one from Shaver Lake and the other from Pine Flat Reservoir; both are very long, slow, and twisty drives.

Campsites, facilities: There are 75 sites for tents or RVs up to 35 feet (no hookups). Picnic tables and fire grills are provided. Vault toilets are available, but there is no drinking water. A boat ramp is nearby. Some facilities are wheelchair-accessible. Leashed pets are permitted.

Reservations, fees: Reservations are not accepted. Sites are $24 per night, $9 per night for additional RV, $3 per night for each additional vehicle, $1 per pet per night. Open June through October.

Directions: From Fresno, drive east on Highway 168 to Dinkey Creek Road (on the right just as you enter the town of Shaver Lake). Turn right and drive 13 miles to McKinley Grove Road/Forest Road 40. Turn right and drive 14 miles to Courtright Road. Turn left (north) and drive 12 miles to the campground entrance road on the right.

Contact: Sierra National Forest, High Sierra Ranger District, 559/855-5355, www.fs.fed.us; PG&E Land Services, 916/386-5164, www.pge.com/recreation.

43 MARMOT ROCK WALK-IN
🏃 🏊 🎣 🚤 🐕 🚐 ⛺

Scenic rating: 8

on Courtright Reservoir in
Sierra National Forest

Courtright Reservoir is in the high country at 8,200 feet elevation. Marmot Rock Walk-In is set at the southern end of the lake, with a boat ramp nearby. This is a pretty Sierra lake that provides options for boaters and hikers. Trout fishing can also be good here. Boaters must observe a 15-mph speed limit, which makes for quiet water. There are two driving routes to this lake, one from Shaver Lake and

the other from Pine Flat Reservoir; both are very long, slow, and twisty drives.

Campsites, facilities: There are 15 sites for tents or small RVs; most sites are walk-in. Picnic tables and fire grills are provided. Vault toilets are available, but there is no drinking water. A boat ramp is nearby. Leashed pets are permitted.

Reservations, fees: Reservations are not accepted. Sites are $24 per night, $3 per night for each additional vehicle, $1 per pet per night. Open July through October.

Directions: From Fresno, drive east on Highway 168 to Dinkey Creek Road (on the right just as you enter the town of Shaver Lake). Turn right and drive 13 miles to McKinley Grove Road/Forest Road 40. Turn right and drive 14 miles to Courtright Road. Turn left (north) and drive 10 miles to the campground entrance road on the right (on the south shore of the lake). Park and walk a short distance to the campground.

Contact: PG&E Land Services, 916/386-5164, www.pge.com/recreation; Sierra National Forest, High Sierra Ranger District, 559/855-5355, www.fs.fed.us.

44 WISHON VILLAGE RV RESORT
🏃 🏊 🎣 🚤 🐕 🚐 ⛺

Scenic rating: 7

near Wishon Reservoir

This privately operated mountain park is set near the shore of Wishon Reservoir, about one mile from the dam. Trout stocks often make for good fishing in early summer, and anglers with boats love the 15-mph speed limit, which keeps personal watercraft off the water. Backpackers and hikers can find a great trailhead at the south end of the lake at Coolidge Meadow, where a trail awaits that is routed to the Woodchuck Creek drainage and numerous lakes in the John Muir Wilderness. The elevation is 6,772 feet.

Campsites, facilities: There are 97 sites with

full hookups (50 amps) for RVs up to 45 feet, and 26 sites for tents. A rental trailer is also available. Picnic tables and fire pits are provided. Restrooms with coin showers, drinking water, a general store, and Sunday church services are available. Coin laundry, ice, boat ramp, motorboat rentals, bait and tackle, boat slips, volleyball, horseshoes, and propane gas are nearby. Leashed pets are permitted.

Reservations, fees: Reservations are recommended. RV sites are $35 per night, tent sites are $25 per night, $3 per person per night for more than two people, $3 per pet per night. Weekly and monthly rates available. Open May through September.

Directions: From Fresno, drive east on Highway 168 to Dinkey Creek Road (on the right just as you enter the town of Shaver Lake). Turn right and drive 13 miles to McKinley Grove Road (Forest Road 40). Turn right and drive 15 miles to the park (66500 McKinley Grove Road/Forest Road 40).

Contact: Wishon Village RV Resort, 559/865-5361, www.wishonvillage.com.

45 LILY PAD

Scenic rating: 7

near Wishon Reservoir in
Sierra National Forest

This is the smallest of the three camps at Wishon Reservoir. It is set along the southwest shore at 6,500 feet elevation, about a mile from both the lake and a good boat ramp. A 15-mph speed limit ensures quiet water, making this an ideal destination for families with canoes or rafts. The conditions at this lake are similar to those at Courtright Reservoir. There are two driving routes to this lake, one from Shaver Lake and the other from Pine Flat Reservoir; both are very long, slow, and twisty drives.

Campsites, facilities: There are 11 sites for tents or RVs up to 35 feet (no hookups), and four hike-in sites. Picnic tables and fire grills

are provided. Vault toilets are available, but there is no drinking water. Groceries, boat rentals, boat ramp, and propane gas are nearby. Some facilities are wheelchair-accessible. Leashed pets are permitted.

Reservations, fees: Reservations are not accepted. Sites are $16 per night, $7 per night for additional RV, $3 per night for each additional vehicle, $1 per pet per night. Open May through October, weather permitting.

Directions: From Fresno, drive east on Highway 168 to Dinkey Creek Road (on the right just as you enter the town of Shaver Lake). Turn right and drive 13 miles to McKinley Grove Road (Forest Road 40). Turn right and drive 16 miles to the campground on the right.

Contact: Sierra National Forest, High Sierra Ranger District, 559/855-5355, www.fs.fed.us; PG&E Land Services, 916/386-5164, www.pge.com/recreation.

46 UPPER KINGS RIVER GROUP CAMP

Scenic rating: 8

on Wishon Reservoir

Wishon Reservoir is a great place for a camping trip. When the lake is full, which is not often enough, the place has great natural beauty, set at 6,400 feet elevation and surrounded by national forest. The fishing is fair enough on summer evenings, and a 15-mph speed limit keeps the lake quiet. Swimming is allowed, but the water is very cold. A side-trip option is hiking from the trailhead at Woodchuck Creek, which within the span of a one-day hike takes you into the John Muir Wilderness and past three lakes—Woodchuck, Chimney, and Marsh. There are two driving routes to this lake, one from Shaver Lake and the other from Pine Flat Reservoir; both are very long, slow, and twisty drives.

Campsites, facilities: There is a group site for tents or RVs up to 40 feet (no hookups) that can accommodate up to 50 people. Picnic tables and fire grills are provided. Drinking water and vault toilets are available. Leashed pets are permitted.

Reservations, fees: Reservations are required at 916/386-5164. Sites are $150 per night. Open June through early October, weather permitting.

Directions: From Fresno, drive east on Highway 168 to Dinkey Creek Road (on the right just as you enter the town of Shaver Lake). Turn right and drive 13 miles to McKinley Grove Road/Forest Road 40. Turn right and drive to the Wishon Dam. The campground is near the base of the dam.

Contact: PG&E Land Services, 916/386-5164, www.pge.com/recreation.

47 HORTON CREEK

Scenic rating: 7

near Bishop

This is a little-known, primitive BLM camp set along Horton Creek, northwest of Bishop. It can make a good base camp for hunters in the fall, with wild, rugged country to the west. The elevation is 4,975 feet.

Campsites, facilities: There are 53 sites for tents or RVs up to 30 feet (no hookups). Picnic tables and fire grills are provided. Pit toilets and garbage containers are available. No drinking water is available. Leashed pets are permitted.

Reservations, fees: Reservations are not accepted. Sites are $5 per night; LTVA season passes are available for $300. There is a 14-day stay limit. Open early May through October, weather permitting.

Directions: Drive on U.S. 395 to Sawmill Road (eight miles north of Bishop). Turn left (northwest, toward the Sierra) and drive a very short distance to Round Valley Road. Turn right and drive approximately five miles to the campground entrance on the left.

Contact: Bureau of Land Management, Bishop Field Office, 760/872-4881, www.blm.gov/ca.

48 BROWN'S MILLPOND CAMPGROUND

Scenic rating: 6

near Bishop

This privately operated camp is adjacent to the Millpond Recreation Area, which offers ball fields, playgrounds, and a swimming lake. No powerboats are allowed. There are opportunities for sailing, archery, tennis, horseshoe games, and fishing.

Campsites, facilities: There are 75 sites for tents or RVs of any length; some sites have partial hookups (30 amps). Picnic tables and fire grills are provided. Restrooms with flush toilets and coin showers, drinking water, and coin laundry are available. A limit of one vehicle per site is enforced. Leashed pets are permitted.

Reservations, fees: Reservations are accepted. Sites are $20–25 per vehicle per night. Open March through October.

Directions: Drive on U.S. 395 to a road signed "Millpond/County Park" (seven miles north of Bishop). Turn southwest (toward the Sierra) at that road (Ed Powers Road) and drive 0.2 mile to Sawmill Road. Turn right and drive 0.8 mile to Millpond Road. Turn left and drive a short distance to the campground.

Contact: Brown's Millpond Campground, 760/873-5342 or 760/937-6775, www.brownscampgrounds.com/millpond.html.

49 BROWN'S TOWN

Scenic rating: 5

near Bishop

This privately operated campground is one of several in the vicinity of Bishop. It's all shade and grass, and it's next to the golf course.

Campsites, facilities: There are 106 sites with no hookups for tents or RVs of any length and 44 sites with partial hookups (30 amps) for tents or RVs. Some sites are pull-through. Picnic tables are provided, and fire grills are provided at most sites. Restrooms with flush toilets and coin showers, drinking water, cable TV at 10 sites, coin laundry, dump station, museum, convenience store, and snack bar are available. Leashed pets are permitted.

Reservations, fees: Reservations are accepted. RV sites are $25–28 per night, tent sites are $20 per night, $1 per person per night for more than two people. One-vehicle limit per site. Fourteen-day stay limit per season. Some credit cards accepted. Open March through Thanksgiving, weather permitting.

Directions: Drive on U.S. 395 to Schober Lane (one mile south of Bishop) and the campground entrance. Turn northwest (toward the Sierra) and into the campground.

Contact: Brown's Town, 760/873-8522, www. brownscampgrounds.com/browns.html.

50 BITTERBRUSH

Scenic rating: 7

near Bishop in the Inyo National Forest

Bitterbrush opened in 2007 and is situated along Bishop Creek with piñon pines and sagebrush providing the scenery. In the fall, the aspens are spectacular in the canyon between here and beautiful Lake Sabrina. The elevation is 7,350 feet.

Campsites, facilities: There are 35 sites for tents or RVs to 40 feet (no hookups). Picnic tables, bear-proof lockers, and fire rings are provided. Drinking water (seasonal), vault toilets, and a dump station are available. Some facilities are wheelchair-accessible. Leashed pets are permitted.

Reservations, fees: Reservations are not accepted. Sites are $21 per night; free when water becomes unavailable. There is a maximum 14-day limit. Open year-round, weather permitting.

Directions: From Bishop drive west on Highway 168 for nine miles to the campground.

Contact: Inyo National Forest, White Mountain Ranger District, 760/873-2500, www. fs.fed.us.

51 FORKS

Scenic rating: 7

near South Lake in Inyo National Forest

After a visit here, it's no mystery how the Forest Service named this camp. It is at the fork in the road, which gives you two options: You can turn south on South Lake Road and drive along the South Fork of Bishop Creek up to pretty South Lake, or you can keep driving on Highway 168 to another beautiful lake, Lake Sabrina, where hikers will find a trailhead that offers access to the John Muir Wilderness. The elevation is 7,800 feet.

Campsites, facilities: There are 21 sites for RVs up to 30 feet (no hookups). Picnic tables and fire grills are provided. Drinking water and flush toilets are available. Supplies are available in Bishop. Leashed pets are permitted.

Reservations, fees: Reservations are not accepted. Sites are $21 per night. Open late April through October, weather permitting.

Directions: Drive on U.S. 395 to Bishop and Highway 168. Turn west (toward the Sierra) on Highway 168 and drive 14 miles to South Lake Road. Turn left and drive 0.25 mile to the campground entrance on the right.

Contact: Inyo National Forest, White Mountain Ranger District, 760/873-2500, www.fs.fed. us; Rainbow Pack Outfitters, 760/873-8877.

52 BIG TREES

Scenic rating: 8

on Bishop Creek in Inyo National Forest

This is a small Forest Service camp on Bishop Creek at 7,500 feet elevation. This section of

the stream is stocked with small trout by the Department of Fish and Game. Both South Lake and Lake Sabrina are about 10 miles away.
Campsites, facilities: There are 16 sites for tents or RVs up to 30 feet (no hookups). Picnic tables and fire grills are provided. Drinking water and flush toilets are available. A dump station is two miles away at Four Jeffrey. Horseback-riding facilities are approximately seven miles away. Supplies are available in Bishop. Leashed pets are permitted.
Reservations, fees: Reservations are not accepted. Sites are $21 per night. Open late April through October, weather permitting.
Directions: Drive on U.S. 395 to Bishop and Highway 168. Turn west (toward the Sierra) on Highway 168 and drive 11 miles to the campground access road on the left. Turn left and drive two miles on a dirt road to the campground.
Contact: Inyo National Forest, White Mountain Ranger District, 760/873-2500, www.fs.fed. us; Rainbow Pack Outfitters, 760/873-8877.

53 BISHOP PARK AND GROUP
🚶 🛶 🎣 ♿ 🚐 ⛺

Scenic rating: 6
near Lake Sabrina in Inyo National Forest

Bishop Park Camp is one in a series of camps along Bishop Creek. This one is set just behind the summer community of Aspendell. It is about two miles from Lake Sabrina, an ideal day trip or jump-off spot for a backpacking expedition into the John Muir Wilderness. The elevation is 8,400 feet.
Campsites, facilities: There are 21 sites for tents or RVs up to 22 feet (no hookups), and a group tent site for up to 25 people. Picnic tables, fire grills, and food lockers are provided. Drinking water and flush toilets are available. Horseback-riding facilities are nearby. Supplies are available in Bishop. Some facilities are wheelchair-accessible. Leashed pets are permitted.

Reservations, fees: Reservations are not accepted for the family sites, but are required for the group site at 877/444-6777 or www.recreation. gov ($9 reservation fee). Sites are $21 per night, $65 per night for group site. Open mid-May through mid-October, weather permitting.
Directions: Drive on U.S. 395 to Bishop and Highway 168. Turn west (toward the Sierra) on Highway 168 and drive 15 miles to the campground.
Contact: Inyo National Forest, White Mountain Ranger District, 760/873-2500, www.fs.fed. us; Rainbow Pack Outfitters, 760/873-8877; campground management, 760/872-7018.

54 INTAKE AND INTAKE WALK-IN
🚶 🛶 🎣 🐕 🚐 ⛺

Scenic rating: 7
on Sabrina Creek in Inyo National Forest

This small camp, set at 8,200 feet elevation at a tiny reservoir on Bishop Creek, is about three miles from Lake Sabrina where a trailhead leads into the John Muir Wilderness. Nearby North Lake and South Lake provide side-trip options. All three are beautiful alpine lakes.
Campsites, facilities: There are eight sites for tents or RVs up to 40 feet (no hookups), and five walk-in tent sites. Picnic tables, food lockers, and fire grills are provided. Drinking water and flush toilets are available. A dump station is available 1.5 miles away at Four Jeffrey. Supplies are available in Bishop. Leashed pets are permitted.
Reservations, fees: Reservations are not accepted. Sites are $21 per night. The walk-in sites are open year-round, weather permitting. Drive-in sites are open April through October, weather permitting.
Directions: Drive on U.S. 395 to Bishop and Highway 168. Turn west (toward the Sierra) on Highway 168 and drive 14.5 miles to the campground entrance.

CAMPING

Contact: Inyo National Forest, White Mountain Ranger District, 760/873-2500, www.fs.fed.us.

55 FOUR JEFFREY

Scenic rating: 8

near South Lake in Inyo National Forest

The camp is set on the South Fork of Bishop Creek at 8,100 feet elevation, about four miles from South Lake. If you can arrange a trip in the fall, make sure you visit this camp. The fall colors are spectacular, with the aspen trees exploding in yellows and oranges. It is also the last camp on South Lake Road to be closed in the fall, and though nights are cold, it is well worth the trip. This is by far the largest of the Forest Service camps in the vicinity. There are three lakes in the area: North Lake, Lake Sabrina, and South Lake. South Lake is stocked with trout and has a 5-mph speed limit.

Campsites, facilities: There are 106 sites for tents or RVs up to 30 feet (no hookups). Picnic tables, food lockers, and fire grills are provided. Drinking water, flush toilets, and a dump station are available. Horseback-riding facilities are available nearby. A café, a small store, and fishing-boat rentals are available at South Lake. Supplies are available in Bishop. Some facilities are wheelchair-accessible. Leashed pets are permitted.

Reservations, fees: Reservations are accepted at 877/444-6777 or www.recreation.gov ($9 reservation fee). Sites are $21 per night. Open mid-April through October, weather permitting.

Directions: Drive on U.S. 395 to Bishop and Highway 168. Turn west (toward the Sierra) on Highway 168 and drive 14 miles to South Lake Road. Turn left and drive 0.5 mile to the campground.

Contact: Inyo National Forest, White Mountain Ranger District, 760/873-2500, www.fs.fed.us; Rainbow Pack Outfitters, 760/873-8877.

56 CREEKSIDE RV PARK

Scenic rating: 7

on the South Fork of Bishop Creek

This privately operated park in the high country is set up primarily for RVs. A lot of folks are surprised to find it here. The South Fork of Bishop Creek runs through the park. A bonus is a fishing pond stocked with Alpers trout. North, Sabrina, and South Lakes are in the area. The elevation is 8,300 feet.

Campsites, facilities: There are 45 sites with full or partial hookups (20 and 30 amps) for RVs up to 35 feet, and four sites for tents. Fourteen rental trailers are also available. Restrooms with flush toilets and coin showers, drinking water, convenience store, propane, horseshoes, and fish-cleaning facilities are available. Leashed pets are permitted.

Reservations, fees: Reservations are accepted. RV sites are $43 per night, tent sites are $32 per night, $1 per person per night for more than two people, $5 per night for each additional vehicle, $5 per pet per night. Open May through October. Some credit cards accepted.

Directions: Drive on U.S. 395 to Bishop and Highway 168. Turn west (toward the Sierra) on Highway 168 and drive 14 miles to South Lake Road. Turn left and drive two miles to the campground entrance on the left (1949 South Lake Road).

Contact: Creekside RV Park, 760/873-4483, www.bishopcreeksidervpark.com.

57 NORTH LAKE

Scenic rating: 8

on Bishop Creek near North Lake in Inyo National Forest

North Lake is a beautiful Sierra lake set at an elevation of 9,500 feet, with good trout fishing much of the season and surrounded by beautiful aspens. No motors are allowed on this 13-acre lake. The camp is set on the North Fork of Bishop Creek near North Lake and close to a trailhead that offers access to numerous lakes in the John Muir Wilderness and eventually connects with the Pacific Crest Trail. There is also an outstanding trailhead that leads to several small alpine lakes in the nearby John Muir Wilderness for day hikes, or all the way up to Bishop Pass and Dusy Basin.

Campsites, facilities: There are 11 sites for tents only. Picnic tables and fire grills are provided. Drinking water and vault toilets are available. Horseback-riding facilities are available nearby. Supplies are available in Bishop. Leashed pets are permitted.

Reservations, fees: Reservations are not accepted. Sites are $21 per night. Open early June through mid-September, weather permitting.

Directions: Drive on U.S. 395 to Bishop and Highway 168. Turn west (toward the Sierra) on Highway 168 and drive 17 miles to Forest Road 8S02 (signed "North Lake"). Turn right (north) on Forest Road 8S02 and drive two miles to the campground.

Contact: Inyo National Forest, White Mountain Ranger District, 760/873-2500, www.fs.fed. us; Bishop Pack Outfitters, 760/873-4785.

58 SABRINA

Scenic rating: 8

near Lake Sabrina in Inyo National Forest

BEST (

You get the best of both worlds at this camp. It is set at 9,000 feet elevation on Bishop Creek, just 0.5 mile from 200-acre Lake Sabrina, one of the prettiest alpine lakes in California that you can reach by car. A 10-mph boat speed limit is in effect. Sabrina is stocked with trout, including some big Alpers trout. Trails nearby are routed into the high country of the John Muir Wilderness. Take your pick. Whatever your choice, it's a good one. By the way, Sabrina is pronounced "Sa-bry-na," not "Sa-bree-na."

Campsites, facilities: There are 18 sites for tents or RVs up to 30 feet (no hookups). Picnic tables and fire grills are provided. Drinking water and pit toilets are available. A boat ramp and boat rentals are nearby. Supplies

© US FOREST SERVICE, INYO NATIONAL FOREST

beautiful Lake Sabrina

CAMPING

are available in Bishop. Leashed pets are permitted.

Reservations, fees: Reservations are not accepted. Sites are $21 per night. Open mid-May through mid-September, weather permitting.

Directions: Drive on U.S. 395 to Bishop and Highway 168. Turn west (toward the Sierra) on Highway 168 and drive 17 miles (signed "Lake Sabrina" at a fork) to the campground.

Contact: Inyo National Forest, White Mountain Ranger District, 760/873-2500, www.fs.fed.us; Bishop Pack Outfitters, 760/873-4785.

59 WILLOW

Scenic rating: 8

on Bishop Creek in Inyo National Forest

This is one in a series of pretty Forest Service camps set along the south fork of Bishop Creek. Willow is located near Mountain Glen (see listing in this chapter) at an elevation of 9,000 feet. Primitive and beautiful, this is a favorite. Just up the road is the trailhead to the Chocolate Lakes and Bishop Pass, as well as low-speed boating and fishing at Lake Sabrina and South Lake. A good spot to set up shop.

Campsites, facilities: There are 10 sites for tents or RVs to 25 feet (no hookups). Picnic tables, bear-proof, lockers, and fire rings are provided. Pit toilets are available. There is no drinking water. A nearby spring has water that looks good but must be treated before use. Leashed pets are permitted.

Reservations, fees: Reservations are not accepted. Sites are $20 per night. There is a 7-day stay limit. Open late May to late September.

Directions: From Bishop drive west 13 miles on Highway 168 to South Lake Road. Turn left and drive 5.5 miles to the campground.

Contact: Inyo National Forest, White Mountain Ranger District, 760/873-2500, www.fs.fed.us.

60 MOUNTAIN GLEN

Scenic rating: 8

on Bishop Creek in Inyo National Forest

Mountain Glen rests along the south fork of Bishop Creek. Jeffrey pines, piñon pines, aspen, and sagebrush green the campground, but come in mid-September when the aspens explode in a riot of colors, bringing the canyon to life. You can often have this place to yourself then. Little Bishop Creek is nearby and is stocked with small trout. The elevation is 8,200 feet.

Campsites, facilities: There are five sites for tents or small RVs (no hookups). Picnic tables, bear-proof lockers, and fire rings are provided. Vault toilets are available, but there is no drinking water. Leashed pets are permitted.

Reservations, fees: Reservations are not accepted. Sites are $20 per night. There is a maximum 7-day limit. Open late May to late September.

Directions: From Bishop drive west 13 miles on Highway 168 to South Lake Road. Turn left and drive three miles to the campground.

Contact: Inyo National Forest, White Mountain Ranger District, 760/873-2500, www.fs.fed.us.

61 KEOUGH'S HOT SPRINGS

Scenic rating: 5

in Owens Valley on U.S. 305

This private facility is the site of the Eastern Sierra's largest natural hot springs pool. The landscape is the stark high desert, but makes for sensational sunsets with colors sometimes refracting across what seems an infinite sky. With the public springs at Hot Creek now off limits, Keough's is a very good choice.

Campsites, facilities: There are 10 tent sites and 10 sites for RVs up to 40 feet (partial

30-amp hookups), plus two furnished tent cabins. Picnic tables are provided, and campers can bring their own above-ground fire pit. Drinking water, flush toilets, a snack bar, and a gift shop are available. Leashed pets are permitted.

Reservations, fees: Reservations are accepted. Sites are $20–25 per night, $1 per person per night for more than two people. There is a maximum 14-day limit. Open year round, weather permitting.

Directions: From Bishop drive south on Highway 395 for seven miles to Keough's Hot Springs Road. Turn right on Keough's Hot Springs Road and drive one mile to the resort.

Contact: Keough's Hot Springs, 760/872-4670, www.keoughshotsprings.com.

62 BAKER CREEK CAMPGROUND

Scenic rating: 4

near Big Pine

Because this is a county-operated RV park, it is often overlooked by campers who consider only camps on reservations systems. That makes this a good option for cruisers touring the eastern Sierra on U.S. 395. It's ideal for a quick overnighter, with easy access from Big Pine. The camp is set along Baker Creek at 4,000 feet elevation in the high plateau country of the eastern Sierra. An option is fair trout fishing during the evening bite on the creek.

Campsites, facilities: There are 70 sites for tents or RVs up to 40 feet (no hookups). Picnic tables and fire grills are provided. Vault toilets and hand-pumped well water are available. You can buy supplies about 1.5 miles away in Big Pine. Leashed pets are permitted.

Reservations, fees: Reservations are not accepted. Sites are $10 per vehicle per night. Open year-round, weather permitting.

Directions: Drive on U.S. 395 to Big Pine and Baker Creek Road. Turn west (toward the Sierra) on Baker Creek Road and drive a mile to the campground.

Contact: Inyo County Parks Department, 760/873-5577, www.inyocountycamping.com.

63 GLACIER VIEW

Scenic rating: 4

near Big Pine

This is one of two county camps near the town of Big Pine, providing U.S. 395 cruisers with two options. The camp is set along the Big Pine Canal at 3,900 feet elevation. It is owned by the county but operated by a concessionaire, Brown's, which runs five small campgrounds in the area: Glacier View, Keough Hot Springs, Millpond, Brown's Owens River, and Brown's Town.

Campsites, facilities: There are 40 sites for tents or RVs of any length; some sites have partial hookups (30 amps) and/or are pull-through. Picnic tables and fire grills are provided. Restrooms with flush toilets and coin showers and drinking water are available. Supplies are available in Big Pine. Leashed pets are permitted.

Reservations, fees: Reservations are not accepted. Tent sites are $12 per night, RV sites (hookups) are $17 per night. Open year-round.

Directions: Drive on U.S. 395 to the park entrance (0.5 mile north of Big Pine) on the southeast side of the road. Turn east (away from the Sierra) and enter the park.

Contact: Inyo County Parks Department, 760/873-5577, www.inyocountycamping.com.

CAMPING

64 PALISADE GLACIER AND CLYDE GLACIER GROUP CAMP

Scenic rating: 8

on Big Pine Creek in Inyo National Forest

This is a trailhead camp set at 7,600 feet elevation, most popular for groups planning to rock-climb the Palisades. This climbing trip is for experienced mountaineers only; it's a dangerous expedition where risk of life can be included in the bargain. Safer options include exploring the surrounding John Muir Wilderness.

Campsites, facilities: There are two group sites for tents or RVs up to 30 feet (no hookups) that can accommodate up to 20 and 25 people respectively. Picnic tables and fire grills are provided. Drinking water and vault toilets are available. Some facilities are wheelchair-accessible. Leashed pets are permitted.

Reservations, fees: Reservations are required at 877/444-6777 or www.recreation.gov ($9 reservation fee). Sites are $65 per night. Open mid-May through mid-October.

Directions: Drive on U.S. 395 to Big Pine and Crocker Street/Glacier Lodge Road. Turn west (toward the Sierra) and drive nine miles (it becomes Glacier Lodge Road) to the campground on the left.

Contact: Inyo National Forest, White Mountain Ranger District, 760/873-2500, www. fs.fed.us.

65 BIG PINE CREEK

Scenic rating: 8

in Inyo National Forest

This is another good spot for backpackers to launch a multiday trip. The camp is set along Big Pine Creek at 7,700 feet elevation, with trails near the camp that are routed to the numerous lakes in the high country of the John Muir Wilderness.

Campsites, facilities: There are 30 sites for tents or RVs up to 22 feet (no hookups). Picnic tables, food lockers, and fire grills are provided. Drinking water and vault toilets are available. Some facilities are wheelchair-accessible. Leashed pets are permitted.

Reservations, fees: Reservations are accepted at 877/444-6777 or www.recreation.gov ($9 reservation fee). Sites are $20 per night. Open early May through October, weather permitting.

Directions: Drive on U.S. 395 to Big Pine and Crocker Street/Glacier Lodge Road. Turn west (toward the Sierra) and drive nine miles (it becomes Glacier Lodge Road) to the campground.

Contact: Inyo National Forest, White Mountain Ranger District, 760/873-2500, www. fs.fed.us.

66 UPPER SAGE FLAT

Scenic rating: 8

on Big Pine Creek in Inyo National Forest

This is one in a series of Forest Service camps in the area set up primarily for backpackers taking off on wilderness expeditions. Several trails are available nearby that lead into the John Muir Wilderness. The best of these is routed west past several lakes to the base of the Palisades, and beyond to John Muir Trail. Even starting at 7,600 feet, expect a steep climb.

Campsites, facilities: There are 21 sites for tents or RVs up to 25 feet (no hookups). Picnic tables, food lockers, and fire grills are provided. Drinking water and vault toilets are available. Some facilities are wheelchair-accessible. Leashed pets are permitted.

Reservations, fees: Reservations are accepted at 877/444-6777 or www.recreation.gov ($9 reservation fee). Sites are $20 per night. Open late April through mid-September, weather permitting.

Directions: Drive on U.S. 395 to Big Pine and Crocker Street/Glacier Lodge Road. Turn west (toward the Sierra) and drive 8.5 miles (it becomes Glacier Lodge Road) to the campground.

Contact: Inyo National Forest, White Mountain Ranger District, 760/873-2500, www. fs.fed.us.

67 SAGE FLAT

Scenic rating: 8

on Big Pine Creek near Big Pine in Inyo National Forest

This camp, like the others in the immediate vicinity, is set up primarily for backpackers who are getting ready to head out on multiday expeditions into the nearby John Muir Wilderness. The trail is routed west past several lakes to the base of the Palisades, and beyond to John Muir Trail. Your hike from here will begin with a steep climb from the trailhead at 7,600 feet elevation. The camp is set along Big Pine Creek, which is stocked with small trout.

Campsites, facilities: There are 28 sites for tents or RVs up to 35 feet (no hookups). Picnic tables, food lockers, and fire grills are provided. Drinking water and pit toilets are available. Leashed pets are permitted.

Reservations, fees: Reservations are not accepted. Sites are $20 per night. Open late mid-April through mid-September, weather permitting.

Directions: Drive on U.S. 395 to Big Pine and Crocker Street/Glacier Lodge Road. Turn west (toward the Sierra) and drive eight miles (it becomes Glacier Lodge Road) to the campground.

Contact: Inyo National Forest, White Mountain Ranger District, 760/873-2500, www. fs.fed.us.

68 TINNEMAHA CAMPGROUND

Scenic rating: 6

near Big Pine

This primitive, little-known (to out-of-towners) county park campground is on Tinnemaha Creek at 4,400 feet elevation. The creek is stocked with Alpers trout. Horse camping is allowed, but call ahead.

Campsites, facilities: There are 55 sites for tents or RVs of any length (no hookups). Picnic tables and fire grills are provided. Vault toilets are available. No drinking water is available so bring your own. Stream water is available and must be boiled or pump-filtered before use. Leashed pets are permitted.

Reservations, fees: Reservations are not accepted. Sites are $10 per vehicle per night. Open year-round.

Directions: Drive on U.S. 395 to Tinnemaha Creek Road (seven miles south of Big Pine and 19.5 miles north of Independence). Turn west (toward the Sierra) on Fish Springs Road and drive 0.5 mile to Tinnemaha Creek Road. Turn west (left) and drive two miles to the park on the right.

Contact: Inyo County Parks Department, 760/873-5577, www.inyocountycamping. com.

69 TABOOSE CREEK CAMPGROUND

Scenic rating: 4

near Big Pine

The eastern Sierra is stark country, but this little spot provides a stream (Taboose Creek) and a few aspens near the campground. The setting is high desert, with a spectacular view to the west of the high Sierra rising up from sagebrush. There is an opportunity for trout

CAMPING

fishing—fair, not spectacular. The easy access off U.S. 395 is a bonus. The hike up to Taboose Pass from here is one of the steepest grinds in the Sierra. Only the deranged need apply—which is why I did it, of course. The route provides one-day access to the interior of the John Muir Wilderness. The elevation is 3,900 feet.

Campsites, facilities: There are 56 sites for tents or RVs up to 40 feet (no hookups). Picnic tables and fire grills are provided. Drinking water (hand-pumped from a well) and vault toilets are available. Supplies are available in Big Pine or Independence. Leashed pets are permitted.

Reservations, fees: Reservations are not accepted. Sites are $10 per vehicle per night. Open year-round.

Directions: Drive on U.S. 395 to Taboose Creek Road (11 miles south of Big Pine and 14 miles north of Independence). Turn west (toward the Sierra) on Taboose Creek Road and drive 2.5 miles to the campground (straight in).

Contact: Inyo County Parks Department, 760/873-5577, www.inyocountycamping.com.

70 GRANDVIEW

Scenic rating: 6

near Big Pine in Inyo National Forest

This is a primitive and little-known camp, and the folks who find this area earn their solitude. It is in the White Mountains east of Bishop at 8,600 feet elevation along White Mountain Road. The road borders the Ancient Bristlecone Pine Forest to the east and leads north to jump-off spots for hikers heading up Mount Barcroft (13,023 feet) or White Mountain (14,246 feet, the third-highest mountain in California). A trail out of the camp leads up to an old mining site.

Campsites, facilities: There are 27 sites for tents or RVs up to 35 feet (no hookups). Picnic tables and fire grills are provided. Vault toilets are available. No drinking water is available. Garbage must be packed out. Leashed pets are permitted.

Reservations, fees: Reservations are not accepted. There is no fee for camping, but donations are accepted. Open year-round, weather permitting.

Directions: From Big Pine on U.S. 395, turn east on Highway 168 and drive 13 miles. Turn north on White Mountain/Bristlecone Forest Road (Forest Road 4S01) and drive 5.5 miles to the campground.

Contact: Inyo National Forest, White Mountain Ranger District, 760/873-2500, www.fs.fed.us.

71 CHOINUMNI

Scenic rating: 7

on lower Kings River

This campground is set in the San Joaquin foothills on the Kings River, a pretty area. Since the campground is operated by Fresno County, it is off the radar of many visitors. Fishing, rafting, canoeing, and hiking are popular. The elevation is roughly 1,000 feet, surrounded by a landscape of oak woodlands and grassland foothills. The park is roughly 33 miles east of Fresno.

Campsites, facilities: There are 79 sites for tents or RVs of any length (no hookups), and one group site for up to 75 people. Some sites are pull-through. Picnic tables and fire rings are provided. Drinking water, flush toilets, and dump station are available. Canoe rentals are available nearby. No facilities within 10 miles. Leashed pets are permitted.

Reservations, fees: Reservations are accepted for the group site only. Sites are $18 per night, $5 per night for each additional vehicle, $110 per night for the group site. Open year-round.

Directions: From Fresno, drive east on Highway 180 for 17.5 miles to Piedra Road. Turn left on Piedra Road and drive eight miles to Trimmer Springs Road. Turn right on Trimmer Springs Road and drive one mile to Pine Flat Road. Turn right and drive 100 yards to the camp entrance on the right.

Contact: Fresno County Parks Department, 559/488-3004, www.co.fresno.ca.us.

72 PINE FLAT RECREATION AREA

Scenic rating: 7

near Pine Flat Lake

This is a county park that is open all year, set below the dam of Pine Flat Lake, actually not on the lake at all. As a county park campground, it is often overlooked by out-of-towners.

Campsites, facilities: There are 52 pull-through sites for tents or RVs of any length (no hookups). Fire grills and picnic tables are provided. Restrooms with flush toilets, drinking water, dump station and a wheelchair-accessible fishing area are available. A store, coin laundry, and propane gas are nearby (within a mile). Leashed pets are permitted.

Reservations, fees: Reservations are not accepted. Sites are $18 per night, $5 per night for each additional vehicle. Open year-round.

Directions: From Fresno, drive east on Highway 180 for 17.5 miles to Trimmer Springs Road. Turn left and drive eight miles to the town of Piedra. Continue on Trimmer Springs Road for one mile to Pine Flat Road. Turn right and drive three miles to the campground on the right.

Contact: Fresno County Parks Department, 559/488-3004, www.co.fresno.ca.us.

73 ISLAND PARK AND DEER CREEK POINT GROUP

Scenic rating: 7

on Pine Flat Lake

These are two of four Army Corps of Engineer campgrounds available at Pine Flat Lake, a popular lake set in the foothill country east of Fresno. When Pine Flat is full, or close to full, it is very pretty. The lake is 21 miles long with 67 miles of shoreline and 4,270 surface acres. Right—a big lake with unlimited potential. Because the temperatures get warm here in spring, then smoking hot in summer, the lake is like Valhalla for boating and water sports. The fishing for white bass is often excellent in late winter and early spring and, after that, conditions are ideal for water sports. The elevation is 1,000 feet.

Campsites, facilities: There are 52 sites for tents or RVs of any length (no hookups), 60 overflow sites (at Island Park), and two group sites for 80 people each for tents or RVs up to 45 feet. Picnic tables and fire grills are provided. Restrooms with flush toilets and coin showers, drinking water, pay telephone, boat ramp, fish-cleaning station, and dump station are available. There is a seasonal store at the campground entrance. Boat rentals are available within five miles. Some facilities are wheelchair-accessible. Leashed pets are permitted.

Reservations, fees: Reservations are accepted for individual sites and required for the group sites at 877/444-6777 or www.recreation.gov ($9 reservation fee). Sites are $20–30 per night, $75 per night for group site. Boat launching is $3 per day. Open year-round.

Directions: From Fresno, drive east on Highway 180 for 17.5 miles to Trimmer Springs Road. Turn left and drive eight miles to the town of Piedra. Continue on Trimmer Springs Road for one mile to Pine Flat Road. Turn right and drive 0.25 mile to the park entrance (signed "Island Park").

CAMPING

Contact: U.S. Army Corps of Engineers, Sacramento District, Pine Flat Field Office, 559/787-2589.

74 LAKERIDGE CAMPING AND BOATING RESORT

Scenic rating: 7

on Pine Flat Lake

Pine Flat Lake is a 20-mile-long reservoir with seemingly unlimited recreation potential. It is an excellent lake for all water sports. It is in the foothills east of Fresno at 970 feet elevation, covering 4,912 surface acres with 67 miles of shoreline. The lake's proximity to Fresno has made it a top destination for boating and water sports. Fishing for white bass can be excellent in the spring and early summer. There are also rainbow trout, largemouth bass, smallmouth bass, bluegill, catfish, and black crappie. Note: A downer is that there are only a few sandy beaches, and the lake level can drop as low as 20 percent full.

Campsites, facilities: There are 107 sites with full or partial hookups (50 amps) for tents or RVs up to 40 feet. Picnic tables and barbecue grills are available at some sites. Restrooms with showers, modem access, coin laundry, ice, horseshoes, and pay phone are available. A convenience store and boat and houseboat rentals are nearby. Leashed pets are permitted.

Reservations, fees: Reservations are recommended at 877/787-2260. RV sites are $35–43 per night, tent sites are $25–30, $5 per pet per night. Some credit cards accepted. Open year-round.

Directions: From Fresno, drive east on Highway 180 for 17.5 miles to Trimmer Springs Road. Turn left and drive eight miles to the town of Piedra. Continue on Trimmer Springs Road for four miles to Sunnyslope Road. Turn right and drive one mile to the resort on the right.

Contact: Lakeridge Camping and Boating Resort, 559/787-2260; Pine Flat Marina, 559/787-2506, www.lakeridgecampground.com.

75 KIRCH FLAT

Scenic rating: 8

on the Kings River in Sierra National Forest

BEST (

Kirch Flat is on the Kings River, about five miles from the head of Pine Flat Lake. This campground is a popular take-out spot for rafters and kayakers running the Middle Kings, putting in at Garnet Dike dispersed camping area and then making the 10-mile, Class III run downstream to Kirch Flat. The camp is set in the foothill country at 1,100 feet elevation, where the temperatures are often hot and the water cold.

Campsites, facilities: There are 17 sites for tents or RVs up to 30 feet (no hookups), and one group camp for up to 50 people and RVs to 35 feet. Picnic tables and fire grills are provided. Vault toilets are available. No drinking water is available. Some facilities are wheelchair-accessible. Leashed pets are permitted.

Reservations, fees: Reservations are not accepted for individual sites, but are required for the group site at 559/855-5355. There is no fee for camping. Reservation applications are open from March through July with a lottery to select the winners. Open year-round.

Directions: From Fresno, drive east on Highway 180 for 17.5 miles to Trimmer Springs Road. Turn left and drive 28 miles to Trimmer. Continue east on Trimmer Springs Road (along the north shore of Pine Flat Lake) and drive 18 miles to the campground on the right.

Contact: Sierra National Forest, High Sierra Ranger District, 559/855-5355, www.fs.fed.us.

76 BLACK ROCK

Scenic rating: 7

on Black Rock Reservoir in
Sierra National Forest

Little Black Rock Reservoir is a little-known spot that can provide a quiet respite compared to the other big-time lakes and camps in the region. The camp is set near the outlet stream on the west end of the lake, created from a small dam on the North Fork Kings River at 4,200 feet elevation.

Campsites, facilities: There are 10 sites for tents or small RVs. Picnic tables and fire grills are provided. Vault toilets are available. There is no drinking water. Garbage must be packed out. Leashed pets are permitted.

Reservations, fees: Reservations are not accepted. Sites are $14 per night, $7 per night per additional RV, $3 per night for additional vehicle, $1 per pet per night. Open June through November.

Directions: From Fresno, drive east on Highway 180 for 17.5 miles to Trimmer Springs Road. Turn left and drive 28 miles to Trimmer. Continue east on Trimmer Springs Road (along the north shore of Pine Flat Lake) and drive 18 miles to Black Road. Turn left and drive 10 miles to the campground.

Contact: Sierra National Forest, High Sierra Ranger District, 559/855-5355, www.fs.fed.us; PG&E Land Services, 916/386-5164, www.pge.com/recreation.

77 CAMP 4 1/2

Scenic rating: 7

on the Kings River in Sequoia National Forest

On my visit to this primitive camp, I found five sites here, not "four and a half." This Sequoia National Forest campground is small, primitive, and usually hot. The elevation is 1,000 feet. It is one in a series of camps just east of Pine Flat Lake along the Kings River, primarily used for rafting access. (See the Kirch Flat and Mill Flat listings in this chapter for more information.) The Forest Service may make improvements to this campground in 2009.

Campsites, facilities: There are five sites for tents only. Picnic tables and fire grills are provided. Vault toilets are available. No drinking water is available. Garbage must be packed out. Leashed pets are permitted.

Reservations, fees: Reservations are not accepted. There is no fee for camping. Open year-round.

Directions: From Fresno, drive east on Highway 180 for 17.5 miles to Trimmer Springs Road. Turn left and drive 28 miles to Trimmer. Continue east on Trimmer Springs Road (along the north shore of Pine Flat Lake) and drive 18 miles (it becomes Forest Road 11S12) to Forest Road 12S01 (crossing the river). Take Forest Road 12S01 for one mile (along the river) to a dirt road on the right (at the junction of the second bridge). Turn right (still Forest Road 12S01) and drive 0.7 mile to the campground. Not advised for trailers or large RVs.

Contact: Sequoia National Forest, Hume Lake Ranger District, 559/338-2251, www.fs.fed.us.

78 CAMP 4

Scenic rating: 7

on the Kings River in Sequoia National Forest

This is one in a series of camps set on the Kings River upstream from Pine Flat Lake, a popular access point for rafters and kayakers. The Kings River is well known for providing some of the best rafting and kayaking water in California. The weather gets so hot that many take a dunk in the river on purpose; non-rafters had better bring a cooler stocked

CAMPING

with ice and drinks. Camp 4 is a mile from Mill Creek Flat.

Campsites, facilities: There are five sites for tents only. Picnic tables and fire grills are provided. Vault toilets are available. No drinking water is available. Garbage must be packed out. Leashed pets are permitted.

Reservations, fees: Reservations are not accepted. There is no fee for camping. Open year-round.

Directions: From Fresno, drive east on Highway 180 for 17.5 miles to Trimmer Springs Road. Turn left and drive 28 miles to Trimmer. Continue east on Trimmer Springs Road (along the north shore of Pine Flat Lake) and drive 18 miles (it becomes Forest Road 11S12) to Forest Road 12S01 (crossing the river). Take Forest Road 12S01 for one mile (along the river) to a dirt road on the right (at the junction of the second bridge). Turn right (still Forest Road 12S01) and drive 1.5 miles to the campground (on the south side of the river). Not advised for trailers and large RVs.

Contact: Sequoia National Forest, Hume Lake Ranger District, 559/338-2251, www.fs.fed.us.

79 MILL FLAT

🏃 🛶 🐕 ⛺

Scenic rating: 7

on the Kings River in Sequoia National Forest

This camp is on the Kings River at the confluence of Mill Creek. It's a small, primitive spot that gets very hot in the summer. The elevation is 1,100 feet. Rafters sometimes use this as an access point for trips down the Kings River. This is best in spring and early summer, when melting snow from the high country fills the river with water.

Campsites, facilities: There are five sites for tents only. Picnic tables and fire grills are provided. Vault toilets are available. No drinking water is available. Garbage must be packed out. Leashed pets are permitted.

Reservations, fees: Reservations are not accepted. There is no fee for camping. Open year-round.

Directions: From Fresno, drive east on Highway 180 for 17.5 miles to Trimmer Springs Road. Turn left and drive 28 miles to Trimmer. Continue east on Trimmer Springs Road (along the north shore of Pine Flat Lake) and drive 18 miles (it becomes Forest Road 11S12) to Forest Road 12S01 (crossing the river). Take Forest Road 12S01 for one mile (along the river) to a dirt road on the right (at the junction of the second bridge). Turn right (still Forest Road 12S01) and drive 2.5 miles to the campground (on the south side of the river). Not advised for trailers and large RVs.

Contact: Sequoia National Forest, Hume Lake Ranger District, 559/338-2251, www.fs.fed.us.

80 PRINCESS

🐕 🚐 ⛺

Scenic rating: 7

on Princess Meadow in
Giant Sequoia National Forest

This mountain camp is at 5,900 feet elevation. It is popular because of its proximity to both Hume Lake and the star attractions at Kings Canyon National Park. Hume Lake is just four miles from the camp. The Grant Grove entrance to Kings Canyon National Park is only six miles away to the south, while continuing on Highway 180 to the east will take you into the heart of Kings Canyon.

Campsites, facilities: There are 90 sites for tents or RVs up to 22 feet (no hookups). Picnic tables and fire grills are provided. Drinking water, vault toilets, amphitheater, and dump station are available. A store is four miles away at Hume Lake. Leashed pets are permitted.

Reservations, fees: Reservations are accepted at 877/444-6777 or www.recreation.gov ($9 reservation fee). Sites are $18 per night, $36 per night for a double site, $5 per night for

each additional vehicle, plus $20 per vehicle national park entrance fee. Prices are higher on holiday weekends. Open May through September, weather permitting.
Directions: From Fresno, drive east on Highway 180 for 55 miles to the Big Stump Entrance Station at Sequoia and Kings Canyon National Parks. Continue 1.5 miles to a junction (signed left for Grant Grove). Turn left and drive 1.5 miles to Grant Grove Village, then continue for 4.5 miles to the campground on the right.
Contact: Sequoia National Forest, Hume Lake Ranger District, 559/338-2251, www.fs.fed.us; California Land Management, 559/335-2232.

81 HUME LAKE

Scenic rating: 8

in Giant Sequoia National Forest

For newcomers, Hume Lake is a surprise: a pretty lake, with great summer camps for teenagers. Canoeing and kayaking are excellent, and so is the trout fishing, especially near the dam. Swimming is allowed. A 5-mph speed limit is in effect on this 85-acre lake, and only electric motors are permitted. Another surprise is the adjacent religious camp center. The nearby access to Kings Canyon National Park adds a bonus. The elevation is 5,200 feet.
Campsites, facilities: There are 60 tent sites and 14 sites for tents or RVs up to 22 feet (no hookups). Picnic tables and fire grills are provided. Drinking water and flush toilets are available. A store, café, bicycle rentals, and boat rentals are nearby. Leashed pets are permitted.
Reservations, fees: Reservations are accepted at 877/444-6777 or www.recreation.gov ($9 reservation fee). Sites are $20–40 per night, $5 per night for each additional vehicle, plus $20 per vehicle national park entrance fee. Rates are higher on holiday weekends.

Open mid-May through September, weather permitting.
Directions: From Fresno, drive east on Highway 180 for 55 miles to the Big Stump Entrance Station at Sequoia and Kings Canyon National Parks. Continue 1.5 miles to a junction (signed left for Grant Grove). Turn left and drive six miles to the Hume Lake Road junction. Turn right and drive three miles to Hume Lake and the campground entrance road. Turn right and drive 0.25 mile to the campground on the left.
Contact: Sequoia National Forest, Hume Lake Ranger District, 559/338-2251, www.fs.fed.us; California Land Management, 559/335-2232.

82 ASPEN HOLLOW GROUP CAMP

Scenic rating: 6

near Hume Lake in Sequoia National Forest

This large group camp is set at 5,200 feet elevation about a mile south of Hume Lake near a feeder to Tenmile Creek, the inlet stream to Hume Lake. Entrances to Kings Canyon National Park are nearby.
Campsites, facilities: This is a group camp for tents or RVs of any length (no hookups) that can accommodate up to 100 people. Picnic tables, food lockers, and fire grills are provided. Drinking water and vault toilets are available. A store is nearby. Some facilities are wheelchair-accessible. Leashed pets are permitted.
Reservations, fees: Reservations are required at 877/444-6777 or www.recreation.gov ($9 reservation fee). The camp is $225 per night, plus $20 per vehicle national park entrance fee. Open mid-May through mid-September, weather permitting.
Directions: From Fresno, drive east on Highway 180 for 55 miles to the Big Stump Entrance Station at Sequoia and Kings Canyon National Parks. Continue 1.5 miles to a

junction (signed left for Grant Grove). Turn left and drive six miles to the Hume Lake Road junction. Turn right and drive three miles to Hume Lake and the campground entrance road. Turn right and drive around Hume Lake. Continue south one mile (past the lake) to the campground entrance road.

Contact: Sequoia National Forest, Hume Lake Ranger District, 559/338-2251, www.fs.fed.us.

83 LOGGER FLAT GROUP CAMP

Scenic rating: 7

on Tenmile Creek in
Giant Sequoia National Forest

This is the group-site alternative to Landslide campground. This camp is set near the confluence of Tenmile Creek and Landslide Creek at 5,300 feet elevation, about two miles upstream from Hume Lake. (For more information, see the Landslide listing in this chapter.)

Campsites, facilities: This is one group campsite for tents or RVs of any length (no hookups) that can accommodate up to 50 people. Picnic tables, food lockers, and fire ring are provided. Drinking water and vault toilets are available. A store is nearby. Some facilities are wheelchair-accessible. Leashed pets are permitted.

Reservations, fees: Reservations are required at 877/444-6777 or www.recreation.gov ($9 reservation fee). The camp is $112.50 per night, plus $20 per vehicle national park entrance fee. Open mid-May through mid-September, weather permitting.

Directions: From Fresno, drive east on Highway 180 for 55 miles to the Big Stump Entrance Station at Sequoia and Kings Canyon National Parks. Continue 1.5 miles to a junction (signed left for Grant Grove). Turn left and drive six miles to the Hume Lake Road junction. Turn right and drive three

miles to Hume Lake and the campground entrance road. Turn right and drive around Hume Lake to Tenmile Road. Continue south three miles to the campground entrance on the right.

Contact: Sequoia National Forest, Hume Lake Ranger District, 559/338-2251, www.fs.fed.us.

84 LANDSLIDE

Scenic rating: 7

on Landslide Creek in
Giant Sequoia National Forest

If you want quiet, you got it; few folks know about this camp. If you want a stream nearby, you got it; Landslide Creek runs right beside the camp. If you want a lake nearby, you got it; Hume Lake is just to the north. If you want a national park nearby, you got it; Kings Canyon National Park is nearby. Add it up: You got it. The elevation is 5,800 feet.

Campsites, facilities: There are eight sites for tents only and one site for RVs up to 22 feet (no hookups). Picnic tables and fire grills are provided. Drinking water and vault toilets are available. A store is nearby. Leashed pets are permitted.

Reservations, fees: Reservations are not accepted. Sites are $16 per night, $32 per night for a double site, $5 per night for each additional vehicle, plus $20 per vehicle national park entrance fee. Open May through September, weather permitting.

Directions: From Fresno, drive east on Highway 180 for 55 miles to the Big Stump Entrance Station at Sequoia and Kings Canyon National Parks. Continue 1.5 miles to a junction (signed left for Grant Grove). Turn right at Generals Highway and drive three miles to Hume Lake Road/Tenmile Road (Forest Road 13S09). Turn left and drive about seven miles (past Tenmile campground) to the campground on the left.

CAMPING

Contact: Sequoia National Forest, Hume Lake Ranger District, 559/338-2251, www.fs.fed.us.

85 TENMILE

Scenic rating: 7
on Tenmile Creek in
Giant Sequoia National Forest

This is one of three small, primitive campgrounds along Tenmile Creek south (and upstream) of Hume Lake. RV campers are advised to use the lower campsites because they are larger. This one is about four miles from the lake at 5,800 feet elevation. It provides an alternative to camping in nearby Kings Canyon National Park.

Campsites, facilities: There are 13 sites for tents or RVs up to 22 feet (no hookups). Picnic tables and fire grills are provided. Vault toilets are available. No drinking water is available. Some facilities are wheelchair-accessible. Leashed pets are permitted.

Reservations, fees: Reservations are not accepted. Sites are $16 per night, $32 per night for a double site, $5 per night for each additional vehicle, plus $20 per vehicle national park entrance fee. Camping fees are higher on holiday weekends. Open May through mid-September, weather permitting.

Directions: From Fresno, drive east on Highway 180 for 55 miles to the Big Stump Entrance Station at Sequoia and Kings Canyon National Parks. Continue 1.5 miles to a junction (signed left for Grant Grove). Turn right at Generals Highway and drive three miles to Hume Lake Road/Tenmile Road (Forest Road 13S09). Turn left and drive about five miles to the campground on the left.

Contact: Sequoia National Forest, Hume Lake Ranger District, 559/338-2251, www.fs.fed.us.

86 AZALEA

Scenic rating: 7
in Kings Canyon National Park

This camp is tucked just inside the western border of Kings Canyon National Park. It is set at 6,600 feet elevation, near the General Grant Grove of giant sequoias. (For information on several short, spectacular hikes among the giant sequoias, see the Sunset listing in this chapter.) Nearby Sequoia Lake is privately owned; no fishing, no swimming, no trespassing. To see the spectacular Kings Canyon, one of the deepest gorges in North America, re-enter the park on Highway 180.

Campsites, facilities: There are 110 sites for tents or RVs up to 30 feet (no hookups). Picnic tables, food lockers, and fire grills are provided. Drinking water and flush toilets are available. Evening ranger programs are often offered. A store and horseback-riding facilities are nearby. Showers are available in Grant Grove Village during the summer. Some facilities are wheelchair-accessible. Leashed pets are permitted, except on trails.

Reservations, fees: Reservations are not accepted. Sites are $18 per night, plus $20 per vehicle national park entrance fee. Open year-round.

Directions: From Fresno, drive east on Highway 180 for 55 miles to the Big Stump Entrance Station at Sequoia and Kings Canyon National Parks. Continue 1.5 miles to a junction (signed left for Grant Grove). Turn left and drive 1.5 miles to Grant Grove Village, then continue for 0.7 mile to the campground entrance on the left.

Contact: Sequoia and Kings Canyon National Parks, 559/565-3341, www.nps.gov/seki; Kings Canyon Visitor Center, 559/565-4307; Grant Grove Horse Stables, 559/335-9292.

CAMPING

87 CRYSTAL SPRINGS

Scenic rating: 5

in Kings Canyon National Park

Directly to the south of this camp is the General Grant Grove and its giant sequoias. But continuing on Highway 180 provides access to the interior of Kings Canyon National Park, and this camp makes an ideal jump-off point. From here you can drive east, passing Cedar Grove Village, cruising along the Kings River, and finally coming to a dead-end loop, taking in the drop-dead gorgeous landscape of one of the deepest gorges in North America. One of the best hikes, but also the most demanding, is the 13-mile round-trip to Lookout Peak, out of the Cedar Grove Village area. It involves a 4,000-foot climb to 8,531 feet elevation, and with it a breathtaking view of Sierra ridges, Cedar Grove far below, and Kings Canyon.

Campsites, facilities: There are 36 sites for tents or RVs up to 22 feet (no hookups) and 14 group sites for 7–15 people each. Picnic tables, food lockers, and fire grills are provided. Drinking water and flush toilets are available. A store and horseback-riding facilities are nearby. Evening ranger programs are often offered in the summer. Showers are available in Grant Grove Village during the summer season. Some facilities are wheelchair-accessible. Leashed pets are permitted, except on trails.

Reservations, fees: Reservations are not accepted. Sites are $18 per night, plus $20 per vehicle national park entrance fee; group sites are $35 per night. Open mid-May through mid-September, weather permitting.

Directions: From Fresno, drive east on Highway 180 for 55 miles to the Big Stump Entrance Station at Sequoia and Kings Canyon National Parks. Continue 1.5 miles to a junction (signed left for Grant Grove). Turn left and drive 1.5 miles to Grant Grove Village, then continue for 0.7 mile to the campground entrance on the right.

Contact: Sequoia and Kings Canyon National Parks, 559/565-3341; Kings Canyon Visitor Center, 559/565-4307, www.nps.gov/seki.

88 SUNSET

Scenic rating: 7

in Kings Canyon National Park

This is the biggest of the camps that are just inside the Sequoia National Park boundaries at Grant Grove Village, at 6,600 feet elevation. The nearby General Grant Grove of giant sequoias is the main attraction. There are many short, easy walks among the sequoias, each breathtakingly beautiful. They include Big Stump Trail, Sunset Trail, North Grove Loop, General Grant Tree, Manzanita and Azalea Loop, and Panoramic Point and Park Ridge Trail. Seeing the General Grant Tree is a rite of passage for newcomers; after a half-hour walk you arrive at a sequoia that is approximately 1,800 years old, 107 feet in circumference, and 267 feet tall.

Campsites, facilities: There are 157 sites for tents or RVs up to 30 feet (no hookups) and two group sites for 15–30 people each. Picnic tables, food lockers, and fire grills are provided. Drinking water and flush toilets are available. In the summer, evening ranger programs are often available. A store and horseback-riding facilities are nearby. Showers are available in Grant Grove Village during the summer. Some facilities are wheelchair-accessible. Leashed pets are permitted, except on trails.

Reservations, fees: Reservations are not accepted for individual sites, but they are required for the group sites (write to Sunset Group Sites, P.O. Box 926, Kings Canyon National Park, CA 93633, or fax 559/565-4391). Sites are $18 per night, plus $20 per vehicle national park entrance fee. Group sites are $40–60 per night. Open late May through mid-September, weather permitting.

Directions: From Fresno, drive east on

Highway 180 for 55 miles to the Big Stump Entrance Station at Sequoia and Kings Canyon National Parks. Continue 1.5 miles to a junction (signed left for Grant Grove). Turn left (still Highway 180) and drive one mile to the campground entrance (0.5 mile before reaching Grant Grove Village).

Contact: Sequoia and Kings Canyon National Parks, 559/565-3341; Kings Canyon Visitor Center, 559/565-4307, www.nps.gov/seki.

89 BUCK ROCK
🏕️ 🚐 ⛺

Scenic rating: 4

near Big Meadows Creek in Giant Sequoia National Monument

This is a remote camp that provides a little-known option to nearby Sequoia and Kings Canyon National Parks. If the national parks are full and you're stuck, this camp provides an insurance policy. The elevation is 7,500 feet.

Campsites, facilities: There are nine primitive sites for tents or RVs up to 25 feet (no hookups). Picnic tables and fire grills are provided. Vault toilets are available. No drinking water is available. Leashed pets are permitted.

Reservations, fees: Reservations are not accepted. There is no fee for camping, but there is a $20 per vehicle national park entrance fee. Open May to early September, weather permitting.

Directions: From Fresno, drive east on Highway 180 for 55 miles to the Big Stump Entrance Station at Sequoia and Kings Canyon National Parks. Continue 1.5 miles to a junction (signed left for Grant Grove). Turn right at Generals Highway and drive about five miles to Big Meadows Road/Forest Road 14S11. Turn left on Big Meadows Road and drive five miles to the campground entrance road on the left. Turn left and drive a short distance to the campground.

Contact: Sequoia National Forest, Hume Lake Ranger District, 559/338-2251, www.fs.fed.us.

90 BIG MEADOWS
🏕️ 🏊 🚻 🚐 ⛺

Scenic rating: 7

on Big Meadows Creek in Giant Sequoia National Monument

This primitive, high-mountain camp (7,600 feet) is beside little Big Meadows Creek. Backpackers can use this as a launching pad, with the nearby trailhead (one mile down the road to the west) leading to the Jennie Lake Wilderness. Kings Canyon National Park, only a 12-mile drive away, is a nearby side trip.

Campsites, facilities: There are 45 sites along Big Meadows Creek and Big Meadows Road for tents or RVs up to 22 feet (no hookups). Picnic tables and fire grills are provided. Vault toilets are available. No drinking water is available. Leashed pets are permitted.

Reservations, fees: Reservations are not accepted. There is no fee for camping, but there is a $20 per vehicle national park entrance fee. Open May through early October, weather permitting.

Directions: From Fresno, drive east on Highway 180 for 55 miles to the Big Stump Entrance Station at Sequoia and Kings Canyon National Parks. Continue 1.5 miles to a junction (signed left for Grant Grove). Turn right at Generals Highway and drive about five miles to Big Meadows Road/Forest Road 14S11. Turn left on Big Meadows Road and drive five miles to the camp.

Contact: Sequoia National Forest, Hume Lake Ranger District, 559/338-2251, www.fs.fed.us.

CAMPING

91 SENTINEL
🚶 ⛵ 🏠 ♿ 🚐 ⛺

Scenic rating: 8

in Kings Canyon National Park

This camp provides an alternative to nearby Sheep Creek (see listing in this chapter). They both tend to fill up quickly in the summer. It's a short walk to Cedar Grove Village, the center of activity in the park. The elevation is 4,600 feet. Hiking and trout fishing are excellent in the vicinity. The entrance road provides stunning rim-of-the-world views of Kings Canyon, and then drops to right along the Kings River.

Campsites, facilities: There are 82 sites for tents or RVs up to 30 feet (no hookups). Picnic tables, food lockers, and fire grills are provided. Restrooms with flush toilets and drinking water are available. A store, coin showers, coin laundry, riding stables, and snack bar are nearby. Some facilities are wheelchair-accessible. Leashed pets are permitted.

Reservations, fees: Reservations are not accepted. Sites are $18 per night, plus $20 per vehicle national park entrance fee. Open late April through October, weather permitting.

Directions: From Fresno, drive east on Highway 180 for 55 miles to the Big Stump Entrance Station at Sequoia and Kings Canyon National Parks. Continue 1.5 miles to a junction (signed left for Grant Grove). Turn left and drive 32 miles to the campground entrance on the left (near Cedar Grove Village).

Contact: Sequoia and Kings Canyon National Parks, 559/565-3341; Cedar Grove Visitor Center, 559/565-3793, www.nps.gov/seki.

92 SHEEP CREEK
🚶 ⛵ 🏠 🚐 ⛺

Scenic rating: 8

in Kings Canyon National Park

This is one of the camps that always fills up quickly on summer weekends. It's a pretty spot and just a short walk from Cedar Grove Village. The camp is set along Sheep Creek at 4,600 feet elevation.

Campsites, facilities: There are 111 sites for tents or RVs up to 30 feet (no hookups). Picnic tables and fire grills are provided. Restrooms with flush toilets and drinking water are available. A store, coin laundry, snack bar, and coin showers are available nearby. Leashed pets are permitted.

Reservations, fees: Reservations are not accepted. Sites are $18 per night, plus $20 per vehicle national park entrance fee. Open late April through mid-November.

Directions: From Fresno, drive east on Highway 180 for 55 miles to the Big Stump Entrance Station at Sequoia and Kings Canyon National Parks. Continue 1.5 miles to a junction (signed left for Grant Grove). Turn left and drive 31.5 miles to the campground entrance on the left (near Cedar Grove Village).

Contact: Sequoia and Kings Canyon National Parks, 559/565-3341; Cedar Grove Visitor Center, 559/565-3793, www.nps.gov/seki.

93 CANYON VIEW GROUP CAMP
🚶 🏠 ⛺

Scenic rating: 8

in Kings Canyon National Park

BEST (

If it weren't for this group camp in the Cedar Grove Village area, large gatherings wishing to camp together in Kings Canyon National Park would be out of luck. The access road leads to dramatic views of the deep Kings River Canyon, one of the deepest gorges in North America. One of the best hikes here, but also one of the most demanding, is the 13-mile round-trip to Lookout Peak out of the Cedar Grove Village area. It involves a 4,000-foot climb to 8,531 feet elevation, and with it, a breathtaking view of Sierra ridges, Cedar Grove far below, and Kings Canyon. The elevation is 4,600 feet.

Campsites, facilities: There are 12 tent-only group sites that accommodate 7–19 people per site, and four sites that accommodate groups of 20–40 per site. Picnic tables, food lockers, and fire grills are provided. Drinking water and flush toilets are available. Coin showers, store, snack bar, and coin laundry are nearby. Leashed pets are permitted.

Reservations, fees: Reservations are not accepted for the 12 tent-only group sites, but they are required for the four sites that accommodate 20–40 people each (write to Canyon View Group Sites, P.O. Box 926, Kings Canyon National Park, CA 93633, or fax 559/565-0314 May–Oct., or 559/565-4391 Nov.–Apr.). Tent-only group sites are $18 per night, the large group sites are $35–40 per night, and there is a $20 per vehicle national park entrance fee. Open May through October (group site: June–Sept.), weather permitting.

Directions: From Fresno, drive east on Highway 180 for 55 miles to the Big Stump Entrance Station at Sequoia and Kings Canyon National Parks. Continue 1.5 miles to a junction (signed left for Grant Grove). Turn left and drive 32.5 miles to the campground entrance (0.5 mile past the ranger station, near Cedar Grove Village).

Contact: Sequoia and Kings Canyon National Parks, 559/565-3341; Cedar Grove Visitor Center, 559/565-3793, www.nps.gov/seki.

94 MORAINE

Scenic rating: 8

in Kings Canyon National Park

This is one in a series of camps in the Cedar Grove Village area of Kings Canyon National Park. This camp is used only as an overflow area. Hikers should drive past the Cedar Grove Ranger Station to the end of the road at Copper Creek, a prime jump-off point for a spectacular hike. The elevation is 4,600 feet.

Campsites, facilities: There are 120 sites for tents or RVs up to 30 feet (no hookups). Picnic tables and fire grills are provided. Drinking water and flush toilets are available. Coin showers, store, snack bar, and coin laundry are nearby. Leashed pets are permitted.

Reservations, fees: Reservations are not accepted. Sites are $18 per night, plus $20 per vehicle national park entrance fee. Open May through October, weather permitting.

Directions: From Fresno, drive east on Highway 180 for 55 miles to the Big Stump Entrance Station at Sequoia and Kings Canyon National Parks. Continue 1.5 miles to a junction (signed left for Grant Grove). Turn left and drive 33 miles to the campground entrance (one mile past the ranger station, near Cedar Village).

Contact: Sequoia and Kings Canyon National Parks, 559/565-3341; Cedar Grove Visitor Center, 559/565-3793, www.nps.gov/seki.

95 ESHOM CREEK

Scenic rating: 7

on Eshom Creek in
Giant Sequoia National Monument

The campground at Eshom Creek is just two miles outside the boundaries of Sequoia National Park. It is well hidden and a considerable distance from the crowds and sights in the park interior. It is set along Eshom Creek at an elevation of 4,800 feet. Many campers at Eshom Creek hike straight into the national park, with a trailhead at Redwood Saddle (just inside the park boundary) providing a route to see the Redwood Mountain Grove, Fallen Goliath, Hart Tree, and Hart Meadow in a sensational loop hike.

Campsites, facilities: There are 23 sites for tents or RVs up to 22 feet (no hookups), and five group sites for up to 12 people each. Picnic tables and fire grills are provided. Drinking water and vault toilets are available. Leashed pets are permitted.

Reservations, fees: Reservations are not accepted. Sites are $18 per night, $5 per night for each additional vehicle, $36 per night for group site. Camping fees are higher on holiday weekends. Open May through early October, weather permitting.

Directions: Drive on Highway 99 to Visalia and the exit for Highway 198 east. Take that exit and drive east on Highway 198 for 11 miles to Highway 245. Turn left (north) on Highway 245 and drive 18 miles to Badger and County Road 465. Turn right and drive eight miles to the campground.

Contact: Sequoia National Forest, Hume Lake Ranger District, 559/338-2251, www.fs.fed.us; California Land Management, 559/335-2232.

96 FIR GROUP CAMPGROUND

Scenic rating: 6

near Stony Creek in
Giant Sequoia National Monument

This is one of two large group camps in the Stony Creek area.

Campsites, facilities: This group camp for tents or RVs up to 30 feet (no hookups) can accommodate up to 100 people. Picnic tables, food lockers, and fire grills are provided. Drinking water and vault toilets are available. A store and coin laundry are nearby. Leashed pets are permitted.

Reservations, fees: Reservations are required at 877/444-6777 or www.recreation.gov ($9 reservation fee). The camp is $225 per night, plus $20 per vehicle national park entrance fee. Fees are higher on holiday weekends. Open mid-May through mid-September, weather permitting.

Directions: From Fresno, drive east on Highway 180 for 55 miles to the Big Stump Entrance Station at Sequoia and Kings Canyon National Parks. Continue 1.5 miles to a

junction (signed left for Grant Grove). Turn right at Generals Highway and drive about 14 miles to the campground entrance on the left.

Contact: Sequoia National Forest, Hume Lake Ranger District, 559/338-2251, www.fs.fed.us.

97 STONY CREEK

Scenic rating: 6

in Giant Sequoia National Monument

Stony Creek Camp provides a good option if the national park camps are filled. It is set creekside at 6,400 feet elevation. Sequoia and Kings Canyon National Parks are nearby.

Campsites, facilities: There are 49 sites for tents or RVs up to 22 feet (no hookups). Picnic tables and fire grills are provided. Drinking water, food lockers, and flush toilets are available. A store and coin laundry are nearby. Leashed pets are permitted.

Reservations, fees: Reservations are accepted at 877/444-6777 or www.recreation.gov ($9 reservation fee). Sites are $20–40 per night, $5 per night for each additional vehicle, plus $20 per vehicle national park entrance fee. Fees are higher on holiday weekends. Open May through early September, weather permitting.

Directions: From Fresno, drive east on Highway 180 for 55 miles to the Big Stump Entrance Station at Sequoia and Kings Canyon National Parks. Continue 1.5 miles to a junction (signed left for Grant Grove). Turn right at Generals Highway and drive about 13 miles to the campground entrance on the right.

Contact: Sequoia National Forest, Hume Lake Ranger District, 559/338-2251, www.fs.fed.us.

98 COVE GROUP CAMP

Scenic rating: 6

near Stony Creek in
Giant Sequoia National Monument

This large group camp is beside Stony Creek. The elevation is 6,500 feet.

Campsites, facilities: There are 204 sites for tents or RVs up to 50 feet (no hookups) and five group sites for 12–50 people each. Picnic tables and fire grills are provided. Drinking water, flush toilets, and dump station are available. A store, coin showers, and coin laundry are eight miles away. Some facilities are wheelchair-accessible. Leashed pets are permitted.

Reservations, fees: Reservations are required at 877/444-6777 or www.recreation.gov ($9 reservation fee). The camp is $112.50 per night, plus $20 per vehicle national park entrance fee. Fees are higher on holiday weekends. Open mid-May through mid-September, weather permitting.

Directions: From Fresno, drive east on Highway 180 for 55 miles to the Big Stump Entrance Station at Sequoia and Kings Canyon National Parks. Continue 1.5 miles to a junction (signed left for Grant Grove). Turn right at Generals Highway and drive about 14 miles to the campground entrance on the left (just past Fir Group Campground).

Contact: Sequoia National Forest, Hume Lake Ranger District, 559/338-2251, www.fs.fed.us.

99 DORST CREEK

Scenic rating: 7

on Dorst Creek in Sequoia National Park

 **BEST (**

This camp is set on Dorst Creek at 6,700 feet elevation, near a trail routed into the backcountry and through Muir Grove. Dorst Creek is a favorite for families because the spacious sites are set beneath a forest canopy and the campground itself is huge. There is plenty of room to run around and youngsters are apt to make friends with kids from other sites. The hike to the Muir Grove of Giant Sequoias is an easy hike, not too hard for children and their parents. It is one in a series of big, popular camps in Sequoia National Park. Bear visits are common here.

Campers must keep food in a bear-proof food locker or you will get a ticket. The reason why? Things that go bump in the night swing through Dorst Creek camp all summer long. That's right, Mr. Bear (a whole bunch of them) makes food raids like UPS drivers on pick-up routes. That's why keeping your food in a bear-proof locker is not only a must, it's the law.

Campsites, facilities: There are 204 sites for tents or RVs up to 30 feet (no hookups) and five group sites for 12–50 people each. Picnic tables and fire grills are provided. Drinking water, flush toilets, and dump station are available. A store, coin showers, and coin laundry are eight miles away. Some facilities are wheelchair-accessible. Leashed pets are permitted.

Reservations, fees: Reservations are accepted at 877/444-6777 or www.recreation.gov ($9 reservation fee). Sites are $20 per night (includes reservation fee), plus $20 per vehicle national park entrance fee, $40–60 per night for group sites. Open Memorial Day through Labor Day, weather permitting.

Directions: From Fresno, drive east on Highway 180 for 55 miles to the Big Stump Entrance Station at Sequoia and Kings Canyon National Parks. Continue 1.5 miles to a junction (signed left for Grant Grove). Turn right at Generals Highway and drive about 25.5 miles to the campground entrance on the right.

Contact: Sequoia and Kings Canyon National Parks, 559/565-3341; Lodgepole Visitor Center, 559/565-4436, www.nps.gov/seki.

100 LODGEPOLE
🏃 🚴 🎣 🐕 🚐 ⛺

Scenic rating: 8

on the Marble Fork of the Kaweah River in
Sequoia National Park

This giant, pretty camp on the Marble Fork
of the Kaweah River is typically crowded. A
bonus here is an excellent trailhead nearby
that leads into the backcountry of Sequoia
National Park. The elevation is 6,700 feet. For
information on backcountry permits, phone
the Mineral King Ranger Station, 559/565-
3135.

Campsites, facilities: There are 204 sites for
tents or RVs up to 40 feet (no hookups). Picnic
tables and fire grills are provided. Restrooms
with flush toilets, drinking water, dump station, gift shop, and evening ranger programs
are available. A store, deli, coin showers, and
coin laundry are nearby. Leashed pets are
permitted.

Reservations, fees: Reservations are accepted
at 877/444-6777 or www.recreation.gov ($9
reservation fee). Sites are $18–20 per night
(includes reservation fee), plus $20 per vehicle
national park entrance fee. Open year-round,
with limited winter services.

Directions: From Fresno, drive east on
Highway 180 for 55 miles to the Big Stump
Entrance Station at Sequoia and Kings Canyon National Parks. Continue 1.5 miles to a
junction (signed left for Grant Grove). Turn
right at Generals Highway and drive about
25 miles to Lodgepole Village and the turnoff
for Lodgepole Campground. Turn left and
drive 0.25 mile (past Lodgepole Village) to
the campground.

Contact: Sequoia and Kings Canyon National
Parks, 559/565-3341; Lodgepole Visitor Center, 559/565-4436, www.nps.gov/seki.

101 POTWISHA
🏃 🚴 🎣 ♿ 🚐 ⛺

Scenic rating: 7

on the Marble Fork of the Kaweah River in
Sequoia National Park

This pretty spot on the Marble Fork of the
Kaweah River is one of Sequoia National
Park's smaller drive-to campgrounds. By
looking at maps, newcomers may think it is a
very short drive farther into the park to see the
General Sherman Tree, Giant Forest, and the
famous trailhead for the walk up Moro Rock.
Nope. It's a slow, twisty drive, but with many
pullouts for great views. A few miles east of the
camp, visitors can find Buckeye Flat and a trail
that is routed along Paradise Creek.

Campsites, facilities: There are 42 sites for
tents or RVs up to 30 feet (no hookups). Picnic
tables, food lockers, and fire grills are provided. Drinking water, flush toilets, dump
station, and evening ranger programs are available. Some facilities are wheelchair-accessible.
Leashed pets are permitted.

Reservations, fees: Reservations are not
accepted. Sites are $18 per night, plus $20
per vehicle national park entrance fee. Open
year-round.

Directions: From Visalia, drive east on Highway 198 for 36 miles to the Ash Mountain
entrance station to Sequoia and Kings Canyon National Parks. Continue into the park
(the road becomes Generals Highway) and
drive four miles to the campground on the
left. Vehicles of 22 feet or longer are not advised on Generals Highway from Potwisha to
Giant Forest Village and are advised to use
Highway 180 through the Big Stump entrance
station.

Contact: Sequoia and Kings Canyon National
Parks, 559/565-3341; Lodgepole Visitor Center, 559/565-4436, www.nps.gov/seki.

CAMPING

102 BUCKEYE FLAT

🏃 🛶 🏕️ ♿ 🔺

Scenic rating: 8

on the Middle Fork of the Kaweah River in
Sequoia National Park

In any big, popular national park such as Sequoia, the smaller the campground, the better.
Well, Buckeye Flat is one of the smaller ones,
set on the Middle Fork of the Kaweah River
with a trail just south of camp that runs beside
pretty Paradise Creek.

Campsites, facilities: There are 28 tent sites.
Picnic tables, food lockers, and fire grills are
provided. Drinking water and flush toilets
are available. Some facilities are wheelchair-
accessible. Leashed pets are permitted.

Reservations, fees: Reservations are not accepted. Sites are $18 per night, plus $20 per vehicle
national park entrance fee. Open mid-April
through mid-September, weather permitting.

Directions: From Visalia, drive east on Highway 198 for 36 miles to the Ash Mountain
entrance station to Sequoia and Kings Canyon
National Parks. Continue into the park (the
road becomes Generals Highway) and drive
6.2 miles to the turnoff (across from Hospital
Rock) for Buckeye Flat Campground. Turn
right and drive 0.6 mile to the campground.
Vehicles of 22 feet or longer are not advised
on Generals Highway from Potwisha to Giant
Forest Village and are advised to use Highway
180 through the Big Stump entrance station.

Contact: Sequoia and Kings Canyon National
Parks, 559/565-3341; Lodgepole Visitor Center, 559/565-4436, www.nps.gov/seki.

103 HORSE CREEK

🏊 🛶 🛥️ 🐕 🚶 ♿ 🚐 🔺

Scenic rating: 6

on Lake Kaweah

Lake Kaweah is a big lake, covering nearly
2,000 acres with 22 miles of shoreline. This

camp is set on the southern shore of the lake.
In the spring when the lake is full and the surrounding hills are green, you may even think
you have found Valhalla. With such hot weather
in the San Joaquin Valley, it's a boater's heaven,
ideal for water-skiers. In spring, when the water
is too cool for water sports, anglers can have the
lake to themselves for good bass fishing. Other
species include trout, catfish, and crappie. By
early summer, it's crowded with personal watercraft and ski boats. The lake level fluctuates
and flooding is a potential problem in some
years. Another problem is that the water level
drops a great deal during late summer, as thirsty
farms suck up every drop they can get, kill-
ing prospects of developing beaches for swimming and wading. The elevation is 300 feet.

Campsites, facilities: There are 80 sites for tents
or RVs up to 30 feet (no hookups). Picnic tables
and fire grills are provided. Restrooms with
flush toilets and showers, drinking water, playground, and a dump station are available. Two
paved boat ramps are available at Kaweah Recreation Area and Lemon Hill Recreation Area.
A store, coin laundry, boat and water-ski rentals,
ice, snack bar, restaurant, gas station, and propane gas are nearby. Some facilities are wheelchair-accessible. Leashed pets are permitted.

Reservations, fees: Reservations are accepted
at 877/444-6777 or www.recreation.gov ($9
reservation fee). Sites are $16 per night. Some
credit cards accepted. Open year-round.

Directions: From Visalia, drive east on Highway 198 for 25 miles to Lake Kaweah's south
shore and the camp on the left.

Contact: U.S. Army Corps of Engineers, Lake
Kaweah, 559/597-2301.

104 ATWELL MILL

🏃 🏕️ ♿ 🔺

Scenic rating: 7

on Atwell Creek in Sequoia National Park

This small, pretty camp in Sequoia National
Park is on Atwell Creek near the East Fork

of the Kaweah River, at an elevation of 6,650 feet. While the road in is paved, it is slow and twisty, with many blind turns. The terrain in this canyon is open and dry, overlooking the East Fork Kaweah River well below. A trail at camp is routed south for a mile down to the Kaweah River, then climbs out of the canyon and along Deer Creek for another two miles through the East Fork Grove, an outstanding day hike.

Campsites, facilities: There are 21 tent sites; no RVs or trailers are permitted. Picnic tables, food lockers, and fire grills are provided. Drinking water and pit toilets are available. A small store is nearby. Some facilities are wheelchair-accessible. Leashed pets are permitted.

Reservations, fees: Reservations are not accepted. Sites are $12 per night, plus $20 per vehicle park entrance fee. Open late May through October, weather permitting.

Directions: From Visalia, drive east on Highway 198 for 36 miles to the town of Three Rivers. Continue east for three miles to Mineral King Road. Turn right on Mineral King Road and drive 19 miles (slow, steep, narrow, and twisty, with blind curves) to the campground. RVs and trailers are not recommended.

Contact: Sequoia and Kings Canyon National Parks, 559/565-3341; Lodgepole Visitor Center, 559/565-4436, www.nps.gov/seki.

105 COLD SPRINGS

Scenic rating: 9

on the East Fork of the Kaweah River in Sequoia National Park

This high-country camp at Sequoia National Park is set at 7,500 feet elevation on the East Fork of the Kaweah River. There is a stellar hiking trail from here, with the trailhead just west of the camp. The hike is routed south along Mosquito Creek, climbing over the course of about three miles to the pretty Mosquito Lakes, a series of four

Marmots think that if they don't move, they're invisible.

© MICHAEL FURNISS

small, beautiful lakes set on the north flank of Hengst Peak (11,127 feet). At road's end, there are two wilderness trailheads for sensational hikes, including one routed out to the Great Western Divide. The Mineral King area is marmot central; those little guyes are everywhere.

Campsites, facilities: There are 44 tent sites. Picnic tables, food lockers, and fire grills are provided. Drinking water and pit toilets are available. A store is nearby. Leashed pets are permitted.

Reservations, fees: Reservations are not accepted. Sites are $12 per night, plus $20 per vehicle national park entrance fee. Open May through October.

Directions: From Visalia, drive east on Highway 198 for 36 miles to the town of Three Rivers. Continue east for three miles to Mineral King Road. Turn right on Mineral King Road and drive 23 miles (slow, steep, narrow, and twisty, with blind curves) to the campground. RVs and trailers are not recommended.

Contact: Sequoia and Kings Canyon National Parks, 559/565-3341; Lodgepole Visitor Center, 559/565-4436, www.nps.gov/seki.

106 SOUTH FORK

Scenic rating: 7

on the South Fork of the Kaweah River in Sequoia National Park

The smallest developed camp in Sequoia National Park might be just what you're looking for. It is set at 3,650 feet elevation on the South Fork of the Kaweah River, just inside the southwestern border of Sequoia and Kings Canyon National Parks. While it is technically in the park, it is nothing like at the Giant Forest. Instead, the road in is twisty and slow, the landscape open and hot. A trail heads east from the camp and traverses Dennison Ridge, eventually leading to Hockett Lakes, a long, demanding overnight trip. This is black-bear habitat, so proper food storage is required.

Campsites, facilities: There are 10 sites for tents only. Picnic tables, food lockers, and fire grills are provided. Pit toilets are available. No drinking water is available. Leashed pets are permitted, except on trails.

Reservations, fees: Reservations are not accepted. Sites are $12 per night from May through October; there is no fee in other months. The national park entrance fee is $20 per vehicle. Open year-round.

Directions: From Visalia, drive east on Highway 198 for 35 miles to South Fork Road (one mile before reaching the town of Three Rivers). Turn right on South Fork Road and drive 13 miles to the campground (the road is dirt for the last four miles).

Contact: Sequoia and Kings Canyon National Parks, 559/565-3341; Lodgepole Visitor Center, 559/565-4436, www.nps.gov/seki.

107 BALCH PARK

Scenic rating: 6

near Mountain Home State Forest

Balch Park is surrounded by Mountain Home State Forest and Giant Sequoia National Monument. A nearby grove of giant sequoias is a feature attraction. The elevation is 6,500 feet. Two stocked fishing ponds are also available.

Campsites, facilities: There are 70 sites for tents or RVs up to 40 feet (no hookups); some sites are pull-through. Picnic tables and fire grills are provided. Drinking water and flush toilets are available. Leashed pets are permitted.

Reservations, fees: Reservations are not accepted. Sites are $16 per night, $5 per night for each additional vehicle, $3 per pet per night. Open May through late October.

Directions: From Porterville, drive east on Highway 190 for 19 miles (a mile past the town of Springville) to Balch Park Road. Turn left (north) at Balch Park Road and drive three miles to Bear Creek Road. Turn east (right) and drive 15 miles (extremely slow and curvy) to the campground (RVs not recommended).

Alternate route for RV drivers: After turning north onto Balch Park Road, drive 40 miles (long and curvy) to the park.

Contact: Balch Park, Tulare County, 559/539-3896, www.co.tulare.ca.us.

108 HIDDEN FALLS WALK-IN

Scenic rating: 7

on the Tule River in Mountain Home State Forest

This small, quiet camp, set at 5,900 feet elevation along the Tule River near Hidden Falls, is one of the prettier camps in Mountain Home

State Forest. It is remote and overlooked by all but a handful of insiders who know its qualities.

Campsites, facilities: There are eight walk-in sites for tents only. Picnic tables, food lockers, and fire grills are provided. Drinking water and pit toilets are available. Leashed pets are permitted.

Reservations, fees: Reservations are not accepted. There is no fee for camping. No trailers are permitted. Open mid-May through early October, weather permitting.

Directions: From Porterville, drive east on Highway 190 for 19 miles (a mile past the town of Springville) to Balch Park Road. Turn left (north) at Balch Park Road and drive about 23 miles to the Mountain Home State Forest sign. Continue on Balch Park Road (the road is long and twisty) and follow the signs to the State Forest Headquarters (where free forest maps are available). From this point, the campgrounds are well signed.

Contact: Mountain Home State Forest, 559/539-2321 (summer) or 559/539-2855 (winter).

109 MOSES GULCH

Scenic rating: 7

on the Tule River in
Mountain Home State Forest

Obscure Moses Gulch sits on the Tule River in a canyon below Moses Mountain (9,331 feet) to the nearby north. A trailhead at the eastern end of the state forest provides access both north and south along the North Fork of the Middle Fork Tule River for a scenic hike. The elevation here is 5,400 feet. Mountain Home State Forest is surrounded by Sequoia National Forest. The cost? State forests provide some of the last free camps in California.

Campsites, facilities: There are 10 sites for tents only. Picnic tables, food lockers, and fire grills are provided. Drinking water and

vault toilets are available. Leashed pets are permitted.

Reservations, fees: Reservations are not accepted. There is no fee for camping. No trailers are permitted. Open mid-May through October, weather permitting.

Directions: From Porterville, drive east on Highway 190 for 19 miles (a mile past the town of Springville) to Balch Park Road. Turn left (north) at Balch Park Road and drive about 23 miles to the Mountain Home State Forest sign. Continue on Balch Park Road (the road is long and twisty) and follow the signs to the State Forest Headquarters (where free forest maps are available). The campgrounds are well signed from this point.

Contact: Mountain Home State Forest, 559/539-2321 (summer) or 559/539-2855 (winter).

110 FRAZIER MILL

Scenic rating: 8

in Mountain Home State Forest

Abundant old-growth sequoias are the prime attraction at this remote camp. The Wishon Fork of the Tule River is the largest of the several streams that pass through this forest. You can't beat the price.

Campsites, facilities: There are 49 sites for tents, with a few of these sites also for RVs up to 35 feet (no hookups). Picnic tables and fire grills are provided. Drinking water, food lockers, and vault toilets are available. Some facilities are wheelchair-accessible. Leashed pets are permitted.

Reservations, fees: Reservations are not accepted, except for the site that is wheelchair-accessible. There is no fee for camping. Open mid-May through early October, weather permitting.

Directions: From Porterville, drive east on Highway 190 for 19 miles (a mile past the town of Springville) to Balch Park Road. Turn left (north) at Balch Park Road and drive about 23 miles to the Mountain Home State Forest sign. Continue on Balch Park Road (the road is long and twisty) and follow the signs to the State Forest Headquarters (where free forest maps are available). The campgrounds are well signed from this point.

Contact: Mountain Home State Forest, 559/539-2321 (summer) or 559/539-2855 (winter).

111 SHAKE CAMP

Scenic rating: 6

in Mountain Home State Forest

This is a little-known spot for horseback riding. Horses can be rented for the day, hour, or night. The camp is set at 6,500 feet elevation and there's a trailhead here for trips into the adjoining Sequoia National Forest and beyond to the east into the Golden Trout Wilderness. Hikers should note that the Balch Park Pack Station, a commercial outfitter, is nearby, so you can expect horse traffic on the trail.

Campsites, facilities: There are 11 sites for tents or RVs up to 20 feet (no hookups). Picnic tables and fire grills are provided. Drinking water, food lockers, and vault toilets are available. A public pack station with corrals is nearby. Some facilities are wheelchair-accessible. Leashed pets are permitted.

Reservations, fees: Reservations are not accepted. There is no fee for camping. Open mid-May through early October, weather permitting.

Directions: From Porterville, drive east on Highway 190 for 19 miles (a mile past the town of Springville) to Balch Park Road. Turn left (north) at Balch Park Road and drive about 23 miles to the Mountain Home State Forest sign. Continue on Balch Park Road (the road is long and twisty) and follow the signs to the State Forest Headquarters (where free forest maps are available). The campgrounds are well signed from this point.

Contact: Mountain Home State Forest, 559/539-2321 (summer) or 559/539-2855 (winter); Balch Park Pack Station, 559/539-2227.

112 HEDRICK POND

Scenic rating: 6

in Mountain Home State Forest

Mountain Home State Forest is highlighted by giant sequoias, and Hedrick Pond provides a fishing opportunity, as it's stocked occasionally in summer with rainbow trout. This camp is set at 6,200 feet elevation, one of five campgrounds in the immediate region. (See the Methuselah Group Camp listing in this chapter for recreation options.)

Campsites, facilities: There are 14 sites for tents or RVs up to 20 feet (no hookups). Picnic tables, food lockers, and fire grills are provided. Drinking water and vault toilets are available. Some facilities are wheelchair-accessible. Leashed pets are permitted.

Reservations, fees: Reservations are not accepted. There is no fee for camping. Open mid-May through October, weather permitting.

Directions: From Porterville, drive east on Highway 190 for 19 miles (a mile past the town of Springville) to Balch Park Road. Turn left (north) at Balch Park Road and drive about 23 miles to the Mountain Home State Forest sign. Continue on Balch Park Road (the road is long and twisty) and follow the signs to the State Forest Headquarters (where free forest maps are available). The campgrounds are well signed from this point.

Contact: Mountain Home State Forest, 559/539-2321 (summer) or 559/539-2855 (winter).

CAMPING

113 METHUSELAH GROUP CAMP

Scenic rating: 6

in Mountain Home State Forest

This is one of the few group campgrounds anywhere in California that is free to users. But hey: Remember to bring water. Mountain Home State Forest is best known for its remoteness, old-growth giant sequoias (hence the name of this camp, Methuselah), trails that provide access to small streams, and horseback trips into the surrounding Sequoia National Forest. It's a primitive camp for self-contained RVs. The elevation is 5,900 feet.

Campsites, facilities: There is one group site for tents or 1–2 RVs up to 20 feet (no hookups) that can accommodate 20–100 people. Fire grills and picnic tables are provided. Vault toilets are available. No drinking water is available. Garbage must be packed out. Leashed pets are permitted.

Reservations, fees: Reservations are required. There is no fee for camping. Open mid-May through early October, weather permitting.

Directions: From Porterville, drive east on Highway 190 for 19 miles (a mile past the town of Springville) to Balch Park Road. Turn left (north) at Balch Park Road and drive about 23 miles to the Mountain Home State Forest sign. Continue on Balch Park Road (the road is long and twisty) and follow the signs to the State Forest Headquarters (where free forest maps are available). The campgrounds are well signed from this point.

Contact: Mountain Home State Forest, 559/539-2321 (summer) or 559/539-2855 (winter).

114 WISHON

Scenic rating: 8

on the Tule River in Giant Sequoia National Monument

Wishon Camp is set at 3,900 feet elevation on the Middle Fork of the North Fork Tule River, just west of the Doyle Springs Summer Home Tract. Just down the road to the east, on the left side, is a parking area for a trailhead. The hike here is routed for a mile to the Tule River and then runs along the stream for about five miles, to Mountain Home State Forest.

Campsites, facilities: There are 39 sites for tents or RVs up to 22 feet (no hookups). Picnic tables and fire grills are provided. Drinking water and vault toilets are available. Leashed pets are permitted.

Reservations, fees: Reservations are accepted at 877/444-6777 or www.recreation.gov ($9 reservation fee). Sites are $18–38 per night, $5 per night for each additional vehicle. Fees are higher on holiday weekends. Open year-round.

Directions: From Porterville, drive east on Highway 190 for 25 miles to County Road 209/Wishon Drive. Turn left at County Road 208/Wishon Drive and drive 3.5 miles (narrow, curvy—RVs not advised).

Contact: Sequoia National Forest and Giant Sequoia National Monument, Western Divide Ranger District, 559/539-2607, www.fs.fed.us/r5/sequoia.

115 COY FLAT

Scenic rating: 4

in Giant Sequoia National Monument

Coy Flat is set between Coy Creek and Bear Creek, small forks of the Tule River, at 5,000 feet elevation. The road out of camp is routed five miles (through Rogers' Camp, which is private property) to the Black Mountain Grove of redwoods, with some giant sequoias set just inside the border of the neighboring Tule River Indian Reservation. From camp, a hiking trail (Forest Trail 31S31) is routed east for two miles through the Belknap Camp Grove of sequoias and then turns and heads south for four miles to Slate Mountain, where it intersects with Summit National Recreation Trail, a steep butt-kicker of a hike that tops out at over 9,000 feet elevation.

Campsites, facilities: There are 20 sites for tents or RVs up to 22 feet (no hookups). Picnic tables and fire grills are provided. Drinking water and vault toilets are available. Leashed pets are permitted.

Reservations, fees: Reservations are accepted at 877/444-6777 or www.recreation.gov ($9 reservation fee). Sites are $17–38 per night, $5 per night for each additional vehicle. Camping fees are higher for holiday weekends. Open mid-April through mid-November.

Directions: From Porterville, drive east on Highway 190 for 34 miles to Camp Nelson and Coy Flat Road. Turn right on Coy Flat Road and drive one mile to the campground.

Contact: Sequoia National Forest and Giant Sequoia National Monument, Western Divide Ranger District, 559/539-2607, www.fs.fed. us/r5/sequoia.

116 BELKNAP

Scenic rating: 7

on the South Fork of Middle Fork Tule River in Giant Sequoia National Monument

The groves of sequoias in this area are a highlight wherever you go. This camp is set on the South Fork of the Middle Fork Tule River near McIntyre Grove and Belknap Camp Grove; a trail from camp is routed east for three miles through Wheel Meadow Grove to the junction with Summit National Recreation Trail at Quaking Aspen camp. The elevation is 5,000 feet.

Campsites, facilities: There are 15 sites for tents only. Picnic tables and fire grills are provided. Drinking water and vault toilets are available. A store is nearby. Leashed pets are permitted.

Reservations, fees: Reservations are accepted at 877/444-6777 or www.recreation.gov ($9 reservation fee). Sites are $18–20 per night, $5 per night for each additional vehicle. Fees are higher on holiday weekends. Open mid-April through mid-November.

Directions: From Porterville, drive east on Highway 190 for 34 miles to Camp Nelson and Nelson Drive. Turn right on Nelson Drive and continue one mile to the camp.

Contact: Sequoia National Forest and Giant Sequoia National Monument, Western Divide Ranger District, 559/539-2607, www.fs.fed. us/r5/sequoia.

117 QUAKING ASPEN

Scenic rating: 4

in Giant Sequoia National Monument

Quaking Aspen sits at a junction of Forest Service roads at 7,000 feet elevation, near the headwaters of Freeman Creek. A trailhead for Summit National Recreation Trail runs right through camp; it's a popular trip on horseback, heading deep into Sequoia National Forest. Another trailhead is 0.5 mile away on Forest Road 21S50. This hike is routed east along Freeman Creek and reaches the Freeman Grove of sequoias in four miles.

Campsites, facilities: There are 32 sites for tents or RVs up to 24 feet (no hookups). Picnic tables and fire grills are provided. Drinking water and vault toilets are available. An amphitheater is available. A store is nearby. Some facilities are wheelchair-accessible. Leashed pets are permitted.

Reservations, fees: Reservations are accepted at 877/444-6777 or www.recreation.gov ($9 reservation fee). Sites are $18–20, $5 per night

CAMPING

for each additional vehicle. Fees are higher on holiday weekends. Open May through mid-November, weather permitting.

Directions: From Porterville, drive east on Highway 190 for 34 miles to Camp Nelson. Continue east on Highway 190 for 11 miles to the campground on the right.

Contact: Sequoia National Forest and Giant Sequoia National Monument, Western Divide Ranger District, 559/539-2607, www.fs.fed.us/r5/sequoia.

118 QUAKING ASPEN GROUP CAMP

Scenic rating: 4

at the headwaters of the South Fork of the Middle Fork Tule River in Giant Sequoia National Monument

For groups, here is an alternative to nearby Peppermint. (See the Peppermint listing in this chapter for recreation options.) The elevation is 7,000 feet. (For details about this area, see the Quaking Aspen listing in this chapter.)

Campsites, facilities: There are seven group sites for tents or RVs up to 24 feet (no hookups) that can accommodate 12–50 people each. Picnic tables and fire grills are provided. Drinking water and vault toilets are available. A lodge with limited supplies is nearby. Some facilities are wheelchair-accessible. Leashed pets are permitted.

Reservations, fees: Reservations are required at 877/444-6777 or www.recreation.gov ($9 reservation fee). Sites are $27–112.50 per night, depending on group size. Open mid-May through mid-November.

Directions: From Porterville, drive east on Highway 190 for 34 miles to Camp Nelson. Continue east on Highway 190 for 11 miles to the campground on the right.

Contact: Sequoia National Forest and Giant Sequoia National Monument, Western Divide

Ranger District, 559/539-2607, www.fs.fed.us/r5/sequoia.

119 HOLEY MEADOW GROUP CAMP

Scenic rating: 7

on Double Bunk Creek in Giant Sequoia National Monument

Holey Meadow is set at 6,400 feet elevation on the western slopes of the Sierra, near Redwood and Long Meadow. Parker Pass is a mile to the west, and if you drive on the Forest Service road over the pass, continue southwest (four miles from camp) to Cold Springs Saddle, and then turn east on the Forest Service spur road, it will take you two miles to Starvation Creek and the Starvation Creek Grove.

Campsites, facilities: There is a group site for tents or RVs up to 16 feet (no hookups) that can accommodate up to 60 people. Fire grills and picnic tables are provided. Vault toilets are available. There is no drinking water; water is available 2.5 miles away at Redwood Meadow campground. Leashed pets are permitted.

Reservations, fees: Reservations are required at 877/444-6777 or www.recreation.gov ($9 reservation fee). The camp is $135–137 per night. Open June through October.

Directions: Drive on Highway 99 to Earlimart (about eight miles north of Delano) and the exit for Avenue 56/County Road J22. Take that exit east and drive 39 miles to the town of California Hot Springs and Parker Pass Road/County Road M50. Turn left on Parker Pass Road and drive 12 miles to Western Divide Highway/County Road M107. Turn left on Western Divide Highway and drive 0.5 mile to the campground entrance.

Contact: Sequoia National Forest and Giant Sequoia National Monument, Western Divide Ranger District, 559/539-2607, www.fs.fed.us/r5/sequoia.

120 REDWOOD MEADOW

Scenic rating: 7

near Parker Meadow Creek in
Giant Sequoia National Monument

The highlight here is the 1.5-mile Trail of the Hundred Giants, which is routed through a grove of giant sequoias and is accessible for wheelchair hikers. This is the site where President Clinton proclaimed the Giant Sequoia National Monument in 2000. The camp is set near Parker Meadow Creek at 6,100 feet elevation. Despite its remoteness, this has become a popular place.

Campsites, facilities: There are 15 sites for tents or RVs up to 16 feet (no hookups). Picnic tables and fire grills are provided. Drinking water and vault toilets are available. Leashed pets are permitted.

Reservations, fees: Reservations are accepted at 877/444-6777 or www.recreation.gov ($9 reservation fee). Sites are $17–20 per night, $5 per night for each additional vehicle. Camping fees are higher on holiday weekends. Open mid-May through October, weather permitting.

Directions: Drive on Highway 99 to Earlimart (about eight miles north of Delano) and the exit for Avenue 56/County Road J22. Take that exit east and drive 39 miles to the town of California Hot Springs and Parker Pass Road/County Road M50. Turn left on Parker Pass Road and drive 12 miles to Western Divide Highway/County Road M107. Turn left on Western Divide Highway and drive three miles to the campground entrance.

Contact: Sequoia National Forest and Giant Sequoia National Monument, Western Divide Ranger District, 559/539-2607, www.fs.fed.us/r5/sequoia.

121 LONG MEADOW GROUP CAMP

Scenic rating: 8

in Giant Sequoia National Monument

Long Meadow is set on little Long Meadow Creek at an elevation of 6,000 feet, within a mile of the remote Cunningham Grove of redwoods to the east. Note that Redwood Meadow is just one mile to the west, where the Trail of the Hundred Giants is a feature attraction.

Campsites, facilities: There is one group site for tents or RVs up to 16 feet (no hookups) that can accommodate up to 36 people. Picnic tables and fire grills are provided. Vault toilets are available. No drinking water is available. Leashed pets are permitted.

Reservations, fees: Reservations are required at 877/444-6777 or www.recreation.gov ($9 reservation fee). The camp is $81–83 per night. Open mid-May through mid-November.

Directions: Drive on Highway 99 to Earlimart (about eight miles north of Delano) and the exit for Avenue 56/County Road J22. Take that exit east and drive 39 miles to the town of California Hot Springs and Parker Pass Road/County Road M50. Turn left on Parker Pass Road and drive 12 miles to Western Divide Highway/County Road M107. Turn left on Western Divide Highway and drive four miles to the campground entrance.

Contact: Sequoia National Forest and Giant Sequoia National Monument, Western Divide Ranger District, 559/539-2607, www.fs.fed.us/r5/sequoia.

122 TULE

Scenic rating: 7

on Lake Success

Lake Success is a big lake with many arms, providing 30 miles of shoreline and making

CAMPING

the place seem like a dreamland for boaters on hot summer days. The lake is set in the foothill country, at an elevation of 650 feet, where day after day of 100-degree summer temperatures are common. That is why boating, waterskiing, and personal-watercraft riding are so popular—anything to get wet. In the winter and spring, fishing for trout and bass is good, including the chance for largemouth bass. No beaches are developed for swimming because of fluctuating water levels, though the day-use area has a decent sloped stretch of shore that is good for swimming. Lake Success is much shallower than most reservoirs, and the water can fluctuate from week to week, with major drawdowns during the summer. The wildlife area along the west side of the lake is worth exploring, and there is a nature trail below the dam. The campground is the centerpiece of the Tule Recreation Area.

Campsites, facilities: There are 104 sites for tents or RVs of any length; some sites have electrical hookups (30 and 50 amps) and some are pull-through. Picnic tables and fire grills are provided. Restrooms with flush toilets and showers, dump station, picnic areas, and playground are available. A store, marina, boat ramp, houseboat, boat and water-ski rentals, bait and tackle, propane gas, restaurant, and gas station are nearby. Leashed pets are permitted.

Reservations, fees: Reservations are accepted at 877/444-6777 or www.recreation.gov ($9 reservation fee). Sites are $16–21 per night. Open year-round.

Directions: Drive on Highway 65 to Porterville and the junction with Highway 190. Turn east on Highway 190 and drive eight miles to Lake Success and the campground entrance on the left.

Contact: U.S. Army Corps of Engineers, Sacramento District, 559/784-0215; Success Marina, 559/781-2078.

123 GOODALE CREEK

Scenic rating: 6

near Independence

This obscure BLM camp is set along little Goodale Creek at 4,000 feet elevation. It is a good layover spot for U.S. 395 cruisers heading north. In hot summer months, snakes are occasionally spotted near this campground.

Campsites, facilities: There are 62 sites for tents or RVs up to 30 feet (no hookups). Picnic tables and fire rings are provided. Pit toilets are available. No drinking water is available. Leashed pets are permitted.

Reservations, fees: Reservations are not accepted. Sites are $5 per night. Maximum stay is 14 days. A LTVA Permit ($300) allows all season access to this and two other BLM campgrounds, Tuttle Creek (see listing in this chapter) and Crowley. Open early April through October, weather permitting.

Directions: Drive on U.S. 395 to Aberdeen Road (12 miles north of Independence). Turn west (toward the Sierra) on Aberdeen Road and drive two miles to the campground on the left.

Contact: Bureau of Land Management, Bishop Field Office, 760/872-4881, www.blm.gov/ca.

124 ONION VALLEY

Scenic rating: 8

in Inyo National Forest

Onion Valley is one of the best trailhead camps for backpackers in the Sierra. The camp is set at 9,200 feet elevation, and from here it's a 2,600-foot climb over the course of about three miles to awesome Kearsarge Pass (11,823 feet). From there you can camp at the Kearsarge Lakes, explore the Kearsarge Pinnacles, or join the John Muir Trail and venture to your choice of many wilderness lakes. A wilderness map and a free wilderness permit (if obtained from the ranger station) are your passports to the high country from this camp. For backpackers, trailhead reservations are required. Note: Bears frequent this camp almost every night of summer. Do not keep your food in your vehicle. Many cars have been severely damaged by bears. Use bear-proof food lockers at the campground and parking area, or use bear-proof food canisters as required in adjacent wilderness area.

Campsites, facilities: There are 29 sites for tents or RVs up to 16 feet (no hookups). Picnic tables and fire grills are provided. Drinking water and vault toilets are available. Leashed pets are permitted.

Reservations, fees: Reservations are accepted at 877/444-6777 or www.recreation.gov ($9 reservation fee). Sites are $14–16 per night, $7 per night for additional vehicle. Maximum stay is 14 days. Open late May through September, weather permitting.

Directions: Drive on U.S. 395 to Independence and Market Street. Turn west (toward the Sierra) at Market Street (becomes Onion Valley Road) and drive 15 miles to the campground at the road's end.

Contact: Inyo National Forest, Mount Whitney Ranger District, 760/876-6200, www. fs.fed.us; Interagency Visitor Center, 760/876-6222.

125 UPPER AND LOWER GRAY'S MEADOW
🥾 🏊 🏕 🚐 ⛺

Scenic rating: 6

on Independence Creek in Inyo National Forest

Gray's Meadow provides two adjacent camps that are set along Independence Creek. Upper Gray's is set at an elevation of 6,200 feet; Lower Gray's is 200 feet lower down canyon. The creek is stocked with small trout by the Department of Fish and Game. The highlight

in the immediate area is the trailhead at the end of the road at Onion Valley camp. For U.S. 395 cruisers looking for a spot, this is a pretty alternative to the camps in Bishop.

Campsites, facilities: Lower Gray's has 52 sites for tents or RVs up to 34 feet (no hookups). Upper Gray's has 35 sites for tents or RVs. Picnic tables, food lockers, and fire grills are provided. Drinking water and flush toilets are available. Supplies and a coin laundry are in Independence. Leashed pets are permitted.

Reservations, fees: Reservations are accepted at 877/444-6777 or www.recreation.gov ($9 reservation fee. look for Grays Meadow). Sites are $14–16 per night, $7 per night for additional vehicle. Open late March through mid-October, with a 14-day limit.

Directions: Drive on U.S. 395 to Independence and Market Street. Turn west (toward the Sierra) at Market Street (becomes Onion Valley Road) and drive five miles to the campground on the right.

Contact: Inyo National Forest, Mount Whitney Ranger District, 760/876-6200, www. fs.fed.us; Interagency Visitor Center, 760/876-6222.

126 INDEPENDENCE CREEK
🏊 🏕 ♿ 🚐 ⛺

Scenic rating: 4

in Independence

This unpublicized county park is often overlooked among U.S. 395 cruisers. It is set at 3,900 feet elevation, one mile outside the town of Independence, which is spiraling downward into something resembling a ghost town. True to form, maintenance is sometimes lacking here. Independence Creek runs through the campground and a museum is within walking distance. At the rate it's going, the whole town could be a museum.

Campsites, facilities: There are 25 sites for tents or RVs up to 30 feet (no hookups). Picnic tables and fire grills are provided. Drinking water and vault toilets are available. Some facilities are wheelchair-accessible. Supplies and a coin laundry are available in Independence. Leashed pets are permitted.

Reservations, fees: Reservations are not accepted. Sites are $10 per vehicle per night. Open year-round.

Directions: Drive on U.S. 395 to Independence and Market Street. Turn west (toward the Sierra) at Market Street and drive one mile (outside the town limits) to the campground.

Contact: Inyo County Parks Department, 760/873-5577, www.inyocountycamping.com.

127 LONE PINE AND LONE PINE GROUP
Scenic rating: 8

near Mount Whitney in Inyo National Forest

This is an alternative for campers preparing to hike Mount Whitney or start the John Muir Trail. It is set at 6,000 feet elevation, 2,000 feet below Whitney Portal (the hiking jump-off spot), providing a lower-elevation location for hikers to acclimate themselves to the altitude. The camp is set on Lone Pine Creek, with decent fishing and spectacular views of Mount Whitney. Because of its exposure to the east, there are also beautiful sunrises, especially in fall.

Campsites, facilities: There are 43 sites for tents or RVs up to 35 feet (no hookups), and one group site for up to 15 people. Picnic tables and fire grills are provided. Drinking water and flush toilets are available. Supplies are available in Lone Pine. Leashed pets are permitted.

Reservations, fees: Reservations are accepted at 877/444-6777 or www.recreation.gov ($9 reservation fee). Sites are $15–17 per night, $5 per night per each additional vehicle, $60 per night for the group site. Open late April through mid-October, with a 14-day limit.

Directions: Drive on U.S. 395 to Lone Pine

and Whitney Portal Road. Turn west (toward the Sierra) on Whitney Portal Road and drive six miles to the campground on the left.

Contact: Inyo National Forest, Mount Whitney Ranger District, 760/876-6200, www.fs.fed.us; Interagency Visitor Center, 760/876-6222.

128 PORTAGEE JOE CAMPGROUND
Scenic rating: 4

near Lone Pine

This small, little-known county park provides an option for both Mount Whitney hikers and U.S. 395 cruisers. The sparse setting is high desert sprinkled with a few aspens, with Mount Whitney and the Sierra crest looming high to the west. The camp is located about five miles from Diaz Lake, set on a small creek at 3,750 feet. Very few out-of-towners know about this spot, a nice insurance policy if you find yourself stuck for a campsite in this region.

Campsites, facilities: There are 15 sites for tents or RVs up to 30 feet (no hookups). Picnic tables and fire grills are provided. Vault toilets and well water are available. Supplies and a coin laundry are available in Lone Pine. Leashed pets are permitted.

Reservations, fees: Reservations are not accepted. Sites are $10 per vehicle per night. Open year-round.

Directions: Drive on U.S. 395 to Lone Pine and Whitney Portal Road. Turn west (toward the Sierra) on Whitney Portal Road and drive one mile to Tuttle Creek Road. Turn left (south) at Tuttle Creek Road and drive 0.1 mile to the campground on the right.

Contact: Inyo County Parks Department, 760/878-0272 or 760/873-5577, www.inyocountycamping.com.

129 WHITNEY TRAILHEAD WALK-IN

🥾 🐕 ⛺

Scenic rating: 9

in Inyo National Forest

BEST

If Whitney Portal is full (common for this world-class trailhead), this camp at 8,300 feet elevation can be reached by hiking in 0.25 mile. Reservations for the summit hike are required. That accomplished, this hike-in camp is an excellent spot for spending a day to become acclimated to the high altitude. The trailhead to the Mount Whitney summit (14,497 feet) is nearby. Mount Whitney is the beginning of the 211-mile John Muir Trail to Yosemite Valley. Food-raiding bears are a common problem here. Campers are required to use bearproof food lockers or food canisters. For information on backcountry permits, phone the ranger district.

Campsites, facilities: There are 10 walk-in tent sites. Picnic tables and fire grills are provided.

hikers on Mount Whitney (14,497 ft.)

© US FOREST SERVICE, INYO NATIONAL FOREST

Drinking water and vault toilets are available. Supplies are available in Lone Pine. Leashed pets are permitted.

Reservations, fees: Reservations are not accepted. Sites are $10 per night. Open mid-May through late October, with a one-night stay limit.

Directions: Drive on U.S. 395 to Lone Pine and Whitney Portal Road. Turn west (toward the Sierra) and drive 13 miles to the parking lot at Whitney Portal. Park and hike 0.25 mile to the campground.

Contact: Inyo National Forest, Mount Whitney Ranger District, 760/876-6200, www.fs.fed.us; Interagency Visitor Center, 760/876-2222.

130 WHITNEY PORTAL AND WHITNEY PORTAL GROUP

🥾 🐕 ♿ 🚐 ⛺

Scenic rating: 9

near Mount Whitney in Inyo National Forest

This camp is home to a world-class trailhead. It is regarded as the number-one jump-off spot for the hike to the top of Mount Whitney, the highest spot in the continental United States, at 14,497.6 feet, as well as the start of the 211-mile John Muir Trail from Mount Whitney to Yosemite Valley. Hikers planning to scale the summit must have a wilderness permit, available by reservation at the Forest Service office in Lone Pine. The camp is at 8,000 feet elevation, and virtually everyone staying here plans to make the trek to the Whitney summit, a climb of 6,500 feet over the course of 10 miles. The trip includes an ascent over 100 switchbacks (often snow-covered in early summer) to top Wotan's Throne and reach Trail Crest (13,560 feet). Here you turn right and take Summit Trail, where the ridge is cut by huge notch windows providing a view down more than 10,000 feet to the little town of Lone Pine and the

CAMPING

© US FOREST SERVICE, INYO NATIONAL FOREST

Whitney Portal Recreation Area,
Inyo National Forest

Owens Valley. When you sign the logbook on top, don't be surprised if you see my name in the registry. A plus at the campground is watching the JMT hikers arrive who are just finishing the trail from north to south—that is, from Yosemite to Whitney. There is no comparing the happy look of success when they drop their packs for the last time, head into the little store, and pick a favorite refreshment for celebration.

Campsites, facilities: There are 43 sites for tents or RVs up to 35 feet (no hookups), and three group sites for up to 15 people each. Picnic tables, food lockers, and fire grills are provided. Drinking water and flush toilets are available. Supplies are available in Lone Pine. Some facilities are wheelchair-accessible. Leashed pets are permitted.

Reservations, fees: Reservations are accepted at 877/444-6777 or www.recreation.gov ($9 reservation fee). Sites are $17–19 per night, $7 per night per each additional vehicle, $45–60 per night for a group site. One-night limit

for walk-in tent sites; seven-day stay limit for group site. Open late May through mid-October.

Directions: Drive on U.S. 395 to Lone Pine and Whitney Portal Road. Turn west (toward the Sierra) on Whitney Portal Road and drive 13 miles to the campground on the left.

Contact: Inyo National Forest, Mount Whitney Ranger District, 760/876-6200; Interagency Visitor Center, 760/876-2222, www.fs.fed.us; California Land Management, 760/937-6070.

131 TUTTLE CREEK

Scenic rating: 4

near Mount Whitney

This primitive BLM camp is set at the base of Mount Whitney along Tuttle Creek at 5,120 feet elevation and is shadowed by several impressive peaks (Mount Whitney, Lone Pine Peak, and Mount Williamson). It is often used as an overflow area if the camps farther up Whitney Portal Road are full. Note: This campground is often confused with a small county campground also on Tuttle Creek Road just off Whitney Portal Road.

Campsites, facilities: There are 85 sites for tents or RVs up to 30 feet (no hookups). Picnic tables and fire rings are provided. Pit toilets are available. No drinking water. Supplies are available in Lone Pine. Leashed pets are permitted.

Reservations, fees: Reservations are not accepted. Sites are $5 per night; season passes are $300. Open year-round.

Directions: Drive on U.S. 395 to Lone Pine and Whitney Portal Road. Turn west (toward the Sierra) on Whitney Portal Road and drive 3.5 miles to Horseshoe Meadow Road. Turn left and drive 1.5 miles to Tuttle Creek Road and the campground entrance (a dirt road) on the right.

Contact: Bureau of Land Management, Bishop Field Office, 760/872-4881, www.blm.gov/ca.

132 DIAZ LAKE

Scenic rating: 7

near Lone Pine

Diaz Lake, set at 3,650 feet elevation in the Owens Valley, is sometimes overlooked by visitors to nearby Mount Whitney. It's a small lake, just 85 acres, and it is popular for trout fishing in the spring when a speed limit of 15 mph is enforced. The lake is stocked with Alpers trout and also has a surprise population of bass. From May through October, when hot weather takes over and the speed limit is bumped up to 35 mph, you can say adios to the anglers and hola to waterskiers. Diaz Lake is extremely popular for waterskiing and swimming and it is sunny most of the year. A 20-foot limit is enforced for boats. A nine-hole golf course is nearby. Boats must be inspected for quagga mussels prior to launching; the launch is closed on Mondays and Tuesdays.

Campsites, facilities: There are 200 sites for tents or RVs of any length; some have partial hookups. Picnic tables and fire grills are provided. Restrooms with flush and vault toilets, drinking water (from a well), playground, and boat ramp are available. Supplies and a coin laundry are in Lone Pine. Leashed pets are permitted.

Reservations, fees: Group reservations are accepted at 760/876-5656. Drive-in sites are $10 per night, RV sites (partial hookups) are $14 per night, boat launch fee is $9. Open year-round.

Directions: Drive on U.S. 395 to the Diaz Lake entrance (three miles south of Lone Pine) on the west side of the road.

Contact: Inyo County Parks Department, 760/878-0272 or 760/873-5577, www.inyocountycamping.com.

133 HORSESHOE MEADOW WALK-IN AND EQUESTRIAN

Scenic rating: 8

near the John Muir Wilderness in Inyo National Forest

Horseshoe Meadow features three trailhead camps, remote and choice, for backpackers heading into the adjacent John Muir Wilderness and Golden Trout Wilderness. The three camps are Cottonwood Pass Walk-In, Cottonwood Lakes Walk-In, and Horseshoe Meadow Equestrian. The camps are set at 10,000 feet elevation near the wilderness border, one of the highest trailheads and drive-to campgrounds in the state. Several trails lead out of camp. The best heads west through Horseshoe Meadow and along a creek, then rises steeply for four miles to Cottonwood Pass, where it intersects with the Pacific Crest Trail. From here backpackers can hike north on the Pacific Crest Trail to Chicken Spring Lake to set up camp, a rewarding overnighter, or drop into Big Whitney Meadow in the Golden Trout Wilderness. Some use this camp as a starting point to climb Mount Whitney from its back side (via Guitar Lake). Trailhead reservations are required. Food-raiding bears mean that campers are required to use bearproof food lockers or bearproof food canisters. The drive in is one of the most spectacular anywhere, with the access road following a cliff edge much of the way, with a 6,000-foot drop to the Owens Valley below. You will also pass fantastic volcanics, the site of many movie settings, including Star Trek with Captain Kirk and a lizard creature. (Can you remember the old episode? My kids, Jeremy and Kris, could, and they simulated a scene playing on the rocks.)

Campsites, facilities: Cottonwood Pass has 18 walk-in sites, Cottonwood Lakes has 12 walk-in sites, and Horseshoe Meadow Equestrian has 10 sites. No hookups. Picnic tables and fire grills are provided. Drinking water and vault toilets are available. A pack station and horse facilities are also available at the equestrian camp; campers are encouraged to pack out all livestock waste. Leashed pets are permitted.

Reservations, fees: Reservations are not accepted. Sites are $6 per night for walk-in sites, $12 per night for equestrian sites. Open late May through mid-October, with a one-night stay limit.

Directions: Drive on U.S. 395 to Lone Pine and Whitney Portal Road. Turn west (toward the Sierra) on Whitney Portal Road and drive 3.5 miles to Horseshoe Meadows Road. Turn left on Horseshoe Meadows Road and drive 19 miles to the end of the road (a nearly 7,000-foot climb) and the parking area. Park and walk a short distance to the campground.

Contact: Inyo National Forest, Mount Whitney Ranger District, 760/876-6200, www.fs.fed.us; Interagency Visitor Center, 760/876-2222.

134 UPPER PEPPERMINT
🚶 🚴 🐕 🚐 🏕

Scenic rating: 6

on Peppermint Creek in
Giant Sequoia National Monument

This is one of two primitive campgrounds at Peppermint Creek, but a road does not directly connect the two camps. Several backcountry access roads snake throughout the area, as detailed on a Forest Service map, and exploring them can make for some self-styled fortune hunts. For the ambitious, hiking the two-mile trail at the end of nearby Forest Road 21S05 leads to a fantastic lookout at The Needles (8,245 feet). The camp elevation is 7,100 feet. There is fire damage in some of the surrounding area.

Campsites, facilities: There is dispersed camping for tents or RVs up to 24 feet (no hookups). Picnic tables and fire rings are provided. Vault toilets are available. No drinking water is available. Garbage must be packed out. A lodge with limited supplies is nearby. Leashed pets are permitted.

Reservations, fees: Reservations are not accepted. There is no fee for camping. A fire permit is required. Open June through September, weather permitting.

Directions: From Porterville, drive east on Highway 190 for 34 miles to Camp Nelson. Continue east on Highway 190 for 15 miles to the campground entrance road.

Contact: Sequoia National Forest and Giant Sequoia National Monument, Western Divide Ranger District, 559/539-2607, www.fs.fed.us/r5/sequoia.

135 LOWER PEPPERMINT
🚶 🚴 🐕 🚐 🏕

Scenic rating: 6

in Giant Sequoia National Monument

This is a little-known camp in Sequoia National Forest, set along Peppermint Creek at 5,300 feet elevation. This area has a vast network of backcountry roads, which are detailed on a Forest Service map. The camp is in the immediate vicinity of the Sequoia forest fire, named the McNally Fire, which burned more than 100,000 acres in the summer of 2002. The fire started in the Kern River Canyon and then burned up the Kern Canyon north to Forks of the Kern.

Campsites, facilities: There are 17 sites for tents or RVs up to 16 feet (no hookups). Picnic tables and fire grills are provided. Drinking water and vault toilets are available. Leashed pets are permitted.

Reservations, fees: Reservations are not accepted. Sites are $16 per night. Open June through September.

Directions: From Bakersfield, drive east on Highway 178 for 40 miles to the town of Lake Isabella and Highway 155/Burlando Way. Turn left (north) and drive 10 miles to Kernville Sierra Way. Turn (north) and drive 24 miles to Johnsondale and Forest Road 22S82/Lloyd Meadow Road. Turn right and drive about 10.5 miles (paved road) to the campground.

Contact: Sequoia National Forest and Giant Sequoia National Monument, Western Divide Ranger District, 559/539-2607, www.fs.fed.us/r5/sequoia.

136 LIMESTONE

Scenic rating: 5

on the Kern River in Sequoia National Forest

Set deep in the Sequoia National Forest at 3,800 feet, Limestone is a small campground along the Kern River, fed by snowmelt from Mount Whitney. This stretch of the Kern is extremely challenging and sensational for white-water rafting, with cold water and many of the rapids rated Class IV and Class V—for experts with guides only. The favored put-in is at the Johnsondale Bridge, and from here it's a 21-mile run to Kernville. The river pours into Isabella Lake many miles later. Two sections are unrunnable: Fairview Dam (Mile 2.5) and Salmon Falls (Mile 8). For nonrafters, South Creek Falls provides a side trip, one mile to the west. There is fire damage in some of the surrounding area.

Campsites, facilities: There are 22 sites for tents or RVs up to 30 feet (no hookups). Picnic tables and fire grills are provided. Vault toilets are available. No drinking water is available. Supplies and a coin laundry are in Kernville. Leashed pets are permitted.

Reservations, fees: Reservations are not accepted. Sites are $16 per night, $5 per night for each additional vehicle. Open April through November, weather permitting.

Directions: From Bakersfield, drive east on Highway 178 for about 40 miles to the town of Lake Isabella and Highway 155/Burlando Way. Turn left (north) and drive 10 miles to Kernville and the Kern River Highway/Sierra Way. Turn left on the Kern River Highway and drive 19 miles (two miles past Fairview) to the campground entrance.

Contact: Sequoia National Forest, Kern River Ranger District, Kernville Office, 760/376-3781, www.fs.fed.us.

137 LEAVIS FLAT

Scenic rating: 7

on Deer Creek in Giant Sequoia National Monument

Leavis Flat is just inside the western border of Sequoia National Forest along Deer Creek, at an elevation of 3,000 feet. The highlight here is the adjacent California Hot Springs.

Campsites, facilities: There are nine sites for tents or RVs up to 16 feet (no hookups). Picnic tables and fire grills are provided. Drinking water and vault toilets are available. A store, coin laundry, and propane gas can be found nearby. Leashed pets are permitted.

Reservations, fees: Reservations are accepted at 877/444-6777 or www.recreation.gov ($9 reservation fee). Sites are $18–20 per night, $5 per night for each additional vehicle. Camping fees are higher on holiday weekends. Open year-round.

Directions: Drive on Highway 99 to Earlimart (about eight miles north of Delano) and the exit for Avenue 56/County Road J22. Take that exit east and drive 39 miles to the town of California Hot Springs and the campground.

Contact: Sequoia National Forest and Giant Sequoia National Monument, Western Divide Ranger District, 559/539-2607, www.fs.fed.us/r5/sequoia.

138 WHITE RIVER

Scenic rating: 7

in Giant Sequoia National Monument

White River is set at 4,000 feet elevation, on the White River near where little Dark

CAMPING

Canyon Creek enters it. A trail from camp follows downstream along the White River to the west for three miles, dropping into Ames Hole and Cove Canyon. The region's hot springs are about a 10-minute drive away to the north.

Campsites, facilities: There are 12 sites for tents or RVs up to 24 feet (no hookups). Picnic tables and fire grills are provided. Drinking water and vault toilets are available. Leashed pets are permitted.

Reservations, fees: Reservations are accepted at 877/444-6777 or www.recreation.gov ($9 reservation fee). Sites are $18–20 per night, $5 per night for each additional vehicle. Camping fees are higher on holiday weekends. Open mid-April through mid-October.

Directions: Drive on Highway 99 to Delano and the exit for Highway 155. Take that exit and drive east for about 40 miles to Jack Ranch Road (just west of Glennville). Turn left on Jack Ranch Road and drive about four miles to White River Road/Sugarloaf Drive. Turn right and drive 1.5 miles to Forest Road 24S05. Bear left and drive 0.75 mile to Idlewild, and continue (on this dirt road) for six miles to the campground.

Contact: Sequoia National Forest and Giant Sequoia National Monument, Western Divide Ranger District, 559/539-2607, www.fs.fed. us/r5/sequoia.

139 FROG MEADOW

Scenic rating: 6

near Giant Sequoia National Monument

This small, primitive camp, set near Tobias Creek at 7,500 feet elevation, is in the center of a network of Forest Service roads that explore the surrounding Sequoia National Forest. The nearby feature destination is the Tobias Peak Lookout (8,284 feet), two miles directly south of the camp.

Campsites, facilities: There are 10 sites for

tents or RVs up to 16 feet (no hookups). Vault toilets are available. No drinking water is available. Garbage must be packed out. Leashed pets are permitted.

Reservations, fees: Reservations are not accepted. There is no fee for camping. Open June through September, weather permitting.

Directions: Drive on Highway 99 to Delano and the exit for Highway 155. Take that exit and drive east for about 40 miles to Jack Ranch Road (just west of Glennville). Turn left on Jack Ranch Road and drive about four miles to White River Road/Sugarloaf Drive. Turn right on Sugarloaf Drive and drive 4.5 miles to Guernsey Mill/Sugarloaf Drive. Continue on Sugarloaf Road/Forest Road 23S16 for about seven miles to Forest Road 24S50 (a dirt road). Turn left on Forest Road 24S50 and drive four miles to Frog Meadow and the campground. The route is long, slow, and circuitous. A map of Sierra National Forest is required.

Contact: Sequoia National Forest and Giant Sequoia National Monument, Western Divide Ranger District, 559/539-2607, www.fs.fed. us/r5/sequoia.

140 FAIRVIEW

Scenic rating: 4

on the Kern River in Sequoia National Forest

BEST (

Fairview is one of six campgrounds set on the Upper Kern River above Isabella Lake and adjacent to the Kern River, one of the prime rafting and kayaking rivers in California. This camp sits at 3,500 feet elevation. Many of the rapids are rated Class IV and Class V—for experts with guides only. The favored put-in is at the Johnsondale Bridge, and from here it's a 21-mile run to Kernville. The river eventually pours into Isabella Lake. Two sections are unrunnable: Fairview Dam (Mile 2.5) and Salmon Falls (Mile 8). There is fire damage in some of the surrounding area.

Campsites, facilities: There are 55 sites for

tents or RVs up to 45 feet (no hookups). Picnic tables and fire grills are provided. Drinking water, vault toilets, and a dump station are available. Supplies and a coin laundry are available in Kernville. Some facilities are wheelchair-accessible. Leashed pets are permitted.

Reservations, fees: Reservations are accepted at 877/444-6777 or www.recreation.gov ($9 reservation fee). Sites are $18–20 per night, $5 per night for each additional vehicle. Camping fees are higher on holiday weekends. Open April through October, weather permitting.

Directions: From Bakersfield, drive east on Highway 178 for about 40 miles to the town of Lake Isabella and Highway 155/Burlando Way. Turn left (north) and drive 10 miles to Kernville and the Kern River Highway/Sierra Way. Turn left on the Kern River Highway and drive 18 miles to the town of Fairview. Continue to the north end of town to the campground entrance.

Contact: Sequoia National Forest, Kern River Ranger District, Kernville Office, 760/376-3781, www.fs.fed.us.

141 HORSE MEADOW

Scenic rating: 8

on Salmon Creek in Sequoia National Forest

This is a little-known spot set along Salmon Creek at 7,600 feet elevation. It is a region known for big meadows, forests, backcountry roads, and plenty of horses. It is just west of the Dome Land Wilderness, and there is a series of three public pastures for horses in the area, as well as trails ideal for horseback riding. From camp, one such trail follows along Salmon Creek to the west to Salmon Falls, a favorite for the few who know of it. A more popular overnight trip is to head to a trailhead about five miles east, which provides a route to Manter Meadows in the Dome Lands.

Campsites, facilities: There are 41 sites for

tents or RVs up to 22 feet (no hookups). Picnic tables and fire grills are provided. Drinking water and vault toilets are available. Garbage must be packed out. Leashed pets are permitted.

Reservations, fees: Reservations are not accepted. Sites are $17 per night, $5 per night for each additional vehicle. Open June through October, weather permitting.

Directions: From Bakersfield, drive east on Highway 178 for about 40 miles to the town of Lake Isabella and Highway 155/Burlando Way. Turn left (north) and drive 10 miles to Kernville and the Kern River Highway/Sierra Way. Turn left on the Kern River Highway for about 20 miles to Sherman Pass Road (signed "Highway 395/Black Rock Ranger Station"). Make a sharp right on Sherman Pass Road and drive about 6.5 miles to Cherry Hill Road/Forest Road 22S12 (there is a green gate with a sign that says "Horse Meadow/Big Meadow"). Turn right and drive about four miles (the road becomes dirt) and continue for another three miles (follow the signs) to the campground entrance road.

Contact: Sequoia National Forest, Kern River Ranger District, Kernville Office, 760/376-3781, www.fs.fed.us.

142 GOLDLEDGE

Scenic rating: 7

on the Kern River in Sequoia National Forest

This is another in the series of camps on the Kern River north of Isabella Lake. This one is set at 3,200 feet elevation.

Campsites, facilities: There are 37 sites for tents or RVs up to 30 feet (no hookups). Picnic tables and fire grills are provided. Drinking water and vault toilets are available. Supplies and a coin laundry are available in Kernville. Leashed pets are permitted.

Reservations, fees: Reservations are accepted at 877/444-6777 or www.recreation.gov ($9 reservation fee). Sites are $18–20 per night, $5 per night for each additional vehicle. Camping fees are higher on holiday weekends. Open May through August.

Directions: From Bakersfield, drive east on Highway 178 for about 40 miles to the town of Lake Isabella and Highway 155/Burlando Way. Turn left (north) and drive 10 miles to Kernville and the Kern River Highway/Sierra Way. Turn left on the Kern River Highway and drive 10 miles to the campground.

Contact: Sequoia National Forest, Kern River Ranger District, Kernville Office, 760/376-3781, www.fs.fed.us.

143 HOSPITAL FLAT

Scenic rating: 8

on the North Fork of the Kern River
in Sequoia National Forest

It's kind of like the old shell game, trying to pick the best of the campgrounds along the North Fork of the Kern River. This one is seven miles north of Isabella Lake. The elevation is 2,800 feet. (For information on rafting on the Kern River, see the Fairview listing in this chapter.)

Campsites, facilities: There are 40 sites for tents or RVs up to 30 feet (no hookups), and one group site for up to 30 people. Picnic tables and fire grills are provided. Drinking water and vault toilets are available. Supplies and a coin laundry are available in Kernville. Some facilities are wheelchair-accessible. Leashed pets are permitted.

Reservations, fees: Reservations are accepted for individual sites and required for the group site at 877/444-6777 or www.recreation.gov ($9 reservation fee). Sites are $18–20 per night, $5 per night for each additional vehicle, $75 per night for the group site. Camping fees are higher on holiday weekends. Open May through August.

Directions: From Bakersfield, drive east on

Highway 178 for about 40 miles to the town of Lake Isabella and Highway 155/Burlando Way. Turn left (north) and drive 10 miles to Kernville and the Kern River Highway/Sierra Way. Turn left on the Kern River Highway and drive 6.5 miles to the campground.

Contact: Sequoia National Forest, Kern River Ranger District, Kernville Office, 760/376-3781, www.fs.fed.us.

144 CAMP THREE

Scenic rating: 9

on the North Fork of the Kern River in
Sequoia National Forest

This is the second in a series of camps along the North Fork Kern River north of Isabella Lake (in this case, five miles north of the lake). If you don't like this spot, Hospital Flat is just two miles upriver and Headquarters is just one mile downriver. The camp elevation is 2,800 feet. Note: In past editions, this was listed as "Camp 3." But if you are making an online reservation, you must spell it out or the camp will not be recognized.

Campsites, facilities: There are 52 sites for tents or RVs up to 30 feet (no hookups), and two group sites for up to 30 people. Picnic tables and fire grills are provided. Drinking water and vault toilets are available. A store and coin laundry are available in Kernville. Some facilities are wheelchair-accessible. Leashed pets are permitted.

Reservations, fees: Reservations are accepted for individual sites and required for the group sites at 877/444-6777 or www.recreation. gov ($9 reservation fee). Sites are $18–20 per night, $5 per night for each additional vehicle, $85–87 per night for a group site. Camping fees are higher on holiday weekends. Open May through August.

Directions: From Bakersfield, drive east on Highway 178 for about 40 miles to the town of Lake Isabella and Highway 155/Burlando

Way. Turn left (north) and drive 10 miles to Kernville and the Kern River Highway/Sierra Way. Turn left on the Kern River Highway and drive five miles to the campground.
Contact: Sequoia National Forest, Kern River Ranger District, Kernville Office, 760/376-3781, www.fs.fed.us.

145 HEADQUARTERS

Scenic rating: 8

on the North Fork of the Kern River in Sequoia National Forest

As you head north from Isabella Lake on Sierra Way, this is the first in a series of Forest Service campgrounds from which to take your pick, all of them set along the North Fork of the Kern River. The North Fork Kern is best known for offering prime white water for rafting and kayaking. The elevation is 2,800 feet.
Campsites, facilities: There are 44 sites for tents or RVs up to 27 feet (no hookups). Picnic tables and fire grills are provided. Drinking water and vault toilets are available. Some facilities are wheelchair-accessible. Supplies and a coin laundry are available in Kernville. Leashed pets are permitted.
Reservations, fees: Reservations are accepted at 877/444-6777 or www.recreation.gov ($9 reservation fee). Sites are $18–20 per night, $5 per night for each additional vehicle. Camping fees are higher on holiday weekends. Open year-round.
Directions: From Bakersfield, drive east on Highway 178 for about 40 miles to the town of Lake Isabella and Highway 155/Burlando Way. Turn left (north) and drive 10 miles to Kernville and the Kern River Highway/Sierra Way. Turn left on the Kern River Highway and drive three miles to the campground.
Contact: Sequoia National Forest, Kern River Ranger District, Kernville Office, 760/376-3781, www.fs.fed.us.

146 PANORAMA

Scenic rating: 7

in Giant Sequoia National Monument

This pretty spot is set at 7,200 feet elevation in a region of Sequoia National Forest filled with a network of backcountry roads. The camp is set in an inconspicuous spot and is easy to miss. A good side trip is to drive two miles south, turn left, and continue a short distance to a trailhead on the right side of the road for Portuguese Peak (a Forest Service map is strongly advised). From here, it's a one-mile butt-kicker to the top of Portuguese Peak, at 7,914 feet elevation.
Campsites, facilities: There is dispersed camping for tents or RVs up to 16 feet (no hookups). No drinking water is available. Garbage must be packed out. Leashed pets are permitted.
Reservations, fees: Reservations are not accepted. There is no fee for camping. Open June through August.
Directions: Drive on Highway 99 to Delano and the exit for Highway 155. Take that exit and drive east for about 40 miles to Jack Ranch Road (just west of Glennville). Turn left on Jack Ranch Road and drive about four miles to White River Road/Sugarloaf Drive. Turn right on Sugarloaf Drive and drive 4.5 miles to Guernsey Mill/Sugarloaf Drive. Continue on Sugarloaf Road/Forest Road 23S16 for about six miles to the campground (paved all the way).
Contact: Sequoia National Forest and Giant Sequoia National Monument, Western Divide Ranger District, 559/539-2607, www.fs.fed.us.

CAMPING

147 CEDAR CREEK

Scenic rating: 7

in Sequoia National Forest

This is a little-known, primitive Forest Service camp set at 4,800 feet elevation on the southwest flank of Sequoia National Forest, right along little Cedar Creek, with easy access off Highway 155. Greenhorn Mountain Park and Alder Creek provide nearby alternatives.

Campsites, facilities: There are 11 sites for tents only. Picnic tables and fire grills are provided. There is no drinking water. Vault toilets are available. Garbage must be packed out. Leashed pets are permitted.

Reservations, fees: Reservations are not accepted. There is no fee for camping. Open May through October.

Directions: Drive on Highway 99 to Delano and the exit for Highway 155. Take that exit and drive east on Highway 155 for 41 miles to Glennville. Continue east for nine miles to the campground.

Contact: Sequoia National Forest, Kern River Ranger District, Lake Isabella Office, 760/379-5646, www.fs.fed.us.

148 GREENHORN MOUNTAIN PARK

Scenic rating: 7

near Shirley Meadows

This county campground is near the Shirley Meadows Ski Area, a small ski park open on weekends in winter when there is sufficient snow. Greenhorn Mountain Park covers 160 acres, set at 6,000 feet elevation. The region is filled with a network of Forest Service roads, detailed on a map of Sequoia National Forest. Isabella Lake is a 15-minute drive to the east.

Campsites, facilities: There are 70 sites for tents or RVs up to 24 feet (no hookups). Fourteen cabins are also available as a group rental. Picnic tables and fire pits or fire rings are provided. Drinking water is available intermittently; check for current status. Restrooms with flush toilets and showers are available. Leashed pets are permitted.

Reservations, fees: Reservations are only accepted for groups of at least 40 people. Sites are $14 per night. Open spring through fall, weather permitting.

Directions: From Bakersfield, drive east on Highway 178 for about 40 miles to the town of Lake Isabella and Highway 155/Burlando Way. Turn left (north) and drive six miles to Wofford Heights. Turn left (west) on Highway 155 and drive 10 miles to the park on the left.

Contact: Kern County Parks, 661/868-7000, www.co.kern.ca.us/parks/.

149 ALDER CREEK

Scenic rating: 7

in Sequoia National Forest

This primitive camp is just inside the western border of Sequoia National Forest, an obscure spot that requires traversing a very twisty and, at times, rough road. It is set at 3,900 feet elevation, just 0.25 mile upstream from where Alder Creek meets Slick Rock Creek. There is a trail out of the camp that runs north for two miles along Slick Rock Creek.

Campsites, facilities: There are 13 sites for tents or RVs up to 20 feet (no hookups). Picnic tables and fire grills are provided. Vault toilets are available. No drinking water is available. Garbage must be packed out. Leashed pets are permitted.

Reservations, fees: Reservations are not accepted. There is no fee for camping. Open May through October.

Directions: Drive on Highway 99 to Delano

and the exit for Highway 155. Take that exit and drive east on Highway 155 for 41 miles to Glennville. Continue east for eight miles to Alder Creek Road. Turn right on Alder Creek Road and drive three miles to the campground.

Contact: Sequoia National Forest, Kern River Ranger District, Lake Isabella Office, 760/379-5646, www.fs.fed.us.

150 EVANS FLAT

Scenic rating: 4

in Sequoia National Forest

Evans Flat is an obscure campground in the southwest region of Sequoia National Forest, about 10 miles west of Isabella Lake, with no other camps in the vicinity. You have to earn this one, but if you want solitude, Evans Flat can provide it. It is set at 6,100 feet elevation, with Woodward Peak 0.5 mile to the east. A natural spring is east of camp within walking distance. Note that this campsite is no longer designed as an equestrian site.

Campsites, facilities: There are 20 sites for tents or RVs up to 20 feet (no hookups), including four equestrian sites. Fire grills and picnic tables are provided. A vault toilet and a fenced pasture are available. No drinking water is available. Garbage must be packed out. Leashed pets are permitted.

Reservations, fees: Reservations are not accepted. There is no fee for camping. Open May through October.

Directions: From Bakersfield, drive east on Highway 178 for about 40 miles to the town of Lake Isabella and Highway 155. Turn left (north) and drive six miles to Wofford Heights. Turn left (west) on Highway 155 and drive seven miles to Rancheria Road. Turn left and drive 8.3 miles (first paved, then dirt) to the campground.

Contact: Sequoia National Forest, Kern River

Ranger District, Lake Isabella office, 760/379-5646, www.fs.fed.us.

151 RIVERNOOK CAMPGROUND

Scenic rating: 7

on the North Fork of the Kern River

This is a large, privately operated park set near Isabella Lake a few miles from the head of the lake. Boat rentals are available at one of the nearby marinas. An optional side trip is to visit Keysville, the first town to become established on the Kern River during the gold rush days. The elevation is 2,665 feet.

Campsites, facilities: There are 30 pull-through sites with full hookups (30 and 50 amps) for RVs, 41 sites with partial hookups for RVs, and 59 sites for tents. Picnic tables, fire rings, and drinking water are provided. Restrooms with flush toilets and showers, three dump stations, and cable TV are available. Some facilities are wheelchair-accessible. Leashed pets are permitted.

Reservations, fees: Reservations are recommended. RV sites are $40–45 per night, tent sites are $35 per night, $5 per person per night for more than two people. Some credit cards accepted. Open year-round.

Directions: From Bakersfield, drive east on Highway 178 for about 40 miles to the town of Lake Isabella and Highway 155/Burlando Way. Turn left (north) and drive 10 miles to Kernville and the Kern River Highway/Sierra Way. Turn left on Sierra Way and drive 0.5 mile to the park entrance (14001 Sierra Way).

Contact: Rivernook Campground, 760/376-2705.

CAMPING

152 LIVE OAK NORTH AND SOUTH

Scenic rating: 8

on Isabella Lake

This is one of two camps set in the immediate area on Isabella Lake's northwest side; the other is Tillie Creek. Live Oak is on the west side of the road, Tillie Creek on the eastern, lake side of the road. (For recreation information, see the Tillie Creek listing in this chapter.)

Campsites, facilities: There are 150 sites for tents or RVs up to 30 feet (no hookups) and one group site for up to 100 people. Picnic tables and fire grills are provided. Drinking water and restrooms with coin showers and flush toilets are available. Supplies are available in nearby Wofford Heights. Leashed pets are permitted.

Reservations, fees: Reservations are accepted for individual sites (Live Oak South) and required for the group site (Live Oak) at 877/444-6777 or www.recreation.gov ($9 reservation fee). Sites are $20–22 per night, $5 per night for each additional vehicle, $300–302 per night for group site for up to 100 people. Open May through September.

Directions: From Bakersfield, drive east on Highway 178 for about 40 miles to the town of Lake Isabella and Highway 155. Turn left (north) and drive six miles to the campground entrance road on the left (0.5 mile before reaching Wofford Heights).

Contact: Sequoia National Forest, Kern River Ranger District, Lake Isabella Office, 760/379-5646, www.fs.fed.us.

153 TILLIE CREEK

Scenic rating: 9

on Isabella Lake

This is one of two camps (the other is Live Oak) near where Tillie Creek enters Isabella Lake, set on the northwest shore of the lake near the town of Wofford Heights. Isabella Lake is a large lake, and with it comes a dynamic array of campgrounds, marinas, and facilities. It is set at 2,650 feet elevation in the foothills east of Bakersfield, fed by the Kern River, and dominated by water sports of all kinds.

Campsites, facilities: There are 159 sites for tents or RVs up to 45 feet and four group sites for tents or RVs up to 45 feet that can accommodate 60–150 people each. No hookups. Picnic tables and fire grills are provided. Drinking water and restrooms with showers and flush toilets are available. Dump station, playground, amphitheater, and a fish-cleaning station are nearby. Supplies are nearby in Wofford Heights. Some facilities are wheelchair-accessible. Leashed pets are permitted.

Reservations, fees: Reservations are accepted for individual sites and required for group sites at 877/444-6777 or www.recreation.gov ($9 reservation fee). Sites are $20–22 per night, $5 per night for each additional vehicle, $150–302 per night for group sites. Open year-round.

Directions: From Bakersfield, drive east on Highway 178 for about 40 miles to the town of Lake Isabella and Highway 155. Turn left (north) and drive five miles to the campground (0.5 mile before reaching Wofford Heights).

Contact: Sequoia National Forest, Kern River Ranger District, Lake Isabella Office, 760/379-5646, www.fs.fed.us.

154 CAMP 9

Scenic rating: 8

on Isabella Lake

This campground is primitive and sparsely covered, but it has several bonus features. It is set along the northeast shore of Isabella Lake, known for good boating, waterskiing in the summer, and fishing in the spring. Other options include great rafting and kayaking waters along the North Fork of the Kern River (north of the lake), a good bird-watching area at the South Fork Wildlife Area (along the east side of the lake), and an off-highway-motorcycle park across the road from this campground. The elevation is 2,650 feet.

Campsites, facilities: There are 109 primitive sites for tents or RVs of any length (no hookups), and 11 group sites that can accommodate 30–50 people each. Picnic tables and fire rings are provided. Drinking water, flush and vault toilets, dump station, boat launch, and fish-cleaning station are available. Supplies and a coin laundry are nearby in Kernville. Some facilities are wheelchair-accessible. Leashed pets are permitted.

Reservations, fees: Reservations are accepted for individual sites and are required for the group site at 877/444-6777 or www.recreation.gov ($9 reservation fee). Sites are $17 per night, $5 per night for each additional vehicle, $75–160 per night for a group site. Open year-round.

Directions: From Bakersfield, drive east on Highway 178 for about 40 miles to the town of Lake Isabella and Highway 155. Turn right (south) and drive six miles to the campground entrance on the right (on the northeast shore of Isabella Lake). The campground entrance is just south of the small airport at Lake Isabella.

Contact: Sequoia National Forest, Kern River Ranger District, Lake Isabella Office, 760/379-5646, www.fs.fed.us.

155 HUNGRY GULCH

Scenic rating: 9

near Isabella Lake in Sequoia National Forest

Hungry Gulch is on the western side of Isabella Lake, but across the road from the shore. Nearby Boulder Gulch camp, directly across the road, is an alternative. There are no boat

ramps in the immediate area. (For details about Isabella Lake, see the Pioneer Point listing in this chapter.)

Campsites, facilities: There are 78 sites for tents or RVs up to 30 feet (no hookups). Picnic tables and fire grills are provided. Drinking water, restrooms with coin showers and flush toilets, and fish-cleaning station are available. A playground is nearby. Supplies and a coin laundry are available in Lake Isabella. Leashed pets are permitted.

Reservations, fees: Reservations are accepted at 877/444-6777 or www.recreation.gov ($9 reservation fee). Sites are $20–22 per night, $5 per night for each additional vehicle. Open April through September.

Directions: From Bakersfield, drive east on Highway 178 for about 40 miles to the town of Lake Isabella and Highway 155. Turn left (north) and drive four miles on Highway 155 to the campground.

Contact: Sequoia National Forest, Kern River Ranger District, Lake Isabella Office, 760/379-5646, www.fs.fed.us.

156 BOULDER GULCH

Scenic rating: 8

on Isabella Lake

Boulder Gulch lies fairly near the western shore of Isabella Lake, across the road from Hungry Gulch. Take your pick. Isabella is one of the biggest lakes in Southern California and a prime destination point for Bakersfield area residents. Fishing for trout and bass is best in the spring. The lake is stocked with trout in winter, and other species are bluegill, catfish, and crappie. By the dog days of summer, when people are bow-wowin' at the heat, water-skiers take over, along with folks just looking to cool off. Like a lot of lakes in the valley, Isabella is subject to drawdowns. The elevation is 2,650 feet. (For more information, see the Pioneer Point listing in this chapter.)

Campsites, facilities: There are 78 sites for tents or RVs up to 45 feet (no hookups). Picnic tables and fire grills are provided. Restrooms with flush toilets and coin showers, drinking water, playground, marina, and fish-cleaning station are available. Supplies and a coin laundry are available in the town of Lake Isabella. Leashed pets are permitted.

Reservations, fees: Reservations are accepted at 877/444-6777 or www.recreation.gov ($9 reservation fee). Sites are $20–22 per night, $5 per night for each additional vehicle. Open April through September.

Directions: From Bakersfield, drive east on Highway 178 for about 40 miles to the town of Lake Isabella and Highway 155. Turn left (north) and drive four miles to the campground entrance.

Contact: Sequoia National Forest, Kern River Ranger District, Lake Isabella Office, 760/379-5646, www.fs.fed.us.

157 FRENCH GULCH GROUP CAMP

Scenic rating: 9

on Isabella Lake

This is a large group camp on Isabella Lake at the southwest end of the lake about two miles north of Pioneer Point and the spillway. (For recreation information, see the Pioneer Point listing in this chapter.) The elevation is 2,700 feet.

Campsites, facilities: There is one large group site for tents or RVs of any length (no hookups) that can accommodate up to 100 people. Picnic tables and fire grills are provided. Drinking water and restrooms with flush toilets and solar-heated showers are available. A store, coin laundry, and propane gas are nearby. Leashed pets are permitted.

Reservations, fees: Reservations are required at 877/444-6777 or www.recreation.gov ($9 reservation fee). The camp is $275–302 per night. Open year-round.

Directions: From Bakersfield, drive east on Highway 178 for about 40 miles to the town of Lake Isabella and Highway 155. Turn left (north) and drive three miles to the campground entrance on the right.

Contact: Sequoia National Forest, Kern River Ranger District, Lake Isabella Office, 760/379-5646, www.fs.fed.us.

158 PIONEER POINT

Scenic rating: 9

on Isabella Lake in Sequoia National Forest

Isabella Lake is one of the largest freshwater lakes in Southern California, and with it comes a dynamic array of campgrounds, marinas, and facilities. It is set at 2,650 feet elevation in the foothills east of Bakersfield, fed by the Kern River, and dominated by boating sports of all kinds. This camp is at the lake's southwest corner, between the spillway and the main dam, with a boat ramp available a mile to the east. Isabella is a first-class lake for waterskiing, but in the spring and early summer sailboarding is also excellent, best just east of the Auxiliary Dam. Boat rentals of all kinds are available at several marinas.

Campsites, facilities: There are 78 sites for tents or RVs up to 30 feet (no hookups). Picnic tables and fire grills are provided. Drinking water and restrooms with coin showers and flush toilets are available. A playground and fish-cleaning station are available nearby. A boat ramp is three miles from camp. Supplies and a coin laundry are available in the town of Lake Isabella. Leashed pets are permitted.

Reservations, fees: Reservations are accepted at 877/444-6777 or www.recreation.gov ($9 reservation fee). Sites are $20–22 per night, $5 per night for each additional vehicle. Open year-round.

Directions: From Bakersfield, drive east on Highway 178 for about 40 miles to the town of Lake Isabella and Highway 155. Turn left (north) and drive 2.5 miles north on Highway 155 to the campground.

Contact: Sequoia National Forest, Kern River Ranger District, Lake Isabella Office, 760/379-5646, www.fs.fed.us.

159 KEYESVILLE SPECIAL MANAGEMENT AREA

🏃 🛶 ⚓ 🐴 🚐 ⛺

Scenic rating: 5

on the Kern River near Lake Isabella

The Keyesville area originally was developed in the 1850s during the California gold rush; gold was first discovered in this area in 1851. Very few historical buildings remain, however, since much of the old town of Keyesville was comprised of tents and small shacks along trails. Today, this camp is used primarily by OHV enthusiasts and miners and is an alternative to the more crowded and developed campgrounds around Lake Isabella. The Kern River runs through this 7,133-acre BLM area and campsites are available near the river; dispersed camping is also allowed. The Sequoia National Forest borders this area to the north and west. Keyesville has multi-use trails and specific areas for recreational mining and OHV use. Hunting is allowed in season. Fishing for trout or bass is another option. Swimming is not recommended because of the swift water, undercurrents, and obstacles. A free permit is required for whitewater rafting and is available at the forest service office in Lake Isabella, 760/379-5646.

Campsites, facilities: There is dispersed camping for tents or RVs up to 30 feet (no hookups). Picnic tables and fire rings are provided. Vault toilets are available. There is no drinking water. Garbage must be packed out. Leashed pets are permitted.

Reservations, fees: Reservations are not accepted. There is no fee for camping. A 14-day stay limit for every 30 days is enforced; 28 camping days maximum per year. Open year-round.

Directions: From Bakersfield, drive east on Highway 178 for approximately 40 miles to the town of Lake Isabella and Highway 155. Turn left (north) on Highway 155 and drive one mile to Keyesville Road. Turn left and drive 0.5 mile to the Special Management Area entrance.

Contact: Bureau of Land Management, Bakersfield Field Office, 661/391-6000, www.blm.gov/ca.

160 AUXILIARY DAM

🏊 🛶 ⚓ 🐴 ♿ 🚐 ⛺

Scenic rating: 8

on Isabella Lake

This primitive camp was designed to be an overflow area if other camps at Isabella Lake are packed. It's the only camp directly on the shore of the lake, and many people like it. In addition, a boat ramp is just a mile east for good lake access, and the sailboarding prospects adjacent to the campground are the best of the entire lake. The winds come up and sail right over the dam, creating a steady breeze in the afternoon that is not gusty. The elevation is 2,650 feet.

Campsites, facilities: There are a number of primitive, undesignated sites for tents or RVs of any length (no hookups). Drinking water and restrooms with flush toilets and coin showers are available. Supplies and a coin laundry are available in the town of Lake Isabella. Some facilities are wheelchair-accessible. Leashed pets are permitted.

Reservations, fees: Reservations are not accepted. Sites are $10 per night per vehicle May through September or $50 for a season pass. There is no fee for camping October through April. Open year-round.

Directions: From Bakersfield, drive east on Highway 178 for about 40 miles to the town of Lake Isabella. Continue east on Highway 178 for one mile to the campground entrance.

Contact: Sequoia National Forest, Kern River Ranger District, Lake Isabella Office, 760/379-5646, www.fs.fed.us.

161 PARADISE COVE

Scenic rating: 6

on Isabella Lake

Paradise Cove is on the southeast shore of Isabella Lake at 2,600 feet elevation. A boat ramp is about two miles away to the west, near the South Fork Picnic Area. While the camp is not directly at the lakeshore, it does overlook the broadest expanse of the lake. This part of the lake is relatively undeveloped compared to the areas near Wofford Heights and the dam.
Campsites, facilities: There are 58 sites for tents and a primitive area for up to 80 RVs of any length (no hookups). Picnic tables and fire grills are provided at some sites. Drinking water, restrooms with flush toilets and coin showers, dump station, and fish-cleaning station are available. A camp host is on-site. Some facilities are wheelchair-accessible. Supplies, dump station, and coin laundry are available in Mountain Mesa. Leashed pets are permitted.
Reservations, fees: Reservations are accepted at 877/444-6777 or www.recreation.gov ($9 reservation fee). Sites are $20–22 per night, $5 per night for each additional vehicle. Open year-round.
Directions: From Bakersfield, drive east on Highway 178 for about 40 miles to the town of Lake Isabella. Continue east on Highway 178 for six miles to the campground entrance.
Contact: Sequoia National Forest, Kern River Ranger District, Lake Isabella Office, 760/379-5646, www.fs.fed.us.

162 KOA LAKE ISABELLA/ KERN RIVER

Scenic rating: 4

on Isabella Lake

This KOA camp provides a good, clean option to the Forest Service camps on the southern end of Isabella Lake, Southern California's largest lake. It is set in South Fork Valley (elevation 2,600 feet), east of the lake off Highway 178. The nearest boat ramp is at South Fork Picnic Area (about a five-minute drive to the west), where there is also a good view of the lake.
Campsites, facilities: There are 70 sites with full or partial hookups (30 amps) for tents or RVs up to 40 feet; some sites are pull-through. Picnic tables and fire rings are provided. Restrooms with flush toilets and showers, drinking water, playground, seasonal swimming pool, coin laundry, recreation room, pub, convenience store, dump station, firewood, and propane gas are available. Leashed pets are permitted with some restrictions.
Reservations, fees: Reservations are accepted at 800/562-2085. RV sites are $42–48 per night, tent sites are $29–37 per night, $5 per person per night for more than two people. Some credit cards accepted. Open year-round.
Directions: From Bakersfield, drive east on Highway 178 for about 40 miles to the town of Lake Isabella. Continue east on Highway 178 for 10 miles to the campground entrance on the left (well signed).
Contact: KOA Lake Isabella/Kern River, 760/378-2001, www.koa.com.

163 SANDY FLAT

Scenic rating: 6

on the Kern River in Sequoia National Forest

This camp is opened as an overflow camp if Hobo is filled. It is about a mile from Hobo. It is a low-use campground, with less shade than Hobo; some sites are shaded, others, well, nope. It is used primarily as a boat launch area for kayakers and rafters. Fishing is fair for catfish, bass, and rainbow trout. The river is stocked with trout in the summer.
Campsites, facilities: There are 35 sites for tents or RVs up to 24 feet (no hookups),

including six walk-in sites. Fire rings and picnic tables are provided. Vault toilets and drinking water are available. Some facilities are wheelchair-accessible. Leashed pets are permitted.

Reservations, fees: Reservations are accepted at 877/444-6777 or www.recreation.gov ($9 reservation fee). Sites are $18 per night, $5 per night for each additional vehicle. Open year-round.

Directions: From Bakersfield, drive east on Highway 178 for 35 miles to Borel Road (five miles from Lake Isabella). Turn right (south) at Borel Road and drive 0.3 mile to Old Kern Canyon Road. Turn right and drive one mile to the campground on your right.

Contact: Sequoia National Forest, Kern River Ranger District, Lake Isabella Office, 760/379-5646, www.fs.fed.us.

164 HOBO

Scenic rating: 7

on the Kern River in Sequoia National Forest

BEST (

The secret is out about Hobo: It is set adjacent to a mineral hot springs, that is, an open-air springs, with room for about 10 people at once. The camp is also situated along the lower Kern River, about 10 miles downstream of the dam at Isabella Lake. Rafters sometimes use this camp as a put-in spot for an 18-mile run to the takeout at Democrat Picnic Area, a challenging Class IV run. The elevation is 2,300 feet.

Campsites, facilities: There are 35 sites for tents or RVs up to 22 feet (no hookups). Fire grills and picnic tables are provided. Drinking water, vault toilets, showers, and dump station are available. Leashed pets are permitted.

Reservations, fees: Reservations are not accepted. Sites are $18 per night, $5 per night for each additional vehicle. Open April through September.

Directions: From Bakersfield, drive east on Highway 178 for 35 miles to Borel Road (five miles from Lake Isabella). Turn right (south) at Borel Road and drive 0.3 mile to Old Kern Road. Turn right and drive two miles to the campground on your right.

Contact: Sequoia National Forest, Kern River Ranger District, Lake Isabella Office, 760/379-5646, www.fs.fed.us.

165 BRECKENRIDGE

Scenic rating: 7

in Sequoia National Forest

This is a popular spot for people to visit with sport utility vehicles. It is a tiny, primitive camp set at 6,600 feet elevation near Breckenridge Mountain (a good lookout here) in a little-traveled southwest sector of the Sequoia National Forest. From camp, it's a two-mile drive south up to the lookout, with sweeping views afforded in all directions. There are no other camps in the immediate area.

Campsites, facilities: There are eight tent sites. Picnic tables and fire grills are provided. Vault toilets are available. No drinking water is available. Garbage must be packed out. Leashed pets are permitted.

Reservations, fees: Reservations are not accepted. There is no fee for camping. Open May through September.

Directions: From Bakersfield, drive east on Highway 178 for about 40 miles to the town of Lake Isabella and Lake Isabella Boulevard. Turn right (south) on Lake Isabella Boulevard and drive two miles to a Y intersection with Kern River Canyon Road and Caliente Bodfish Road. Bear left on Caliente Bodfish Road and drive nine miles to the town of Havilah. Continue on Caliente Bodfish Road for two miles to Forest Road 28S06. Turn right and drive about 10 miles to the campground.

Contact: Sequoia National Forest, Kern River Ranger District, Lake Isabella Office, 760/379-5646, www.fs.fed.us.

CAMPING

166 KERN RIVER CAMPGROUND

🏊 🚐 🏕 🎣 ♿ 🚙 ⛺

Scenic rating: 6

at Lake Ming

The campground is set at Lake Ming, a small but exciting place. The lake covers just 205 surface acres, and with the weather so hot, the hot jet boats can make it a wild affair here. It's become a popular spot for southern valley residents, only a 15-minute drive from Bakersfield. It is so popular for water sports that every year, beginning in March, the lake is closed to the public one weekend per month for private boat races and waterskiing competitions. The lake is restricted to sailing and sailboarding on the second weekend of every month and on Tuesday and Thursday afternoons. All other boating, including waterskiing, is permitted on the remaining days. All boats are required to have a permit; boaters may buy one at the park. Swimming is not allowed because there is a parasite in the water that has been known to cause swimmer's itch. Yikes. The lake is stocked with rainbow trout in the winter months, and they join a sprinkling of bluegill, catfish, crappie, and bass. The elevation is 450 feet. Maximum stay is 10 days.

Campsites, facilities: There are 50 sites for tents or RVs up to 28 feet. Picnic tables and fire rings are provided. Restrooms with flush toilets and coin showers, drinking water, dump station, playground, concession stand, picnic area, and boat ramp are available. Some facilities are wheelchair-accessible. A store is nearby. Leashed pets are permitted.

Reservations, fees: Reservations are not accepted. Sites are $22 per night, $10 per night for a second vehicle, $5 per night for a towed vehicle, $4 per night per pet. Discounted prices in winter. Open year-round.

Directions: From Bakersfield, drive east on Highway 178 for 11 miles to Alfred Harrell Highway. Turn left (north) on Alfred Harrell Highway and drive four miles to Lake Ming Road. Turn right on Lake Ming Road and follow the signs to the campground on the right, 0.25 mile west of the lake.

Contact: Kern County Parks and Recreation Department, 661/868-7000, www.co.kern.ca.us/parks.

167 TROY MEADOWS

🥾 🏊 🏕 ♿ 🚙 ⛺

Scenic rating: 7

on Fish Creek in Sequoia National Forest

Obscure? Yes, but what the heck, it gives you an idea of what is possible out in the boondocks. The camp is set at 7,800 feet elevation right along Fish Creek. Black Rock Ranger Station is available two miles northwest. You are advised to stop there before any backcountry trips. Note that off-highway vehicles (OHVs) are allowed in this area. Also note that Jackass National Recreation Trail is a short drive to the east; it runs north aside Jackass Creek to its headwaters just below Jackass Peak (9,245 feet).

Campsites, facilities: There are 73 sites for tents or RVs up to 20 feet (no hookups). Picnic tables and fire grills are provided. Drinking water and vault toilets are available. Garbage must be packed out. Some facilities are wheelchair-accessible. Leashed pets are permitted.

Reservations, fees: Reservations are not accepted. Sites are $17 per night, $5 per night per each additional vehicle. Open June through October, weather permitting.

Directions: Drive on U.S. 395 to Ninemile Canyon Road (four miles north of the town of Pearsonville, 48 miles south of Lone Pine). Turn west on Ninemile Canyon Road and drive 31 miles (the road becomes Sherman Pass Road) to the campground.

Contact: Sequoia National Forest, Kern River Ranger District, Kernville Office, 760/376-3781, www.fs.fed.us.

CAMPING

168 FISH CREEK

Scenic rating: 8

in Sequoia National Forest

This is a pretty spot set at the confluence of Fish Creek and Jackass Creek. The elevation is 7,500 feet. The nearby trails are used by off-highway vehicles, which can make this a noisy campground during the day.

Campsites, facilities: There are 40 sites for tents or RVs up to 27 feet (no hookups). Picnic tables and fire grills are provided. Drinking water and vault toilets are available. Garbage must be packed out. Leashed pets are permitted.

Reservations, fees: Reservations are not accepted. Sites are $17 per night, $5 per night per each additional vehicle. Open June through October, weather permitting.

Directions: Drive on U.S. 395 to Ninemile Canyon Road (four miles north of the town of Pearsonville, 48 miles south of Lone Pine). Turn west on Ninemile Canyon Road and drive 28 miles (the road becomes Sherman Pass Road) to the campground.

Contact: Sequoia National Forest, Kern River Ranger District, Kernville Office, 760/376-3781, www.fs.fed.us.

169 KENNEDY MEADOWS

Scenic rating: 8

on the South Fork of the Kern River in Sequoia National Forest

This is a pretty Forest Service campground set amid piñon pine and sage country, with the Pacific Crest Trail running by the camp. That makes it a great trailhead camp, as well as a refreshing stopover for PCT through-hikers. A highlight is the nearby South Fork Kern River, which provides fishing for rainbow trout. The camp receives moderate use and is a lifesaver for PCT through-hikers.

Campsites, facilities: There are 35 sites for tents or RVs up to 30 feet (no hookups) and three sites for RVs of any length. Picnic tables and fire rings are provided. Drinking water (seasonal) and vault toilets are available. Garbage must be packed out. Leashed pets are permitted.

Reservations, fees: Reservations are not accepted. Sites are $17 per night, $5 per night per each additional vehicle. Open year-round, weather permitting.

Directions: Drive on U.S. 395 to Ninemile Canyon Road (four miles north of the town of Pearsonville, 48 miles south of Lone Pine). Turn west on Ninemile Canyon Road and drive 21 miles to a small store. Bear right at the store (still Ninemile Canyon Road) and continue for three miles to the campground.

Contact: Sequoia National Forest, Kern River Ranger District, Kernville Office, 760/376-3781, www.fs.fed.us.

170 LONG VALLEY

Scenic rating: 5

near the Dome Land Wilderness

This one is way out there. It's set at road's end in Long Valley, a mile from the border of the Dome Land Wilderness to the east, and the camp is used primarily as a jump-off spot for hikers. A trail from camp leads 2.5 miles west, climbing along a small stream and reaching the South Fork of the Kern River, in rugged and remote country. The elevation is 5,200 feet.

Campsites, facilities: There are 13 tent sites. Picnic tables and fire grills are provided. Vault toilets are available. No drinking water is available. Garbage must be packed out. Leashed pets are permitted.

Reservations, fees: Reservations are not accepted. There is no fee for camping, but donations are encouraged. Open year-round.

Directions: Drive on U.S. 395 to Ninemile Canyon Road (four miles north of the town of Pearsonville, 48 miles south of Lone Pine).

Turn west on Ninemile Canyon Road and drive 11 miles to the BLM Work Station and Cane Brake Road. Turn left on Cane Brake Road (the dirt road opposite the BLM station) and drive six miles to Long Valley Road. Turn right and drive eight miles to the campground entrance road on the left. Turn left and drive one mile to the campground.

Contact: Bureau of Land Management, Bakersfield Field Office, 661/391-6000, www. blm.gov/ca.

171 CHIMNEY CREEK

Scenic rating: 5

on the Pacific Crest Trail

This BLM camp is set at 5,900 feet elevation along the headwaters of Chimney Creek, on the southern flank of Chimney Peak (7,990 feet) two miles to the north. This is a trailhead camp for the Pacific Crest Trail, one of its relatively obscure sections. The PCT heads north from camp and in 10 miles skirts the eastern border of Dome Land Wilderness.

Campsites, facilities: There are 32 sites for tents or RVs up to 25 feet (no hookups). Picnic tables and fire grills are provided. Vault toilets are available. Drinking water is seasonally available at the campground. Garbage must be packed out. Horses and leashed pets are permitted.

Reservations, fees: Reservations are not accepted. There is no fee for camping, but donations are encouraged. Open year-round.

Directions: Drive on U.S. 395 to Ninemile Canyon Road (four miles north of the town of Pearsonville, 48 miles south of Lone Pine). Turn west on Ninemile Canyon Road and drive 11 miles to the BLM Work Station and Cane Brake Road. Turn left on Cane Brake Road (the dirt road opposite the BLM station) and drive three miles to the camp on the left.

Contact: Bureau of Land Management, Bakersfield Field Office, 661/391-6000, www. blm.gov/ca.

172 WALKER PASS WALK-IN

Scenic rating: 6

on the Pacific Crest Trail southwest of Death Valley National Park

Long-distance hikers on the Pacific Crest Trail treat this camp as if they were arriving at Valhalla. That's because it is set right on the trail. The camp is set at 5,200 feet elevation, southwest of Death Valley National Park. And if you guessed it was named for Joe Walker, the West's greatest trailblazer and one of my heroes, well, right you are. If you arrive by car instead of on the PCT, use this spot as a base camp. Because of its desert remoteness, very few hikers start trips from this location.

Campsites, facilities: There are two sites for tents or RVs up to 20 feet (no hookups) with limited parking and 11 walk-in sites for tents only. Picnic tables and fire rings are provided. No drinking water is available at the campground, but a spring development is located 0.1 mile west on Highway 178, in the bottom of the drainage by the 30-mph sign. Pit toilets are available. Hitching racks and corrals are available. Garbage must be packed out. Leashed pets are permitted.

Reservations, fees: Reservations are not accepted. There is no fee for camping, but donations are encouraged. A 14-day stay limit is enforced. Open year-round.

Directions: From Bakersfield, drive east on Highway 178 for about 40 miles to the town of Lake Isabella. Continue east on Highway 178 to Onyx and continue 14 miles to Walker Pass and the right side of the road (where a sign is posted for the Pacific Crest Trail). Park and walk 0.25 mile to the campground.

Contact: Bureau of Land Management, Bakersfield Field Office, 661/391-6000, www. blm.gov/ca.

SEQUOIA AND KINGS CANYON HIKING

© LANDIS BENNETT

BEST HIKES

Located on the western slope of the Sierra
Nevada, Sequoia and Kings Canyon National Parks are famous for their
giant sequoia groves, tall mountains, deep canyons, roaring rivers, and
spectacular hiking trails with views of the jagged peaks of the Great Western Divide. Often referred to as "Yosemite without the masses," these
two side-by-side national parks offer classic Sierra scenery without the
infamous overcrowding that plagues that great park to the north. Kings
Canyon and Sequoia have been managed jointly by the National Park
Service since 1943.

The parks abound with superlatives. The highest peak in the contiguous United States – Mount Whitney, at 14,496 feet – is located in Sequoia
National Park, although most people hike to it from the east side, in Inyo
National Forest. Several other park summits top out at more than 14,000
feet. The largest living tree in the world, the Sherman Tree, is found in
Sequoia National Park. At 275 feet tall and with a 103-foot circumference
at the ground, the massive tree is still growing; every year it adds enough
wood to make another 60-foot-tall tree. The second- and third-largest
trees in the world, named Washington and General Grant, respectively,
are also found in Sequoia and Kings Canyon. No nature experience is
quite as awe-inspiring or as humbling as hiking through a grove of these
giant trees.

Three powerful rivers course through the boundaries of Sequoia and
Kings Canyon: the Kings, Kern, and Kaweah. The canyon of the Kings
River is carved to a depth of 8,000 feet below the summit of neighboring
Spanish Mountain, making Kings Canyon deeper than the Grand Canyon
or any other canyon in North America. Hikers who make the long drive on
Highway 180 alongside this dramatic river eventually find themselves at

Roads End, where civilization ends and the wilderness begins. To continue through the Sierra from here, your only choice is to walk. Trail options range from easy strolls along the riverbanks to long, steep treks into the Monarch Wilderness.

A less-visited area of the parks, but a mecca for hikers, is the Mineral King region. A glacier-carved bowl surrounded by massive peaks, Mineral King Valley is crowned by the distinct, pointed pinnacle known as Sawtooth Peak. Reaching the 7,800-foot valley requires a circuitous 25-mile drive from the foothills of Three Rivers. Once the drive is accomplished, hikers can choose from a wide variety of day-hiking and backpacking trails, many of which lead to 10,000-foot-plus alpine lakes.

In December 2000 a new park was tacked on to the borders of Sequoia and Kings Canyon: Giant Sequoia National Monument. Administered by the U.S. Forest Service, not the National Park Service, the national monument contains two noncontiguous land areas, both designated to increase protection for the last remaining giant sequoia groves in the world.

The recreation options don't stop at the national park and monument borders. Hikers can walk through much-less-visited giant sequoia groves in national forest and state forest lands near Dinkey Lakes (McKinley Grove) and Springville (Mountain Home State Forest). Visitors seeking the polished granite landscape of the national parks without the accompanying crowds can find it along the trails of the Kaiser Wilderness area, near Huntington Lake. And far across the Sierra Nevada, on the U.S. 395 corridor in the Eastern Sierra, hikers can access one trailhead after another at the end of almost every road leading west off the highway. From Bishop to Big Pine to Independence to Lone Pine, each westward-bound road is a gateway to a world of hiking opportunities.

HIKING

HIKING

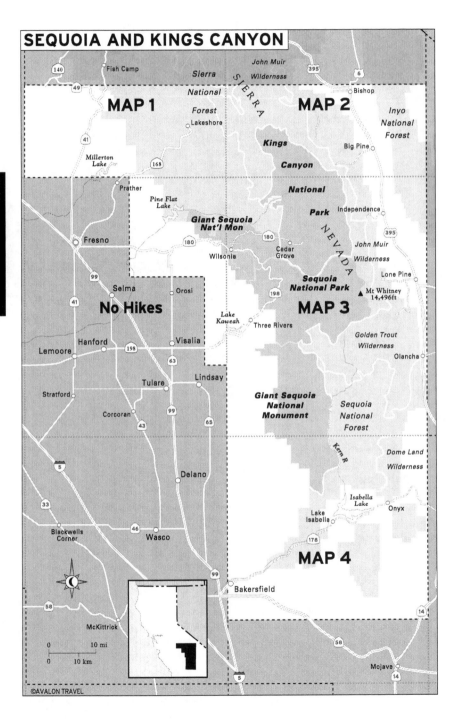

Map 1

Hikes 1-10

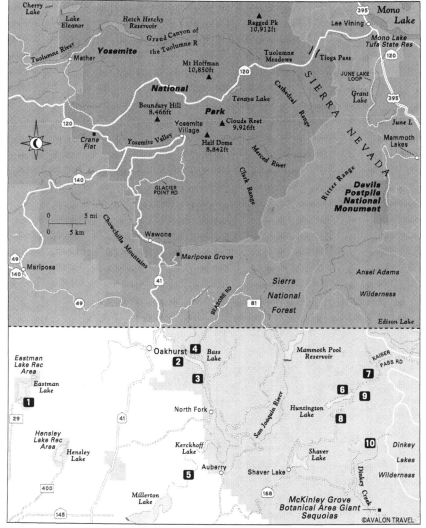

Map 2

Hikes 11-20

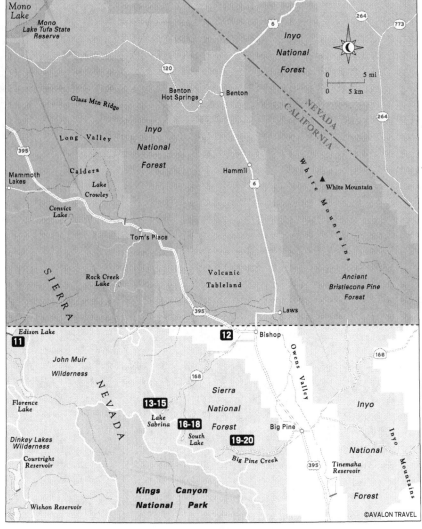

Map 3

Hikes 21-105

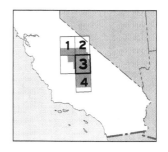

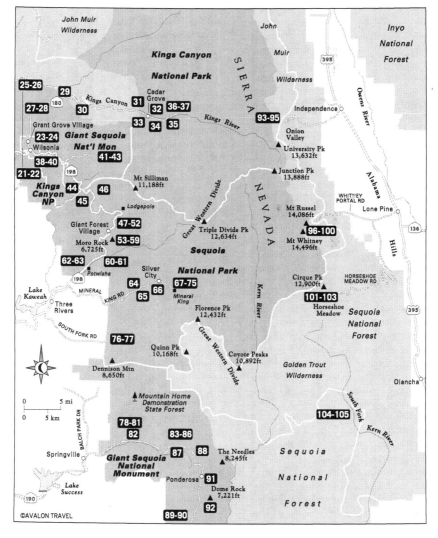

John Muir Wilderness

Kings Canyon National Park

Cedar Grove

25-26
29
27-28
180
30
Kings Canyon
31
32 36-37
Kings River
33 34 35
93-95

John Muir Wilderness

Independence

SIERRA

Inyo National Forest

Owens River

Grant Grove Village
23-24 *Giant Sequoia*
Wilsonia **Nat'l Mon**
38-40
21-22
198
Kings Canyon NP
44 46
45

Onion Valley
University Pk 13,632ft

Junction Pk 13,888ft

NEVADA

41-43

Mt Silliman 11,188ft

Lodgepole

Great Western Divide

WHITNEY PORTAL RD
Lone Pine

Mt Russel 14,086ft

Alabama

Giant Forest Village
47-52
Moro Rock 53-59
6,725ft
62-63 60-61
198 Potwisha
64 66
65
Silver City
Mineral King
67-75
76-77
Quinn Pk 10,168ft

Triple Divide Pk 12,634ft

Sequoia

National Park

Florence Pk 12,432ft

Great Western Divide

Coyote Peaks 10,892ft

96-100
Mt Whitney 14,496ft

Kern River

Cirque Pk 12,900ft
101-103
Horseshoe Meadow

136

HORSESHOE MEADOW RD

Sequoia National Forest

395

Lake Kaweah
MINERAL
KING RD
Three Rivers
SOUTH FORK RD

Dennison Mtn 8,650ft

Golden Trout Wilderness

Olancha

0   5 mi
0   5 km

Mountain Home Demonstration State Forest

78-81
82
83-86
87 88
The Needles 8,245ft

104-105
South Fork
Kern River

BALCH PARK DR

Springville
Giant Sequoia National Monument
Ponderosa 91
Dome Rock 7,221ft

S e q u o i a

N a t i o n a l

Lake Success
190
89-90
92

F o r e s t

©AVALON TRAVEL

Map 4

Hikes 106-119

HIKING

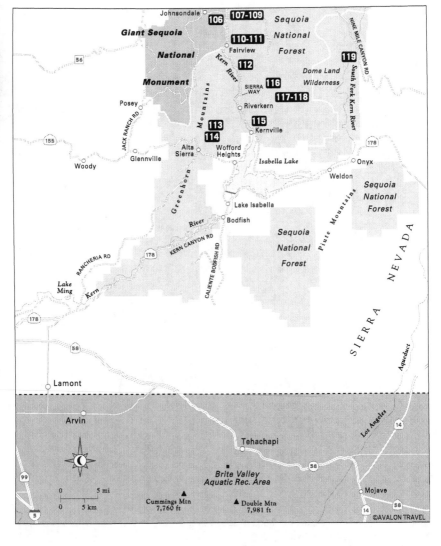

1 LAKEVIEW TRAIL
4.2 mi one-way / 2.0 hr   👫2   ⛰8

**on the southeast shore of
Eastman Lake east of Chowchilla**

Let's get one thing straight: You don't want to hike here at midday in July. Got it? Good. But if it's spring and the wildflowers are in bloom, you'd be wise to head out here to Eastman Lake, then hike the Lakeview Trail that leads along its south and east sides. Sure, a reservoir is a reservoir, but when the water level is high, the grasslands are green, and the flowers are blooming, this reservoir can seem like a little slice of paradise in the Central Valley. The Lakeview Trail leads a total of 4.2 miles one-way from the trailhead at the group campground to Raymond Bridge. Hike as little or as much of it as you please, watching for birds and identifying the wildflowers as you go. Bald eagle sightings are not uncommon; in the spring of 2007, part of this trail was temporarily closed to protect a family of bald eagles nesting along the lakeshore. You probably won't have a lot of company on this trail; after all, most people come to Eastman Lake to fish, not hike. In addition to its trophy bass fishery, the lake also boasts populations of crappie, bluegill, and catfish. They even stock rainbow trout here in the winter when the temperature cools down.

User Groups: Hikers, dogs, horses, and mountain bikes. No wheelchair facilities.

Permits: No permits are required. A $5 day-use fee is charged.

Maps: A free map of Eastman Lake is available at the visitors center. For a topographic map, ask the USGS for Raymond.

Directions: From Merced, drive south on Highway 99 for 20 miles to Chowchilla. Take the Avenue 26 exit and head east for 17 miles. Turn north on County Road 29 and drive eight miles to the lake entrance. Turn right and drive to the parking area by Cordorniz Group Campground.

Contact: U.S. Army Corps of Engineers, Eastman Lake, P.O. Box 67, Raymond, CA 93653, 559/689-3255.

2 WAY OF THE MONO
0.5 mi / 0.5 hr   👫1   ⛰6

**on the northwest end of
Bass Lake near Oakhurst**

The Way of the Mono is an educational trail that teaches about the Mono Indians, who were the first people to live in the Bass Lake area. They inhabited the area for more than 1,000 years. The interpretive displays along the trail point out grinding holes in the rocks, where the Mono people pounded acorns into meal, and describe different methods they used to live through the area's seasonal changes. In addition to a cultural history lesson, the trail also offers beautiful vistas of Bass Lake and its surroundings. Check out the view from the large granite outcrop of Bass Lake and surrounding peaks. This great loop hike takes only about 20 minutes to walk, but leaves you with a much greater understanding of the Bass Lake area.

User Groups: Hikers and dogs. No horses or mountain bikes. No wheelchair facilities.

Permits: No permits are required. Parking and access are free at the trailhead; parking in the day-use area is $3.

Maps: A Sierra National Forest map is available from the U.S. Forest Service. For a topographic map, ask the USGS for Bass Lake.

Directions: From Oakhurst, drive north on Highway 41 for four miles and then turn right on Road 222. Drive four miles and bear right to stay on Road 222. The signed trailhead parking area is across from Little Denver Church Day Use Area, between the Forks Resort and the California Land Management Office.

Contact: Sierra National Forest, Bass Lake Ranger District, 57003 Road 225, North Fork, CA 93643, 559/877-2218, www.fs.fed.us/r5/sierra.

HIKING

HIKING

3 GOAT MOUNTAIN FIRE LOOKOUT
8.0 mi / 4.0 hr   🥾3 ⛰8

on the south end of Bass Lake near Oakhurst

The route to Goat Mountain Fire Lookout can be hiked from trailheads at either Forks Campground or Spring Cove Campground. This is a must-do hike for the legions of campers who spend their summer vacations at Bass Lake. Both trails intersect in about two miles, then join and form one path for the last two miles to the lookout. No matter how you do it, the grade is memorably steep, but also rewarding. As you climb up the trail, you have nearly nonstop views of Bass Lake and the forested valleys surrounding it. You'll also be breathing hard. If you can talk someone into driving a second car to the other trailhead and campground, you can turn this into a pleasant semi-loop trip by hiking up one trail and down the other. Note that this trail has become increasingly popular with mountain bikers in the last few years. If you don't like sharing the trail with them, plan your hike for a weekday, when you're more likely to be out here by yourself. The fire lookout is perched at 4,675 feet in elevation, set on top of a 20-foot steel tower, and offers a 360-degree view.

User Groups: Hikers, dogs, horses, and mountain bikes. No wheelchair facilities.

Permits: No permits are required. Parking and access are free in the campgrounds, but $3 if you park in the day-use area.

Maps: A Sierra National Forest map is available from the U.S. Forest Service. For a topographic map, ask the USGS for Bass Lake.

Directions: From Oakhurst, drive north on Highway 41 for four miles and turn right on Road 222. Drive four miles and bear right to stay on Road 222. Continue along the western shore of Bass Lake for about five miles to Spring Cove Campground. The Spring Cove Trail begins on the east side of the campground entrance. If there is no parking there, you can park at Rocky Point Picnic Area ($3

fee). You can also hike to Goat Mountain Fire Lookout from Forks Campground, three miles north on Road 222.

Contact: Sierra National Forest, Bass Lake Ranger District, 57003 Road 225, North Fork, CA 93643, 559/877-2218, www.fs.fed.us/r5/sierra.

4 WILLOW CREEK
4.8 mi / 2.5 hr   🥾2 ⛰8

on the northeast end of Bass Lake near Oakhurst

Most people hike Willow Creek Trail with one of two things in mind: fishing or swimming. You can't blame them, since the moderately steep trail runs alongside Willow Creek and offers myriad quiet pools and fast, granite-lined cascades. The Forest Service requests that visitors don't swim upstream of Angel Falls, a wide cascade that looks like angel wings, because the creek is used as a domestic water supply. Downstream swimming is allowed, but be wary of the slippery granite. At 2.4 miles from the trailhead, be sure to take the left spur for Devils Slide, at a junction where the main trail continues to its end (0.4 mile farther) at McLeod Flat Road. Devils Slide is a remarkable granite water slide, with large rounded indentations in the rock. A chain-link fence keeps hikers off the dangerously slick granite. From Devils Slide, head back to the main trail and retrace your steps downhill. Expect to see some great views of bright-blue Bass Lake on the return trip.

User Groups: Hikers and dogs. No horses or mountain bikes. No wheelchair facilities.

Permits: No permits are required. Parking and access are free.

Maps: A Sierra National Forest map is available from the U.S. Forest Service. For a topographic map, ask the USGS for Bass Lake.

Directions: From Oakhurst, drive north on Highway 41 for four miles and turn right on Road 222. Drive four miles and bear left on

Road 274. Drive one mile to the trailhead parking area, on the left side of the road, on the west side of the highway bridge over Willow Creek. Alternatively, you can park near Falls Beach Picnic Area on Road 222 by Bass Lake's dam and access the trail via a connector route alongside Willow Creek.

Contact: Sierra National Forest, Bass Lake Ranger District, 57003 Road 225, North Fork, CA 93643, 559/877-2218, www.fs.fed.us/r5/sierra.

5 SQUAW LEAP LOOP
7.8 mi / 4.0 hr

near Millerton Lake

The Squaw Leap area, managed by the Bureau of Land Management, straddles the San Joaquin River upstream of Millerton Lake State Park. This pretty foothill country is best visited in winter or spring, primarily due to the cooler temperatures but also for a chance to see wildflowers. The well-built Six-Mile Loop Trail, which is actually 7.8 miles as described here, rolls through chaparral country. Ceanothus and manzanita line the hillsides; gray pines and blue oaks dot the landscape. The trail begins with a one-mile stretch that leads you down to the river and the start of the loop. A surprisingly well-built footbridge takes you across the river canyon, where you have fine views of whitewater cascades, both upstream and down. On the far side of the bridge, go left on River Trail for 0.7 mile, then bear right on Ridge Trail. At mileage marker No. 3, you have a fine view of the river canyon; this is the best place to stop for a snack. Ridge Trail brings you right back downhill to the bridge you crossed earlier; cross it again and head back to your car to finish out the trip.

User Groups: Hikers, dogs, horses, and mountain bikes. No wheelchair facilities.

Permits: No permits are required. Parking and access are free.

Maps: For a topographic map, ask the USGS for Millerton Lake East.

Directions: From Fresno, drive 37 miles east on Highway 168 and turn left on Auberry Road. Drive through Auberry and turn left on Powerhouse Road. Drive 1.9 miles and turn left on Smalley Road at the sign for Squaw Leap Management Area. Park by the campground and signed trailhead.

Contact: Bureau of Land Management, Bakersfield Field Office, 3801 Pegasus Drive, Bakersfield, CA 93308, 661/391-6000, www.ca.blm.gov/bakersfield.

6 KAISER PEAK
10.6 mi / 6.0 hr or 2 days

in the Kaiser Wilderness north of Huntington Lake near Lakeshore

While many visitors to Huntington Lake take the short strolls to Rancheria Falls or the Indian Pools on Big Creek, far fewer attempt the ascent of Kaiser Peak. Why? Because it's a butt-kicking, 5.3-mile climb to the top, gaining 3,000 feet of elevation on the way to the 10,320-foot peak. Luckily, you get many excellent views of Huntington Lake on the way up, and at the halfway point, you can scramble up for a view and a rest on huge College Rock. Then it's up, up, and up some more, for what seems like an eternity. Finally, you gain the rocky summit, and at last you know why you came. You're wowed by incredible 360-degree views, which take in Mammoth Pool Reservoir, Huntington Lake, Shaver Lake, Mount Ritter, and Mount Goddard. Wow. Backpackers looking for more mileage can turn the hike into a 14-mile loop trip.

User Groups: Hikers, dogs, and horses. No mountain bikes. No wheelchair facilities.

Permits: A free wilderness permit is required for overnight stays and is available from the High Sierra/Prather Ranger Station. Quotas are in effect year-round; permits are available in advance for a $5 reservation fee per person.

Maps: A Sierra National Forest or Kaiser Wilderness map is available from the U.S. Forest Service. For a topographic map, ask the USGS for Kaiser Peak.

Directions: From Fresno, drive northeast on Highway 168 through Clovis for 70 miles to Huntington Lake, turn left on Huntington Lake Road, and drive one mile. Look for the large sign for the horse stables and pack station, and turn right. Follow the pack station road (Deer Creek Road) for 0.5 mile to the hikers' parking area. The trailhead is signed Kaiser Loop Trail.

Contact: Sierra National Forest, High Sierra Ranger District, P.O. Box 559, Prather, CA 93651, 559/855-5360, www.fs.fed.us/r5/sierra.

7 TWIN LAKES AND GEORGE LAKE
8.0-9.8 mi /
6.0-7.0 hr or 2 days   🏃3 ⛰9

in the Kaiser Wilderness north of
Huntington Lake near Lakeshore

Trails into the Kaiser Wilderness always seem to come with a climb, and the route to Twin Lakes and George Lake is no exception. But if you're willing to work your heart and lungs, your reward is a spectacular day hike or backpacking trip to three scenic alpine lakes. Along the way, you must ascend to Kaiser Ridge and cross over it through Potter Pass. You're witness to wildflower-filled meadows, dense conifer forests, and a classic Sierra view from the pass. You can easily make out the jagged outline of the Minarets. It's a great spot to stop and catch your breath. Then it's downhill from the pass to the granite-lined Twin Lakes, at three miles out. Many people make this their destination, then turn around for a six-mile round-trip. If you do, make sure you visit the second Twin Lake, which is much prettier than the first. For those continuing onward, it's uphill again to George Lake, 1.3

miles from Upper Twin Lake. The final push is definitely worth it. Trailhead elevation is 8,200 feet, Twin Lakes are at 8,800 feet, and George Lake is at 9,300 feet. Another good route to these lakes is from the trailhead near Sample Meadow Campground, farther north on Kaiser Pass Road. If you're willing to drive farther, this trail has less of a climb.

User Groups: Hikers, dogs, and horses. No mountain bikes. No wheelchair facilities.

Permits: A free wilderness permit is required for overnight stays and is available from the High Sierra/Prather Ranger Station. Quotas are in effect year-round; permits are available in advance for a $5 reservation fee per person.

Maps: A Sierra National Forest or Kaiser Wilderness map is available from the U.S. Forest Service. For a topographic map, ask the USGS for Kaiser Peak.

Directions: From Fresno, drive northeast on Highway 168 through Clovis for 70 miles to Huntington Lake; turn right on Kaiser Pass Road and drive 4.8 miles to a large parking area on the south side of the road. The trail begins across the road from the parking area. Look for a trail sign for Trail 24E03, Twin Lakes and Potter Pass. Park on the south side of the road; the trail begins on the north side of the road.

Contact: Sierra National Forest, High Sierra Ranger District, P.O. Box 559, Prather, CA 93651, 559/855-5360, www.fs.fed.us/r5/sierra.

8 INDIAN POOLS
1.5 mi / 1.0 hr   🏃1 ⛰8

off Highway 168 near Huntington Lake

When campers at Huntington Lake's many campgrounds are looking for a place to cool off in the afternoon, Indian Pools is where they go. The hike is really a walk, suitable for all ages and abilities. You can stop almost anywhere you like along Big Creek, pick a pool, and wade in. The trailhead is a bit tricky to find; it's all the way at the far end of the Sierra Summit Ski Area parking lot, near some mobile homes and trailers. Ignore the wide dirt road and instead look for the single-track trail signed for Indian Pools. It's a smooth, dirt path that quickly meets up with Big Creek. Flowers bloom in profusion along the stream and the rocky areas of the trail. The official path ends 0.7 mile east of the trailhead, at a huge, clear pool that is big enough to jump into and swim across. A use trail continues farther upstream, marked by trail cairns. If you follow it, you can reach quieter, more private pools.

User Groups: Hikers and dogs. No horses or mountain bikes. No wheelchair facilities.

Permits: No permits are required. Parking and access are free.

Maps: A Sierra National Forest map is available from the U.S. Forest Service. For a topographic map, ask the USGS for Huntington Lake.

Directions: From Fresno, drive northeast on Highway 168 through Clovis for 70 miles, past Shaver Lake. One mile before reaching Huntington Lake, turn right at the signed Sierra Summit Ski Area. Drive 0.5 mile to the far end of the ski area parking lot and look for the signed trailhead for Indian Pools. Occasionally the Sierra Summit parking lot is closed, and you must park on Highway 168 and walk the short distance into the ski area.

Contact: Sierra National Forest, High Sierra Ranger District, P.O. Box 559, Prather, CA 93651, 559/855-5360, www.fs.fed.us/r5/sierra.

🄈 RANCHERIA FALLS
2.0 mi / 1.0 hr

off Highway 168 near Huntington Lake

At 7,760 feet in elevation in Sierra National Forest, the air is clean and fresh, butterflies flutter amid the wildflowers, and a 150-foot waterfall sparkles in the sunlight. Wanna go?

It's an easy trip, with the trailhead located close to popular Huntington Lake. The hike to Rancheria Falls is a well-graded one mile on a National Recreation Trail, suitable for hikers of all levels. The route leads through a fir forest with an understory of wildflowers and gooseberry, and it delivers you at Rancheria Falls' base, where you watch the creek tumble over a 50-foot-wide rock ledge. On weekends the destination can be a little crowded, but you can pick a boulder downstream from the falls and call it your own. Then have a seat and watch the watery spectacle unfold.

User Groups: Hikers, dogs, horses, and mountain bikes. No wheelchair facilities.

Permits: No permits are required. Parking and access are free.

Maps: A Sierra National Forest map is available from the U.S. Forest Service. For a topographic map, ask the USGS for Huntington Lake.

Directions: From Fresno, drive northeast on Highway 168 through Clovis for 70 miles, past Shaver Lake. A half mile before reaching Huntington Lake, take the right turnoff signed for Rancheria Falls (Road 8S31). Follow the dirt road for 1.3 miles to the signed trailhead, at a sharp curve in the road. Park off the road.

Contact: Sierra National Forest, High Sierra Ranger District, P.O. Box 559, Prather, CA 93651, 559/855-5360, www.fs.fed.us/r5/sierra.

🄉 DINKEY LAKES
7.0 mi / 4.0 hr or 2 days

in Dinkey Lakes Wilderness off Highway 168 near Shaver Lake

We've never met anybody who doesn't love the Dinkey Lakes. What's not to love? The small wilderness area has dozens of lakes, and most are so easily accessible that you can see them in a day hike rather than packing along all your gear for an overnight stay. The trip begins with a stream crossing over Dinkey Creek, where you are immediately awed by the incredible array of colors in the rock streambed. Walk on level trail through a flower-filled forest, recross the creek, and start to climb. At 1.3 miles, you reach the junction for the start of the loop. Go right and meet Mystery Lake at 1.6 miles, Swede Lake at 2.3 miles, South Lake at 3.2 miles, and finally First Dinkey Lake at 3.8 miles. First Dinkey Lake is the most beautiful of them all. After taking in the scenery, continue on the loop, now heading westward back to the parking lot. One caveat: Don't expect much solitude. The easy hiking here makes this area extremely popular. Note that the loop described here works as either a day hike or backpacking trip, but if you choose to backpack, you can explore much farther, taking the spurs off the end of the main loop, between South Lake and First Dinkey Lake, to Second Dinkey Lake, Island Lake, Rock Lake, and so on.

User Groups: Hikers, dogs, and horses. No mountain bikes. No wheelchair facilities.

Permits: A wilderness permit is required for overnight stays and is available from the High Sierra/Prather Ranger Station. Quotas are in effect year-round; permits are available in advance for a $5 reservation fee per person.

Maps: A Dinkey Lakes Wilderness map is available from Tom Harrison Maps or the U.S. Forest Service. For topographic maps, ask the USGS for Huntington Lake and Dogtooth Peak.

Directions: From Fresno, drive northeast on Highway 168 through Clovis for 50 miles to the town of Shaver Lake. Turn right on Dinkey Creek Road and drive nine miles. Turn left on Rock Creek Road/9S09, drive 6 miles, turn right on 9S10, and drive 4.7 miles. Turn right at the sign for Dinkey Lakes, on Road 9S62, and drive 2.2 miles to the trailhead. These last two miles are very rough road. Stay left at the fork to bypass the four-wheel-drive area and go straight to the trailhead.

Contact: Sierra National Forest, High Sierra Ranger District, P.O. Box 559, Prather, CA 93651, 559/855-5360, www.fs.fed.us/r5/sierra.

11 LAKE THOMAS EDISON TO AGNEW MEADOWS (JMT / PCT)

38.0 mi one-way / 3 days 🏃4 ⛰10

from Lake Thomas Edison north to Agnew Meadows

The world is not perfect, but the scene from Silver Pass comes close. At 10,900 feet, you scan a bare, high-granite landscape sprinkled with alpine lakes. Just north of the pass are five small lakes: Chief, Papoose, Warrior, Squaw, and Lake of the Lone Indian. This is the highlight on this 38-mile section of the Pacific Crest Trail. The trip starts at Mono Creek, with a good resupply point at Edison Lake (7,650 feet), just two miles away. From the Mono Creek junction, you head north toward Silver Pass, climbing along Silver Pass Creek much of the way. Before you get to Silver Pass, there's a stream crossing that can be dangerous in high-runoff conditions. Top Silver Pass at 10,900 feet, and enjoy a five-mile descent and then a quick ascent to Tully Hole (9,250 feet). Climbing north, you pass Deer Creek, Purple Lake, and Lake Virginia. You head up to Red Cones and then make a steady descent toward Devils Postpile National Monument. A good resupply point is at nearby Reds Meadows Pack Station.

To continue north on the John Muir Trail/Pacific Crest Trail (JMT/PCT), see the *Agnew Meadows to Tuolumne Meadows (JMT/PCT)* hike in the *Yosemite and Mammoth Lakes* chapter. If you are walking this trail in reverse, see the *Whitney Portal to Lake Thomas Edison (JMT/PCT)* hike in this chapter.

Special Note: For food drop information, call the Vermillion Valley Resort. It is open only in summer and fall.

User Groups: Hikers, dogs, and horses. No mountain bikes. No wheelchair facilities.

Permits: A wilderness permit is required for traveling through various wilderness and special-use areas the trail traverses. Contact the Inyo National Forest or Sierra National Forest at the addresses below.

Maps: A John Muir Trail Map Pack is available from Tom Harrison Maps. For topographic maps, ask the USGS for Mammoth Mountain, Crystal Crag, Bloody Mountain, Graveyard Peak, Mount Ritter, and Coip Peak.

Directions: From Fresno, drive northeast on Highway 168 for about 68 miles to the Lakeshore Resort Area, at Huntington Lake. Turn northeast onto Kaiser Pass Road/Forest Service 4S01. Kaiser Pass Road becomes Edison Lake Road at Mono Hot Springs. Drive another five miles north, past the Vermillion Resort and Campground, and beyond to the parking area for backcountry hikers. The trail begins near the west end of the lake.

Contact: Inyo National Forest, Mammoth Ranger Station, P.O. Box 148, Mammoth Lakes, CA 93546, 760/924-5500 or 760/873-2400 (permits), www.fs.usda.gov/inyo; Sierra National Forest, High Sierra Ranger District, P.O. Box 559, Prather, CA 93651, 559/855-5360, www.fs.fed.us/r5/sierra; Vermillion Valley Resort, 559/855-6558 (food drop).

🔢 HONEYMOON LAKE
12.0 mi / 1-2 days

in the John Muir Wilderness

Since the trailhead elevation in Pine Creek Canyon is only 7,400 feet, the best destinations must be gained with a climb. That includes Honeymoon Lake, six miles and a 3,000-foot ascent away. Luckily, you pass Upper and Lower Pine Lake along the route, and there's enough spectacular scenery to keep you motivated as you huff and puff. The route begins by the pack station in the trees along Pine Creek, then joins a mining road that leads to the Brownstone Mine. (Don't be put off by the mining activity at this trailhead. You soon leave it behind as you enter the John Muir Wilderness.) As you switchback up and out of the trees, you gain views of the Owens River Valley and the desertlike White Mountains. Above the mine, the road becomes a trail and

also becomes extremely rocky as it ascends more switchbacks to meet first Lower and then Upper Pine Lake, at 4.7 and 5.7 miles. The upper lake is at 10,400 feet and is reached by following the trail along the lower lake's northwest shore. A quarter mile beyond the upper lake, you reach a trail junction and take the right fork toward Italy Pass, heading west to Honeymoon Lake (in 0.1 mile). Many campsites are found near the granite-bound lake, set at 10,400 feet.

User Groups: Hikers, dogs, and horses. No mountain bikes. No wheelchair facilities.

Permits: A free wilderness permit is required year-round for overnight stays and is available from the Bishop/White Mountain Ranger Station. Quotas are in effect from May 1 to November 1; permits are available in advance for a $5 reservation fee per person.

Maps: A John Muir Wilderness map is available from the U.S. Forest Service. A map of the Mono Divide High County is available from Tom Harrison Maps. For topographic maps, ask the USGS for Bishop and Tungsten Hills.

Directions: From Bishop, drive north on U.S. 395 for seven miles and turn left (west) on Pine Creek Road. Drive 9.5 miles to the trailhead parking area, near the pack station, on the left side of the road.

Contact: Inyo National Forest, White Mountain Ranger Station, 798 North Main Street, Bishop, CA 93514, 760/873-2500, www.fs.usda.gov/inyo.

🔢 BLUE LAKE
6.0 mi / 3.0 hr or 2 days

in the John Muir Wilderness

BEST (

The Sabrina Basin Trail leads to a series of gorgeous alpine lakes set below lofty, 13,000-foot granite peaks. Of these, one of the easiest to reach is scenic Blue Lake, a popular spot for photographers, trout anglers, and cold-water swimmers. If you catch the light just right, you can take pictures of Blue Lake with towering Mount Thompson and the Thompson Ridge mirrored on its surface. It's a 1,250-foot climb to the lake (at 10,400 feet), but it is spread out gradually over three miles. Nonetheless, be prepared for the thin air here, which can make the climb seem pretty strenuous if you're not acclimated. Start by hiking along the shore of Lake Sabrina, then switchback your way uphill to Blue Lake. The trail is very rocky in places; wear good boots. If you get inspired to see more of this high-alpine scenery, you can bear left from Blue Lake to Donkey Lake and the Baboon Lakes (1.5 miles farther), or bear right and hike eastward to the Emerald Lakes and Dingleberry Lake (1.8 miles farther). Any of these are likely to have fewer visitors than Blue Lake.

User Groups: Hikers, dogs, and horses. No mountain bikes. No wheelchair facilities.

Permits: A free wilderness permit is required year-round for overnight stays and is available from the Bishop/White Mountain Ranger Station. Quotas are in effect from May 1 to November 1; permits are available in advance for a $5 reservation fee per person.

Maps: A John Muir Wilderness map is available from the U.S. Forest Service. A Bishop Pass map is available from Tom Harrison Maps. For topographic maps, ask the USGS for Mount Thompson and Mount Darwin.

Directions: From Bishop on U.S. 395, turn west on Line Street/Highway 168 and drive 18.5 miles to Lake Sabrina. Day-use parking is located near the end of the road, just before the boat launch area. Backpackers' parking is located at a turnout near the road to North Lake, 0.5 mile before the end of the road.

Contact: Inyo National Forest, White Mountain Ranger Station, 798 North Main Street, Bishop, CA 93514, 760/873-2500, www.fs.usda.gov/inyo.

14 LAMARCK LAKES

6.0 mi / 3.0 hr or 2 days

in the John Muir Wilderness

The only downer on the Lamarck Lakes Trail is that from the trailhead parking area, you have to walk 0.5 mile down the road to get to the actual trailhead, which is located in North Lake Campground. No problem, though; the scenery is so lovely around here you won't mind the extra walk. Once you access the trailhead, the path heads through the aspens and crosses Bishop Creek on a footbridge. You'll climb gently for one mile through a lodgepole pine forest, gaining only 600 feet to the left fork for Grass Lake, a small and shallow lake in a wide meadow. Grass Lake is worth a brief glance, but it doesn't hold a candle to the Lamarck Lakes. Back on the main trail, the climb begins in earnest, but it's less than a mile more to the short right spur to Lower Lamarck Lake. The lower lake is quite scenic, set in a rock-lined granite basin. Look for Mount Emerson, Mount Lamarck, and the red-colored Piute Crags in the background. Many people make this their destination for the day, but if you want to see more, cross the lake's outlet creek and continue 0.5 mile farther to the Upper Lamarck Lake, which is nearly double in size. There isn't much in the way of a formal trail to Upper Lamarck; you just make your way by following the course of the outlet creek. Those looking for an adventure can make their way from the Lower Lamarck Lake to the Wonder Lakes, set in the basin northwest of Lower Lamarck. Trailhead elevation for this hike is 9,300 feet, the lower lake is at 10,662 feet, and the upper lake is at 10,918 feet.

User Groups: Hikers, dogs, and horses. No mountain bikes. No wheelchair facilities.

Permits: A free wilderness permit is required year-round for overnight stays and is available from the Bishop/White Mountain Ranger Station. Quotas are in effect from May 1 to November 1; permits are available in advance for a $5 reservation fee per person.

Maps: A John Muir Wilderness map is available from the U.S. Forest Service. A Bishop Pass map is available from Tom Harrison Maps. For topographic maps, ask the USGS for Mount Thompson and Mount Darwin.
Directions: From Bishop on U.S. 395, turn west on Line Street/Highway 168 and drive 18 miles toward Lake Sabrina. Just before reaching the lake, turn right at the turnoff for North Lake. Drive 1.5 miles and turn right to park in the hiker parking lot by North Lake, near the pack station. Then walk 0.5 mile down the road to the trailhead, at the edge of North Lake Campground.
Contact: Inyo National Forest, White Mountain Ranger Station, 798 North Main Street, Bishop, CA 93514, 760/873-2500, www.fs.usda.gov/inyo.

15 LOCH LEVEN LAKE
5.0 mi / 3.0 hr

in the John Muir Wilderness

If you're in the mood for a shorter hike in the Bishop Creek and North Lake area, Loch Leven Lake could fit the bill. After walking 0.5 mile from the trailhead parking area to North Lake Campground's trailhead, take the trail marked for Piute Pass. A steep climb in the first mile will leave you panting. Luckily, the route is shaded by lodgepole pines. After you leave the forest, the grade lessens. You traverse a series of switchbacks that take you to the top of a high ridge, where Loch Leven Lake is nestled at 10,740 feet. As you curve your way up the ridge, be sure to stop occasionally and look back at the incredible valley below and the reddish-colored Piute Crags towering above. You'll say "wow" a bunch of times.

Loch Leven Lake is set right alongside the trail in a rocky glacial bowl. It is very long and narrow, with little accessible shoreline. A steep talus slope, usually snow covered, frames its back side. There are a few campsites on the far side of the lake in the whitebark pines.

Ambitious hikers can continue another 1.2 miles to Piute Lake, with little additional elevation gain. A bonus on this trip: In autumn, the quaking aspens along the lower reaches of the route can take your breath away. Total elevation gain to Loch Leven Lake is 1,400 feet.

User Groups: Hikers, dogs, and horses. No mountain bikes. No wheelchair facilities.
Permits: No permits are required. Parking and access are free.
Maps: A John Muir Wilderness map is available from the U.S. Forest Service. A Bishop Pass map is available from Tom Harrison Maps. For topographic maps, ask the USGS for Mount Thompson and Mount Darwin.
Directions: From Bishop on U.S. 395, turn west on Line Street/Highway 168 and drive 18 miles toward Lake Sabrina. Just before reaching the lake, turn right at the turnoff for North Lake. Drive 1.5 miles and turn right to park in the hiker parking lot by North Lake, near the pack station. Walk 0.5 mile down the road to the trailhead, at the edge of North Lake Campground.
Contact: Inyo National Forest, White Mountain Ranger Station, 798 North Main Street, Bishop, CA 93514, 760/873-2500, www.fs.usda.gov/inyo.

16 TYEE LAKES
7.0 mi / 4.0 hr or 2 days

in the John Muir Wilderness

BEST (

There's so much excellent hiking in the South Fork Bishop Creek Canyon, it's hard to choose where to go. Since so many backpackers opt for Bishop Pass Trail and its many lakes (see listing in this chapter), day hikers might do well to choose this trail to the Tyee Lakes instead. Just make sure that you are in the mood for hiking up, because you'll do plenty of that, with a total 2,000-foot elevation gain to the highest lakes. From the bridge over Bishop Creek, your climb begins immediately as you

HIKING

tromp up a hillside covered with sagebrush and aspens, gradually making your way through a few dozen switchbacks. You get great views of the Bishop Creek Canyon as you climb, which is an especially beautiful sight when the aspens are putting on their autumn color show. Finally you enter a lodgepole pine forest, and after two miles of climbing, the grade eases up. You reach one of the smaller, lower Tyee Lakes at 2.3 miles. Another 0.5 mile of climbing brings you to the next small lake (called Tyee Lake number two). These first two lakes are small and pondlike, edged with grass, and not worth much more than a second glance. But keep pushing onward, and in another 0.5 mile, you reach one of the larger Tyee Lakes (number three). The fourth and fifth lakes are only 0.25 mile farther and are separated by a small boulder field. The fifth lake is very small, but the fourth lake (elevation 11,015 feet) is large and beautiful. Backpackers usually set up their tent at the third lake and then day hike to the fourth and fifth lakes. Named for a brand of salmon eggs, the Tyee Lakes offer dependably good trout fishing and the chance to enjoy plenty of classic high Sierra scenery. Backpackers looking to make a semiloop can arrange to have a car waiting at Lake Sabrina in Bishop Creek Canyon, then continue from the Tyee Lakes to George Lake and then Lake Sabrina.

User Groups: Hikers, dogs, and horses. No mountain bikes. No wheelchair facilities.

Permits: A free wilderness permit is required year-round for overnight stays and is available from the Bishop/White Mountain Ranger Station. Quotas are in effect from May 1 to November 1; permits are available in advance for a $5 reservation fee per person.

Maps: A John Muir Wilderness map is available from the U.S. Forest Service. A Bishop Pass map is available from Tom Harrison Maps. For a topographic map, ask the USGS for Mount Thompson.

Directions: From Bishop on U.S. 395, turn west on Line Street/Highway 168 and drive 14 miles to the junction for South Lake. Go left and drive 4.5 miles on South Lake Road to the footbridge that crosses Bishop Creek. It is on the right, just before Willow Campground, and it is signed as Tyee Lakes and George Lake trailhead. Park alongside the road.

Contact: Inyo National Forest, White Mountain Ranger Station, 798 North Main Street, Bishop, CA 93514, 760/873-2500, www.fs.usda.gov/inyo.

🔢 GREEN AND BROWN LAKES
6.6 mi / 3.0 hr　　🏃3 ⛰9

in the John Muir Wilderness

Brown Lake and Green Lake are two excellent day-hiking destinations from the South Lake trailhead in Bishop Creek's South Fork Canyon. With only a 1,500-foot climb, you can visit both lakes, maybe do a little fishing for rainbow trout, and be home in time for supper. Access the trail from the pack station trailhead, and follow a stock trail as it climbs along Bishop Creek through a conifer forest and joins the main Green Lake Trail at one mile. Bear left and level out to an alpine meadow at two miles, where you have a spectacular view of Mount Tom behind you. Soon you'll meet Brown Lake's outlet stream and the little lake itself (really a pond), at 2.5 miles and 10,750 feet. Pay a brief visit, then continue another 0.5 mile to much larger and prettier Green Lake, at 11,050 feet, surrounded by wildflowers and ancient-looking whitebark pines. Both lakes host an abundance of rainbow trout, who might just invite themselves to dinner.

User Groups: Hikers, dogs, and horses. No mountain bikes. No wheelchair facilities.

Permits: No permits are required. Parking and access are free.

Maps: A John Muir Wilderness map is available from the U.S. Forest Service. A Bishop Pass map is available from Tom Harrison Maps. For a topographic map, ask the USGS for Mount Thompson.

Directions: From Bishop on U.S. 395, turn west on Line Street/Highway 168 and drive 14 miles to the junction for South Lake. Go left and drive six miles on South Lake Road to Parchers Resort and pack station, on the left side of the road, just beyond Willow Campground.

Contact: Inyo National Forest, White Mountain Ranger Station, 798 North Main Street, Bishop, CA 93514, 760/873-2500, www.fs.usda.gov/inyo.

18 RUWAU AND CHOCOLATE LAKES LOOP
6.6 mi / 3.5 hr or 2 days 🏃3 ⛺10

In the John Muir Wilderness

Lakes, lakes, lakes everywhere. That's how it is on Bishop Pass Trail, where in the space of only five miles you can access Long Lake, Spearhead Lake, Saddlerock Lake, Bishop Lake, and so on. But if you prefer a loop trip to an out-and-back hike, Bishop Pass Trail provides another lake-filled option: a two-mile hike to Long Lake, then a circular route to Ruwau Lake, the Chocolate Lakes, and Bull Lake. It's the kind of trip that fills your mind with precious memories of blue-sky Sierra scenery and gemlike, rock-lined lakes. Still, the trip is not for everyone; some of the trail is an indistinct route with steep, rocky sections that are not an official trail. Bring a good map with you.

The trail begins on the south side of the parking lot, and you head uphill along the eastern shore of South Lake. The views begin almost immediately, particularly of South Lake, Mount Thompson, and Mount Goode. Take the left fork at 0.75 mile, heading for Long Lake and Bishop Pass. Continue straight, ignoring all turnoffs as you hike up around the spectacular western shore of Long Lake, popular with anglers and backpackers. At 2.5 miles (before you reach the lake's far end), instead of continuing straight to Saddlerock

Lake and Bishop Pass, take the left fork for Ruwau Lake, a steep but short 0.5 mile away. Skirt the edge of Ruwau Lake for about 75 yards, then look for a use trail leading uphill to your left. Make a steep uphill climb for 0.5 mile to the ridgetop, where you'll look down and see the Chocolate Lakes, set below Chocolate Peak. Make the steep descent to the lakes, picking your way along the rocky slope. Once you're there, the hard part is over. You'll find an easy-to-follow trail at the Chocolate Lakes, and then you'll walk downhill for 0.5 mile to Bull Lake, which is big, round, and beautiful. From Bull Lake, you keep on hiking, and in less than 0.25 mile, you rejoin Bishop Pass Trail. Turn right and walk just under two miles back to the parking lot. Wow, what a day.

User Groups: Hikers, dogs, and horses. No mountain bikes. No wheelchair facilities.

Permits: A free wilderness permit is required year-round for overnight stays and is available from the Bishop/White Mountain Ranger Station. Quotas are in effect from May 1 to November 1; permits are available in advance for a $5 reservation fee per person.

Maps: A John Muir Wilderness map is available from the U.S. Forest Service. A Bishop Pass map is available from Tom Harrison Maps. For a topographic map, ask the USGS for Mount Thompson.

Directions: From Bishop on U.S. 395, turn west on Line Street/Highway 168 and drive 14 miles to the junction for South Lake. Go left and drive 7.5 miles on South Lake Road to the end of the road and the trailhead parking area. This parking is for day-use only. If you are backpacking, you must park 1.5 miles from the trailhead, east of Parchers Resort.

Contact: Inyo National Forest, White Mountain Ranger Station, 798 North Main Street, Bishop, CA 93514, 760/873-2500, www.fs.usda.gov/inyo.

19 FIRST AND SECOND FALLS
3.0 mi / 1.5 hr

in the John Muir Wilderness

If you're camping or fishing in Big Pine Canyon, or maybe just wandering around exploring the area, there's a great walk to take starting from the end of the road near Glacier Lodge. Since it's just a day hike, you can park in the parking area right by the lodge and save yourself the long walk from the backpackers' parking lot.

Head west from the trailhead on the wide road, passing some private cabins, and in seconds you cross a bridge over First Falls, a noisy, 200-foot-long whitewater cascade. Bear right onto a narrower trail and start switchbacking uphill, paralleling the cascade. As you climb, you get awesome views into Big Pine Canyon's South Fork. At the top of the falls, cross another bridge over the creek and take a hard left onto a dirt road, staying along the creek. Now it's a flat stroll into the north fork of Big Pine Canyon. Your goal is Second Falls, a larger, more impressive cascade than First Falls; it's less than a mile away and clearly visible from the trail. Since the route is set along the canyon bottom, you get many interesting vistas along the way, from the tall surrounding canyon walls to occasional lodgepole pines and many mountain wildflowers. When the trail starts to climb out of the canyon, take the left spur cutoff to head closer to the waterfall, or just pick a big rock to sit on and admire the scenery.

User Groups: Hikers, dogs, and horses. No mountain bikes. No wheelchair facilities.

Permits: No permits are required. Parking and access are free.

Maps: A John Muir Wilderness map is available from the U.S. Forest Service. A Palisades map is available from Tom Harrison Maps. For a topographic map, ask the USGS for Coyote Flat.

Directions: From Bishop, drive 15 miles south on U.S. 395 to Big Pine. Turn right (west) on Crocker Street, which becomes Glacier Lodge Road, and drive 10.5 miles to Glacier Lodge and the Big Pine Canyon trailhead, at the end of the road. Day hikers may park in the day-use area near the lodge, but backpackers must park 0.5 mile east, on Glacier Lodge Road, in the backpackers' parking lot.

Contact: Inyo National Forest, White Mountain Ranger Station, 798 North Main Street, Bishop, CA 93514, 760/873-2500, www.fs.usda.gov/inyo.

20 FIRST AND SECOND LAKES
9.6 mi / 6.0 hr or 2 days

in the John Muir Wilderness

The trail to First and Second Lakes in Big Pine Canyon follows the same route as the trail to First and Second Falls, above, but then continues onward, climbing up and over Second Falls on the well-graded trail to Cienaga Mirth, at three miles out. Off to the left of the trail you'll see a magnificent stone cabin (now sometimes used as a backcountry ranger residence) built by movie star Lon Chaney. Wildflowers are excellent at the swampy, spring-fed mirth. You reach First Lake at 4.5 miles, and Second Lake is just a few hundred yards farther. By Second Lake, you've climbed to over 10,000 feet, and the lake water is a stunning glacial blue-green. Those who wish to see more lakes can continue on a loop past Second Lake to Third, Fourth, Fifth, and Black Lakes, making a long, 14-mile day. Fifth Lake, just off the loop by a third of a mile, is the most scenic. You'll see hardy mountaineer-types with climbing equipment turning left beyond Third Lake. They're hiking a full nine miles one-way to the edge of Palisade Glacier, the southernmost glacier in the Sierra. Considering it has a 5,000-foot elevation gain, the route to the glacier is not for everybody.

User Groups: Hikers, dogs, and horses. No mountain bikes. No wheelchair facilities.

Permits: A free wilderness permit is required year-round for overnight stays and is available from the Bishop/White Mountain Ranger Station. Quotas are in effect from May 1 to November 1; permits are available in advance for a $5 reservation fee per person.

Maps: A John Muir Wilderness map is available from the U.S. Forest Service. A Palisades map is available from Tom Harrison Maps. For topographic maps, ask the USGS for Coyote Flat and Split Mountain.

Directions: From Bishop, drive 15 miles south on U.S. 395 to Big Pine. Turn right (west) on Crocker Street, which becomes Glacier Lodge Road, and drive 10.5 miles to Glacier Lodge and the Big Pine Canyon trailhead, at the end of the road. Day hikers may park in the day-use area near the lodge, but backpackers must park 0.5 mile east, on Glacier Lodge Road, in the backpackers' parking lot.

Contact: Inyo National Forest, White Mountain Ranger Station, 798 North Main Street, Bishop, CA 93514, 760/873-2500, www.fs.usda.gov/inyo.

21 BIG STUMP TRAIL
1.0 mi / 0.5 hr

in the Grant Grove area of
Kings Canyon National Park

Normally it would be hard for us to get excited about a trail called the Big Stump Trail. In fact, this sort of thing could be quite depressing. But Big Stump Trail, at the entrance to Kings Canyon National Park, is a pleasant nature walk and provides an excellent history lesson as well. The size of the mammoth trees—oops, make that stumps—just blows you away. Most of the big trees were cut for timber in the 1880s, and you'll see the remains of logging activities. Be sure to pick up an interpretive brochure at the Kings Canyon Visitors Center or at the trailhead. The trail is a short loop that circles a meadow. A few mature sequoias still thrive along the route,

including one in the first 50 feet from the parking lot. The path's highlights include the Burnt Monarch, a shell of a giant sequoia that has been ravaged by fire but still stands, and the Mark Twain Stump. The latter belonged to a 26-foot-wide tree that took two men 13 days to cut down.

User Groups: Hikers only. No dogs, horses, or mountain bikes. No wheelchair facilities.

Permits: No permits are required. There is a $20 entrance fee per vehicle at Sequoia and Kings Canyon National Parks, good for seven days.

Maps: A Sequoia and Kings Canyon map is available from Tom Harrison Maps. For a topographic map, ask the USGS for Hume.

Directions: From Fresno, drive east on Highway 180 for 55 miles to the Big Stump Entrance at Kings Canyon National Park. The trail begins 0.5 mile past the entrance station, at the Big Stump Picnic Area.

Contact: Sequoia and Kings Canyon National Parks, 47050 General Highway, Three Rivers, CA 93271-9651, 559/565-3341 or 559/565-4307, www.nps.gov/seki.

22 SUNSET TRAIL
5.0 mi / 2.5 hr

in the Grant Grove area of
Kings Canyon National Park

The Sunset Trail leaves Sunset Campground (elevation 6,590 feet) and heads gently downhill for 2.25 miles to Ella Falls, a pretty 40-foot cascade on Sequoia Creek. At 1.5 miles down the trail, you reach a junction with South Boundary Trail and can take a short side trip to the left to Viola Falls, which isn't much of a waterfall but is a memorably scenic spot on granite-sculpted Sequoia Creek. Most people just mosey down the trail, enjoying the big pines and firs and the flowering western azaleas, and maybe stealing a kiss on one of the wooden footbridges. If you like, you can follow the trail for its entire 2.5-mile length to

Sequoia Lake. Although the lake is privately owned, hikers are allowed to walk along its edge. While you're enjoying the lake, don't forget that the return trip is all uphill with a 1,300-foot elevation gain, so save some water and energy.

User Groups: Hikers only. No dogs, horses, or mountain bikes. No wheelchair facilities.

Permits: No permits are required. There is a $20 entrance fee per vehicle at Sequoia and Kings Canyon National Parks, good for seven days.

Maps: A Sequoia and Kings Canyon map is available from Tom Harrison Maps. For topographic maps, ask the USGS for Hume and General Grant Grove.

Directions: From Fresno, drive east on Highway 180 for 55 miles to the Big Stump Entrance at Kings Canyon National Park. Continue 1.5 miles and turn left, following signs for Kings Canyon. Drive 1.5 miles to Grant Grove Village, and park in the large parking lot near the visitors center. Cross the road and walk on the paved trail toward Sunset Campground's amphitheater. Continue heading left through the camp to site No. 118, where the trail begins.

Contact: Sequoia and Kings Canyon National Parks, 47050 General Highway, Three Rivers, CA 93271-9651, 559/565-3341 or 559/565-4307, www.nps.gov/seki.

Park Ridge. Near the top, you'll parallel the dirt road that leads to the Park Ridge Fire Lookout. Then Manzanita Trail meets up with Azalea Trail, and you'll descend on a much shadier, moister slope. The azaleas bloom bright white with prolific, showy blossoms in June and July. Azalea Trail ends at Wilsonia, a private community within the national park, so just retrace your steps to return back to your car.

User Groups: Hikers only. No dogs, horses, or mountain bikes. No wheelchair facilities.

Permits: No permits are required. There is a $20 entrance fee per vehicle at Sequoia and Kings Canyon National Parks, good for seven days.

Maps: A Sequoia and Kings Canyon map is available from Tom Harrison Maps. For a topographic map, ask the USGS for Hume.

Directions: From Fresno, drive east on Highway 180 for 55 miles to the Big Stump Entrance at Kings Canyon National Park. Continue 1.5 miles and turn left, following signs for Kings Canyon. Drive 1.5 miles to Grant Grove Village and park in the large parking lot near the visitors center. Walk on the service road near the tent cabins to reach the start of the Manzanita Trail.

Contact: Sequoia and Kings Canyon National Parks, 47050 General Highway, Three Rivers, CA 93271-9651, 559/565-3341 or 559/565-4307, www.nps.gov/seki.

23 MANZANITA AND AZALEA TRAILS

3.3 mi / 2.0 hr   👫2 ⛰️7

in the Grant Grove area of
Kings Canyon National Park

This hike is a good exercise route for vacationers staying in Grant Grove Village or in the nearby campgrounds. It climbs 800 feet, which gives your heart and lungs a workout, and it's pretty every step of the way. From the edge of the dirt service road by the tent cabins, Manzanita Trail climbs a dry slope uphill to

24 PANORAMIC POINT AND PARK RIDGE LOOKOUT

4.7 mi / 3.0 hr   👫2 ⛰️9

in the Grant Grove area of
Kings Canyon National Park

Start your trip by taking the 300-yard paved walk from the parking area to Panoramic Point, which delivers what its name implies. An interpretive display names the many peaks and valleys you can see, including the big pointy one, which is Mount Goddard at

13,560 feet. From Panoramic Point, take the dirt Park Ridge Trail that leads to the right along the ridge. Your views continue as you contour along the ridgeline, climbing gently uphill. The trail intersects a dirt road, which you follow for about 50 yards; then bear left onto the trail again. You'll intersect this dirt road once more about 100 yards before the Park Ridge Fire Lookout. Follow the road to the lookout tower, and check out the nifty outdoor shower at its base. If someone is stationed in the tower and gives you permission to come up, do so and sign the visitors register. (The lookout person rarely gets visitors on cloudy days, but he or she gets a good number of them when it's sunny, and you can see for miles around.) The lookout is operated by volunteers during the fire season, which is usually May to October. For your return trip, you can walk down the trail back to Panoramic Point or take the shorter fire road, which also leads back to the parking lot. Views are far better along the trail than on the fire road.

User Groups: Hikers only. No dogs, horses, or mountain bikes. No wheelchair facilities.

Permits: No permits are required. There is a $20 entrance fee per vehicle at Sequoia and Kings Canyon National Parks, good for seven days.

Maps: A Sequoia and Kings Canyon map is available from Tom Harrison Maps. For a topographic map, ask the USGS for Hume.

Directions: From Fresno, drive east on Highway 180 for 55 miles to the Big Stump Entrance at Kings Canyon National Park. Continue 1.5 miles and turn left, following signs for Kings Canyon. Drive 1.5 miles to Grant Grove Village and turn right by the visitors center and store. Follow the road past the cabins, and just before the John Muir Lodge, turn right on the road signed for Panoramic Point. It's 2.3 miles from the visitors center to Panoramic Point.

Contact: Sequoia and Kings Canyon National Parks, 47050 General Highway, Three Rivers, CA 93271-9651, 559/565-3341 or 559/565-4307, www.nps.gov/seki.

25 GENERAL GRANT TREE TRAIL

0.6 mi / 0.5 hr　　🏃1 ⛰8

in the Grant Grove area of
Kings Canyon National Park

BEST (

This paved loop through a giant sequoia grove allows visitors a look at the General Grant Tree, the second-largest tree in the world. Estimated to be 1,800 to 2,000 years old, the General Grant is 267 feet tall and 107 feet in circumference at its base. Every year since 1926, the City of Sanger has held a Christmas celebration around its base, and so the tree is known as "the Nation's Christmas Tree." Its neighbors include the Fallen Monarch, a hollow downed tree that is so wide, it was once used as a park employee camp. Also nearby is a group of big sequoias named after various U.S. states. It may seem a little campy, but there are many excellent photo opportunities in the grove. A bonus: Most, but not all, of this trail is accessible to wheelchair users.

User Groups: Hikers. No dogs, horses, or mountain bikes. Partial wheelchair accessibility.

Permits: No permits are required. There is a $20 entrance fee per vehicle at Sequoia and Kings Canyon National Parks, good for seven days.

Maps: A Sequoia and Kings Canyon map is available from Tom Harrison Maps. For topographic maps, ask the USGS for Hume and General Grant Grove.

Directions: From Fresno, drive east on Highway 180 for 55 miles to the Big Stump Entrance at Kings Canyon National Park. Continue 1.5 miles and turn left, following signs for Kings Canyon. Drive one mile, passing Grant Grove Village, to the left turnoff for General Grant Tree. Turn left and follow the access road for 0.75 mile to the parking lot.

Contact: Sequoia and Kings Canyon National Parks, 47050 General Highway, Three Rivers, CA 93271-9651, 559/565-3341 or 559/565-4307, www.nps.gov/seki.

HIKING

26 NORTH GROVE AND DEAD GIANT LOOP

3.0 mi / 1.5 hr   👣 2 ⛰ 7

in the Grant Grove area of
Kings Canyon National Park

For people who want a little more hiking than what the General Grant Tree Trail (see listing in this chapter) provides, the combined North Grove and Dead Giant Loop Trails are the answer. The walk begins at the oversized vehicle parking at the General Grant Tree parking lot. Past the gate, follow an old dirt road that leads downhill through a mixed forest of sequoia, sugar pine, white fir, and dogwood. Don't expect to see dense groves of sequoias here; the big trees are few and far between. However, the forest is pleasant, quiet, and shady.

Stay to the right at the first junction to follow the posted North Grove Loop Trail. At the bottom of the hill, you'll pass an obscure junction with an old wagon road that was used to take logged sequoias to the mill. Continue to a more obvious junction at one mile out. Turn right and walk 0.25 mile downhill to Lion Meadow. Turn right on a single-track trail and circle around the meadow, heading for the Dead Giant. This sequoia, like some others in the park, is a nearly hollow, dead tree that somehow keeps standing. From the Dead Giant, it's a short tromp to the Sequoia Lake Overlook, a tranquil high point where you can have a snack and enjoy the view of the large, private lake in Sequoia National Forest. From the overlook, backtrack a few yards and turn right to finish out the loop, returning uphill on the wide dirt road. There is a 400-foot gain on the return.

User Groups: Hikers only. No dogs, horses, or mountain bikes. No wheelchair facilities.

Permits: No permits are required. There is a $20 entrance fee per vehicle at Sequoia and Kings Canyon National Parks, good for seven days.

Maps: A Sequoia and Kings Canyon map is available from Tom Harrison Maps. For topographic maps, ask the USGS for Hume and General Grant Grove.

Directions: From Fresno, drive east on Highway 180 for 55 miles to the Big Stump Entrance at Kings Canyon National Park. Continue 1.5 miles and turn left, following signs for Kings Canyon. Drive two miles, passing Grant Grove Village, to the left turnoff for General Grant Tree. Turn left and follow the access road for one mile to the parking lot. The North Grove Loop starts from the far end of the lower parking lot.

Contact: Sequoia and Kings Canyon National Parks, 47050 General Highway, Three Rivers, CA 93271-9651, 559/565-3341 or 559/565-4307, www.nps.gov/seki.

27 CHICAGO STUMP TRAIL

0.5 mi / 0.5 hr   👣 1 ⛰ 7

in Giant Sequoia National Monument
north of the Grant Grove area of
Kings Canyon National Park

Before the loggers extracted their toll, the Converse Basin once sheltered one of the largest and finest groves of giant sequoias in the world. Where the giants once stood, second-growth sequoias have now taken hold. This short and easy stroll takes you through a regenerated mixed forest to the Chicago Stump, a massive stump that belonged to one of the largest trees in the area. The General Noble tree was cut down in 1893, and the lower portion of the tree was reassembled and exhibited at the Chicago World's Fair. The stump that remains is at least 10 feet high and over 25 feet wide. In addition to its historical interest, this easy trail provides a pleasant, peaceful change from the hustle and bustle of the neighboring national parks.

User Groups: Hikers, horses, and dogs. No mountain bikes. No wheelchair facilities.

Permits: No permits are required. There is a $20 entrance fee per vehicle at Sequoia and Kings Canyon National Parks, good for seven days.

HIKING

Maps: A Sequoia National Forest map is available from the U.S. Forest Service. A map of Sequoia and Kings Canyon is available from Tom Harrison Maps. For a topographic map, ask the USGS for Hume.

Directions: From Fresno, drive east on Highway 180 for 55 miles to the Big Stump Entrance at Kings Canyon National Park. Continue 1.5 miles and turn left, following signs for Kings Canyon. Drive approximately 4.5 miles, passing Grant Grove Village, and turn left at the sign for Forest Road 13S03. Drive two miles, turn right on Road 13S65, and continue 0.1 mile to the Chicago Stump trailhead.

Contact: Giant Sequoia National Monument/Sequoia National Forest, Hume Lake Ranger District, 35860 East Kings Canyon Road, Dunlap, CA 93621, 559/338-2251, www.fs.fed.us/r5/sequoia.

28 BOOLE TREE LOOP
2.5 mi / 1.0 hr

in Giant Sequoia National Monument north of the Grant Grove area of Kings Canyon National Park

The drive in to the Boole Tree trailhead is worth the trip by itself, as you pass through a beautiful, ghostly meadow filled with giant sequoia stumps. The sight of them is so otherworldly that it may stay engrained in your memory for a long time. The Boole Tree hike is a loop, and it's a good idea to take the right side of the loop first, making the ascent more gradual. You climb 500 feet to the top of a ridge, then descend the other side, reaching the Boole Tree in one mile. (It's just off the main loop, accessible via a short, obvious spur.) At 269 feet tall and with a diameter of 35 feet, the Boole Tree is the largest tree in any of the national forests, and it's one of the largest trees in the world. It is one of a very few giant sequoias left standing in the Converse Basin grove, as the rest were clear-cut in the late 1800s. Although some people go see the Boole Tree and then turn around, it's better to finish out the loop. You'll be rewarded with a stellar view of Spanish Mountain and the Kings River Canyon.

User Groups: Hikers, horses, and dogs. No mountain bikes. No wheelchair facilities.

Permits: No permits are required. There is a $20 entrance fee per vehicle at Sequoia and Kings Canyon National Parks, good for seven days.

Maps: A Sequoia National Forest map is available from the U.S. Forest Service. A map of Sequoia and Kings Canyon is available from Tom Harrison Maps. For a topographic map, ask the USGS for Hume.

Directions: From Fresno, drive east on Highway 180 for 55 miles to the Big Stump Entrance at Kings Canyon National Park. Continue 1.5 miles and turn left, following signs for Kings Canyon. Drive approximately six miles, passing Grant Grove Village. Turn left at the sign for Forest Road 13S55, Boole Tree, Converse Basin, and Stump Meadow. Drive 2.6 miles, and park in the wide parking pullout.

Contact: Giant Sequoia National Monument/Sequoia National Forest, Hume Lake Ranger District, 35860 Kings Canyon Road, Dunlap, CA 93621, 559/338-2251, www.fs.fed.us/r5/sequoia.

29 YUCCA POINT
4.0 mi / 2.25 hr

in Giant Sequoia National Monument west of the Cedar Grove area of Kings Canyon National Park

The Yucca Point Trail is an upside-down hike—the kind where you go down on the way in (so easy) and up on the way back (not so easy). The path descends from Highway 180 to the Kings River, dropping 1,200 feet along the way. As long as you don't climb uphill at high noon, the hike back is not as bad as it looks from the top. The trail is well graded; the only

HIKING

hardship is that the terrain is all chaparral, so there's almost no shade, just the occasional tall yucca plant. The path is mostly used by anglers heading down to the wild trout section of the Kings River, but hikers like the excellent views it provides and the access to the river's cool, emerald green pools.

User Groups: Hikers only. No dogs, horses, or mountain bikes. No wheelchair facilities.

Permits: No permits are required. There is a $20 entrance fee per vehicle for access to this section of Sequoia National Forest, payable at any of the entrance stations to Kings Canyon and Sequoia National Parks. The fee is good for seven days in both the national forest and the national parks.

Maps: A Sequoia National Forest map is available from the U.S. Forest Service. A map of Sequoia and Kings Canyon is available from Tom Harrison Maps. For a topographic map, ask the USGS for Wren Peak.

Directions: From Fresno, drive east on Highway 180 for 55 miles to the Big Stump Entrance at Kings Canyon National Park. Continue 1.5 miles and turn left, following signs for Kings Canyon. Drive another 16 miles on Highway 180, past Grant Grove and Kings Canyon Lodge, to the Yucca Point trailhead, on the left. Park in the pullouts alongside Highway 180.

Contact: Giant Sequoia National Monument/ Sequoia National Forest, Hume Lake Ranger District, 35860 Kings Canyon Road, Dunlap, CA 93621, 559/338-2251, www.fs.fed.us/r5/ sequoia.

30 WINDY CLIFFS

3.0 mi / 1.5 hr

in Giant Sequoia National Monument
west of the Cedar Grove area of
Kings Canyon National Park

The Forest Service concessionaire charges a fee for tours of Boyden Cave, one of many limestone caverns in the vicinity of Kings Canyon

and Sequoia National Parks, and the parking lot is always busy with carloads and busloads of people waiting to take the tour. The cave is fascinating and worth a visit, but if you're low on cash, you can take this stellar hike instead and get million-dollar views of Kings Canyon for free. From the cave gift shop, walk up the paved path and take the left fork near the entrance to the cave (you'll need to go under the rope that borders the trail to the cave). The trail has a metal bar across it, but the Forest Service says it's perfectly legal to hike it; they just don't want to encourage casual visitors because the trail is unmaintained with very steep drop-offs. Once on the trail, in no time you'll climb a little higher and see a sweeping panorama of Highway 180 and the fast-flowing Kings River below. In one mile, Boulder Creek cascades down the hillside. The path ends when it reaches creekside at 1.5 miles. (A faint path continues, but it's badly overgrown.) Note that poison oak is prolific along this trail, so it might be a good idea to wear long pants and long sleeves.

User Groups: Hikers only. No dogs, horses, or mountain bikes. No wheelchair facilities.

Permits: No permits are required. There is a $20 per vehicle entrance fee for access to this section of Sequoia National Forest, payable at any of the entrance stations to Kings Canyon and Sequoia National Parks. The fee is good for seven days in both the national forest and the national parks.

Maps: A Sequoia National Forest map is available from the U.S. Forest Service. A map of Sequoia and Kings Canyon is available from Tom Harrison Maps. For a topographic map, ask the USGS for Wren Peak.

Directions: From Fresno, drive east on Highway 180 for 55 miles to the Big Stump Entrance at Kings Canyon National Park. Continue 1.5 miles and turn left, following signs for Kings Canyon. Drive 22 miles on Highway 180, passing Grant Grove and Kings Canyon Lodge, to the parking area for Boyden Cave, on the right side of the road.

Contact: Giant Sequoia National Monument/

Sequoia National Forest, Hume Lake Ranger District, 35860 Kings Canyon Road, Dunlap, CA 93621, 559/338-2251, www.fs.fed.us/r5/sequoia.

31 LEWIS CREEK TRAIL
11.6 mi / 6.0 hr or 2 days 🏃4 ⛰9

off Highway 180 in the Cedar Grove area of Kings Canyon National Park

Up, up, and up. If you're willing to climb 3,200 feet over the course of 5.5 miles, your reward is pristine Frypan Meadow, at 7,800 feet in elevation. In early summer, the meadow is green and littered with wildflowers, creating a glorious vision after the hot, sunny climb. But there's no way to see it without first putting in some effort on the Lewis Creek Trail. The good news is that if the first mile or so proves to be too demanding, or too hot if you don't start first thing in the morning, you can always take the right fork at 1.6 miles and head back downhill on Hotel Creek Trail, making a seven-mile loop out of the trip. If you push onward on Lewis Creek Trail, you cross lovely Comb Creek (at 3.2 miles), then Lewis Creek one mile farther. Many day hikers make the Lewis Creek crossing their destination; its pools make fine swimming holes. Backpackers continue another 1.5 miles to Frypan Meadow. If you have your wilderness permit, campsites are available there.

User Groups: Hikers and horses. No dogs or mountain bikes. No wheelchair facilities.

Permits: There is a $20 entrance fee per vehicle at Sequoia and Kings Canyon National Parks, good for seven days. Wilderness permits are required for overnight stays. They are available on a first-come, first-served basis at the wilderness permit station at Roads End or the Kings Canyon Visitor Center. For advanced wilderness permits or information on trail conditions, go to www.nps.gov/seki. Trailhead quotas are in effect from May to September.

Maps: A Sequoia and Kings Canyon map is available from Tom Harrison Maps. For a topographic map, ask the USGS for Cedar Grove.

Directions: From Fresno, drive east on Highway 180 for 55 miles to the Big Stump Entrance at Kings Canyon National Park. Continue 1.5 miles and turn left, following signs for Kings Canyon and Cedar Grove. Drive 31 miles on Highway 180 to the Lewis Creek Trail parking area, on the north side of the road, before you reach Cedar Grove Village.

Contact: Sequoia and Kings Canyon National Parks, 47050 General Highway, Three Rivers, CA 93271-9651, 559/565-3341 or 559/565-4307, www.nps.gov/seki.

32 HOTEL CREEK TRAIL TO CEDAR GROVE OVERLOOK
5.0 mi / 2.5 hr 🏃3 ⛰9

off Highway 180 in the Cedar Grove area of Kings Canyon National Park

The destination on this trip is a stunning overlook of Kings Canyon, the deepest canyon in the continental United States with a plunge of 8,200 feet at its deepest point. In truth, the canyon vistas are continual for most of the hike, so if you don't make it to the overlook, you'll still get an eyeful. The Hotel Creek Trail consists of dozens of switchbacks over open, sunny slopes, climbing 1,200 feet over two miles to a trail junction with Overlook Trail. Turn left to head to the overlook, which peers down on Cedar Grove and the length of Kings Canyon. Some of the best views are of Monarch Divide's high peaks to the north. We hope you came with picnic supplies. For a five-mile round-trip, retrace your steps back to Cedar Grove. If you want to walk farther, you can continue from the overlook junction for another 1.5 miles and turn left, hiking downhill on Lewis Creek Trail and making a seven-mile loop out of the trip. This stretch of Lewis Creek Trail is lined with sweet-smelling ceanothus. Unfortunately, the final 1.2 miles of the loop parallels a park road. Along the way, the trail overlooks a level area next to the South Fork Kings River where wildlife can often be spotted among the meadows and shrubs.

User Groups: Hikers and horses. No dogs or mountain bikes. No wheelchair facilities.

Permits: No permits are required. There is a $20 entrance fee per vehicle at Sequoia and Kings Canyon National Parks, good for seven days.

Maps: A Sequoia and Kings Canyon map is available from Tom Harrison Maps. For a topographic map, ask the USGS for Cedar Grove.

Directions: From Fresno, drive east on Highway 180 for 55 miles to the Big Stump Entrance at Kings Canyon National Park. Continue 1.5 miles and turn left, following signs for Kings Canyon and Cedar Grove. Drive 31.5 miles on Highway 180 to Cedar Grove Village. Turn left at the sign for the visitors center and Cedar Grove Lodge. Continue on the main road past the lodge for 0.25 mile and turn right. The Hotel Creek trailhead is on the left after a few hundred feet.

Contact: Sequoia and Kings Canyon National Parks, 47050 General Highway, Three Rivers, CA 93271-9651, 559/565-3341 or 559/565-4307, www.nps.gov/seki.

🔳 DON CECIL TRAIL TO LOOKOUT PEAK

12.0 mi / 7.0 hr   🏃5 △10

off Highway 180 in the Cedar Grove area of Kings Canyon National Park

Lookout Peak, at 8,531 feet in elevation, is a summit worth ascending, even though it's an all-day trip with a 3,900-foot elevation gain. From the top, you get an unforgettable Sierra view, with Cedar Grove far below you and peaks and ridges all around. In addition, just a few hundred yards from the summit is

Summit Meadow, filled with summer wildflowers. The key is to carry plenty of water and plan on an early-morning start to beat the heat. You can filter water from Sheep Creek, one mile in. Luckily, there's a decent amount of shade in the first few miles. Even though this trailhead is located right by the Cedar Grove campgrounds, few people hike all the way to the peak, so you have a chance at peace and quiet along the trail. The only downer on this hike is that when you near the summit, you see that other people have driven their cars on an alternate route to Lookout Peak (from the Big Meadows area of Giant Sequoia National Monument), and they are gaining the summit after only a 0.25-mile hike. Hey, at least you earned it.

User Groups: Hikers and horses. No dogs or mountain bikes. No wheelchair facilities.

Permits: No permits are required. There is a $20 entrance fee per vehicle at Sequoia and Kings Canyon National Parks, good for seven days.

Maps: A Sequoia and Kings Canyon map is available from Tom Harrison Maps. For a topographic map, ask the USGS for Cedar Grove.

Directions: From Fresno, drive east on Highway 180 for 55 miles to the Big Stump Entrance at Kings Canyon National Park. Continue 1.5 miles and turn left, following signs for Kings Canyon and Cedar Grove. Drive 31.5 miles on Highway 180 and take the right fork for Cedar Grove. The Don Cecil trailhead is on the right side of the road, just beyond the turnoff for Cedar Grove Village and the visitors center. If you reach Canyon View and Moraine Campgrounds, you've gone too far.

Contact: Sequoia and Kings Canyon National Parks, 47050 General Highway, Three Rivers, CA 93271-9651, 559/565-3341 or 559/565-4307, www.nps.gov/seki.

34 ROARING RIVER FALLS

0.4 mi / 0.25 hr   👥1 ⛰8

off Highway 180 in the Cedar Grove area of
Kings Canyon National Park

BEST (

It's an easy stroll to Roaring River Falls, a pretty waterfall that drops through a narrow gorge into the South Fork Kings River. It's the only waterfall in Sequoia and Kings Canyon National Parks that is partially accessible via wheelchair. (The trail is paved and accessible for most of its length, but one section may be too steep for some wheelchair users.) If hikers want a longer walk, they can continue downstream on the River Trail to Zumwalt Meadow in 1.6 miles or Road's End in 2.7 miles. What's extraordinary about the waterfall is not the cascade itself, but the giant rocky pool into which it falls; it's at least 50 feet wide. From where the paved trail ends, at the edge of the pool, the waterfall is perfectly framed by two big conifers. Many beautiful photos have been snapped here.

User Groups: Hikers and wheelchairs. No dogs, horses, or mountain bikes.

Permits: No permits are required. There is a $20 entrance fee per vehicle at Sequoia and Kings Canyon National Parks, good for seven days.

Maps: A Sequoia and Kings Canyon map is available from Tom Harrison Maps. For a topographic map, ask the USGS for Sphinx.

Directions: From Fresno, drive east on Highway 180 for 55 miles to the Big Stump Entrance at Kings Canyon National Park. Continue 1.5 miles and turn left, following signs for Kings Canyon and Cedar Grove. Continue 35 miles on Highway 180 to the sign for Roaring River Falls and the River Trail, three miles past Cedar Grove Village. The trailhead is on the right side of the road.

Contact: Sequoia and Kings Canyon National Parks, 47050 General Highway, Three Rivers, CA 93271-9651, 559/565-3341 or 559/565-4307, www.nps.gov/seki.

35 ZUMWALT MEADOW LOOP

2.0 mi / 1.0 hr   👥1 ⛰9

off Highway 180 in the Cedar Grove area of
Kings Canyon National Park

BEST (

What's the prettiest easy hike in Kings Canyon National Park? The Zumwalt Meadow Loop Trail wins hands down. A scenic two-mile walk along the South Fork Kings River, the Zumwalt Meadow Loop is a delight for hikers of all abilities. Many people bring their fishing rods along to try their luck in the river, but for most, the hiking is better than the fishing. From the parking area, walk downstream along the river to an old suspension footbridge, cross it, and walk back upstream. The loop begins at an obvious fork, and you can hike it in either direction. The south side traverses a boulder field of jumbled rocks that have tumbled down from the Grand Sentinel (elevation 8,504 feet). The north side cuts through a thick, waist-high fern forest and follows a wooden walkway over a marsh. Views of 8,717-foot North Dome are awe inspiring. Trees, meadow, rock, stream, river, canyon walls—Zumwalt Meadow Trail has it all.

User Groups: Hikers only. No dogs, horses, or mountain bikes. No wheelchair facilities.

Permits: No permits are required. There is a $20 entrance fee per vehicle at Sequoia and Kings Canyon National Parks, good for seven days.

Maps: A Sequoia and Kings Canyon map is available from Tom Harrison Maps. For a topographic map, ask the USGS for Cedar Grove.

Directions: From Fresno, drive east on Highway 180 for 55 miles to the Big Stump Entrance at Kings Canyon National Park. Continue 1.5 miles and turn left, following signs for Kings Canyon and Cedar Grove. Continue 36 miles on Highway 180 to the parking area for Zumwalt Meadow, on the right side of the road.

Contact: Sequoia and Kings Canyon National Parks, 47050 General Highway, Three Rivers, CA 93271-9651, 559/565-3341 or 559/565-4307, www.nps.gov/seki.

36 MIST FALLS

9.2 mi / 5.0 hr   2 △9

off Highway 180 in the Cedar Grove area of
Kings Canyon National Park

The Mist Falls Trail is probably the most well-used pathway in Kings Canyon National Park, with good reason. It's a stellar 4.6-mile walk to an impressive cascade on the South Fork Kings River, with only a 650-foot gain in elevation along the way. Many backpackers use this trail to access Paradise Valley and points beyond, while most day hikers turn around at Mist Falls. The first two miles are a flat walk up the Kings River Valley, with canyon walls towering above you on both sides. You spend a lot of time craning your neck, looking up at the high canyon rims, from which springtime waterfalls cascade down. You're in a dry, open forest much of the time.

At two miles, you'll reach a trail junction. Bear left, then start to climb over granite. The farther you go, the more expansive the views become; make sure you keep turning around so you can take in the whole panorama. At four miles, the river starts to look more waterfall-like, with crashing pools and rocky granite slides becoming increasingly vertical. A quarter mile later you reach Mist Falls, which fans out over a 45-foot wide granite ledge and crashes into a boulder-lined pool. It creates a tremendous spray and mist in early summer, and mellows out as the season goes on. Take a look at the falls, then walk back down the trail 0.2 mile to the obvious, immense slab of granite you just passed. This is a favorite spot to have lunch, with its wide-open view of 10,007-foot Avalanche Peak. Look carefully and you can pick out the stone face of The Sphinx.

There are two ways to beat the crowds on this path. First, start early in the morning. Second, hike part of the route on an alternate trail on the river's south side. This trail travels from the Road's End parking lot to the Bailey Bridge at the trail intersection mentioned

above. If you get an early start, save this alternate route for the return trip. By then, the day hikers will be out in full force.

User Groups: Hikers and horses. No dogs or mountain bikes. No wheelchair facilities.

Permits: No permits are required. There is a $20 entrance fee per vehicle at Sequoia and Kings Canyon National Parks, good for seven days.

Maps: A Sequoia and Kings Canyon map is available from Tom Harrison Maps. For a topographic map, ask the USGS for Sphinx.

Directions: From Fresno, drive east on Highway 180 for 55 miles to the Big Stump Entrance at Kings Canyon National Park. Continue 1.5 miles and turn left, following signs for Kings Canyon and Cedar Grove. Continue 38 miles on Highway 180 to Road's End, six miles past Cedar Grove Village. The trailhead is at the east end of the parking lot, near the wilderness ranger station.

Contact: Sequoia and Kings Canyon National Parks, 47050 General Highway, Three Rivers, CA 93271-9651, 559/565-3341 or 559/565-4307, www.nps.gov/seki.

37 COPPER CREEK TRAIL

21.0 mi / 3-4 days   5 △9

off Highway 180 in the Cedar Grove area of
Kings Canyon National Park

The Copper Creek trailhead is at 5,000 feet, and Granite Lake is at 9,972 feet, so it's not hard to do the math. If you're up for a backpacking trip with a 5,000-foot elevation gain over 10 miles, the Granite Lake Basin is your ticket to happiness. But keep in mind that the route can be hot and dry as it switchbacks up manzanita-covered slopes; this trail is considered one of the most strenuous in the Cedar Grove area. Your first night's camp is at Lower Tent Meadow, four miles in and at 7,800 feet. After that, things start to get really good. With Mount Hutchings looming over your left shoulder, the second day's six miles will go easier, bringing you to rocky, jewel-like Granite Lake in only a few hours. You must have a backpacking stove for camping by the lake or anywhere above 10,000 feet.

User Groups: Hikers and horses. No dogs or mountain bikes. No wheelchair facilities.

Permits: There is a $20 entrance fee per vehicle at Sequoia and Kings Canyon National Parks, good for seven days. Wilderness permits are required for overnight stays. They are available on a first-come, first-served basis at the wilderness permit station at Roads End or the Kings Canyon Visitor Center. For advanced wilderness permits or information on trail conditions, go to www.nps.gov/seki. Trailhead quotas are in effect from May to September.

Maps: A Sequoia and Kings Canyon map is available from Tom Harrison Maps. For a topographic map, ask the USGS for Sphinx.

Directions: From Fresno, drive east on Highway 180 for 55 miles to the Big Stump Entrance at Kings Canyon National Park. Continue 1.5 miles and turn left, following signs for Kings Canyon and Cedar Grove. Continue 38 miles on Highway 180 to Road's End, six miles past Cedar Grove Village. The trail begins at the long-term parking area.

Contact: Sequoia and Kings Canyon National Parks, 47050 General Highway, Three Rivers, CA 93271-9651, 559/565-3341 or 559/565-4307, www.nps.gov/seki.

38 REDWOOD CANYON
4.0 mi / 2.0 hr   2 △ 10

southeast of the Grant Grove area of Kings Canyon National Park

BEST

Several loop trips are possible in the Redwood Mountain area of Kings Canyon National Park, but one of the prettiest and simplest trips is just an out-and-back walk on Redwood Canyon Trail, paralleling Redwood Creek. The beauty begins before you even start walking; on the last mile of the drive to the trailhead,

the dirt access road winds through giant sequoias that are so close, you can reach out your car window and touch them. The trail leads downhill from the parking area, and in just over 0.3 mile, you reach a junction and follow Redwood Creek Trail to the right. You'll find that this sequoia grove is far denser than many. Because they are situated by Redwood Creek, the sequoias grow amid a thriving background of dogwoods, firs, ceanothus, and mountain misery. Though the standing sequoias are impressive, some of the fallen ones are really amazing, because you get a close-up look at their immense size. Make sure you hike the full two miles to the stream crossing of Redwood Creek. Some of the best tree specimens are found there, near the junction with Sugar Bowl Loop Trail. The return trip is all uphill but easier than you'd expect.

User Groups: Hikers only. No dogs, horses, or mountain bikes. No wheelchair facilities.

Permits: No permits are required. There is a $20 entrance fee per vehicle at Sequoia and Kings Canyon National Parks, good for seven days.

Maps: A Sequoia and Kings Canyon map is available from Tom Harrison Maps. For a topographic map, ask the USGS for General Grant Grove.

Directions: From Fresno, drive east on Highway 180 for 55 miles to the Big Stump Entrance at Kings Canyon National Park. Continue 1.5 miles and turn right on the Generals Highway, heading for Sequoia National Park. Drive approximately three miles on the Generals Highway to Quail Flat, signed for Hume Lake to the left, and turn right on the dirt road to Redwood Saddle. Drive 1.5 miles and park in the parking lot. Take the trail signed for the Hart Tree and Redwood Canyon.

Contact: Sequoia and Kings Canyon National Parks, 47050 General Highway, Three Rivers, CA 93271-9651, 559/565-3341 or 559/565-4307, www.nps.gov/seki.

39 REDWOOD MOUNTAIN LOOP

10.0 mi / 5.0 hr   3 10

southeast of the Grant Grove area of Kings Canyon National Park

If you have most of a day to hike in the Redwood Mountain area of Kings Canyon National Park, you're in luck. This is one of the best day hikes in all of Kings Canyon. The Redwood Mountain Loop combines the best highlights of the area into one long trail, on which you'll wander in near solitude among the giant sequoias. If the paved, crowded trails to the General Grant Tree and the General Sherman Tree turn you off, this trail will turn you on. Start by hiking on the signed Burnt Grove/Sugar Bowl Loop Trail, which leads uphill from the parking lot. It's one mile to Burnt Grove and 2.5 miles to Sugar Bowl Grove; both are very dense stands of sequoias. Beyond the groves you descend for two miles to intersect with Redwood Canyon Trail. Head downhill and cross Redwood Creek, then proceed to the Fallen Goliath, a mammoth downed tree. One mile farther, you reach the Hart Tree, the largest tree in this area and a real show-stopper. In the final three miles, you get to walk through the Tunnel Log, a hollowed sequoia, and pass by pretty Hart Meadow. Note that if you tire out halfway through this loop, you can always follow the Redwood Canyon Trail uphill back to the start, cutting three miles off your round-trip.

User Groups: Hikers only. No dogs, horses, or mountain bikes. No wheelchair facilities.

Permits: No permits are required. There is a $20 entrance fee per vehicle at Sequoia and Kings Canyon National Parks, good for seven days.

Maps: A Sequoia and Kings Canyon map is available from Tom Harrison Maps. For a topographic map, ask the USGS for General Grant Grove.

Directions: From Fresno, drive east on Highway 180 for 55 miles to the Big Stump Entrance at Kings Canyon National Park.

Continue 1.5 miles and turn right on the Generals Highway, heading for Sequoia National Park. Drive approximately three miles on the Generals Highway to Quail Flat, signed for Hume Lake to the left, and turn right on the dirt road to Redwood Saddle. Drive 1.5 miles and park in the parking lot. Take the trail signed as Burnt Grove/Sugar Bowl Loop.

Contact: Sequoia and Kings Canyon National Parks, 47050 General Highway, Three Rivers, CA 93271-9651, 559/565-3341 or 559/565-4307, www.nps.gov/seki.

40 BUENA VISTA PEAK

2.0 mi / 1.0 hr   1 9

southeast of the Grant Grove area of Kings Canyon National Park

Forget driving to the Kings Canyon Overlook, because just across the road is a trailhead with an easy walk and even better views, plus a chance at a private picnic spot. Buena Vista Peak is not a summit but a rocky dome, peaking at 7,603 feet, and it is one of the highest points west of Generals Highway. It offers far-reaching views of what looks like a million conifers at your feet and the hazy foothills to the southwest. But the best vistas are to the east of the snowcapped peaks of the John Muir and Monarch Wildernesses. An easy half-hour walk takes you up the back side of the dome, passing through pine and fir forest, manzanita, and sage, and walking by some interesting rock formations. Don't miss the giant boulder sculptures in the trail's first 0.25 mile. At the top of Buena Vista Peak, you can wander all around the spacious granite summit, enjoying different perspectives on the vista, before heading back to the parking lot. It's downhill all the way.

User Groups: Hikers only. No dogs, horses, or mountain bikes. No wheelchair facilities.

Permits: No permits are required. There is a $20 entrance fee per vehicle at Sequoia and Kings Canyon National Parks, good for seven days.

Maps: A Sequoia and Kings Canyon map is available from Tom Harrison Maps. For a topographic map, ask the USGS for General Grant Grove.

Directions: From Fresno, drive east on Highway 180 for 55 miles to the Big Stump Entrance at Kings Canyon National Park. Continue 1.5 miles and turn right on the Generals Highway, heading for Sequoia National Park. Drive approximately five miles on the Generals Highway to the Buena Vista trailhead on the right, just across the road and slightly beyond the large pullout for the Kings Canyon Overlook, on the left.

Contact: Sequoia and Kings Canyon National Parks, 47050 General Highway, Three Rivers, CA 93271-9651, 559/565-3341 or 559/565-4307, www.nps.gov/seki.

41 WEAVER LAKE

6.2 mi / 3.0 hr or 2 days

in the Jennie Lakes Wilderness

Tucked into a corner just outside the border of Kings Canyon and Sequoia National Parks, the Jennie Lakes Wilderness is a 10,500-acre wilderness area that is often overlooked by park visitors. It offers much of the same scenery as the national parks, with beautiful lakes, meadows, forests, and streams, but without all the fanfare and crowds. Weaver Lake is the easiest-to-reach destination in the wilderness, and it makes a perfect family backpacking trip or an equally nice day hike. The trail is well signed and passes through a mix of fir forest and meadows. At 1.7 miles, take the left fork for Weaver Lake, climbing uphill to the lake's basin. You'll spy the shelflike slabs of Shell Mountain peeking out above the trees. At just over three miles and at 8,700 feet in elevation, shallow but pretty Weaver Lake is set at the base of Shell Mountain's high, rounded ridge. You can try your luck fishing, or just find a lakeside seat and gaze at the view. On warm days, the brave go swimming.

Note that the road to Big Meadows is usually the last road to open in the area after snowmelt. If you're planning an early season trip, call to check on road and trail conditions.

User Groups: Hikers, dogs, and horses. No mountain bikes. No wheelchair facilities.

Permits: A free campfire permit is required for overnight stays and is available from the Hume Lake Ranger Station. There is a $20 entrance fee per vehicle at Sequoia and Kings Canyon National Parks, good for seven days in both the national forest and the national parks.

Maps: A Jennie Lakes Wilderness map is available from the U.S. Forest Service. A map of Sequoia and Kings Canyon is available from Tom Harrison Maps. For a topographic map, ask the USGS for Muir Grove.

Directions: From Fresno, drive east on Highway 180 for 55 miles to the Big Stump Entrance at Kings Canyon National Park. Continue 1.5 miles and turn right on the Generals Highway, heading for Sequoia National Park. Drive seven miles and turn left on Forest Road 14S11, at the sign for Big Meadows and Horse Corral. Drive three miles to the Big Meadows trailhead.

Contact: Giant Sequoia National Monument/ Sequoia National Forest, Hume Lake Ranger District, 35860 Kings Canyon Road, Dunlap, CA 93621, 559/338-2251, www.fs.fed.us/r5/sequoia.

42 JENNIE ELLIS LAKE

12.0 mi / 6.0 hr or 2 days   🚶3 ▲10

in the Jennie Lakes Wilderness

This trail into the Jennie Lakes Wilderness offers more of a challenge than the route to Weaver Lake, climbing 1,500 feet over six miles with some short, steep pitches. The rewards are also greater, because Jennie Ellis Lake is a beauty and receives fewer visitors than Weaver Lake. The trail is the same as the Weaver Lake Trail for 1.7 miles, but at the fork, you bear right for Jennie Ellis Lake. The trail climbs and dips through fir, pine,

HIKING

and manzanita forest, then crosses Poop Out Pass at 4.7 miles, the highest point on this trip. At nearly six miles, you reach the outlet stream for Jennie Ellis Lake. Follow the short spur trail to the lake, set at 9,000 feet. With a white granite backdrop and some sparse trees, the shoreline looks austere and barren, but beautiful just the same. Campsites are found around the lake, and catching fish for dinner is a fair possibility. If you only came for the day, find a comfortable spot to sit and admire the scenery before you head back.

Note that there is a somewhat shorter trail to reach Jennie Ellis Lake from Stony Creek Campground (10 miles round-trip instead of 12), but shorter doesn't necessarily mean easier. The shorter trail requires a 2,500-foot climb over the first 3.5 miles to Poop Out Pass, with several noticeably steep pitches along the way. At the pass, the two trails join and are one and the same on the final stretch to the lake.

User Groups: Hikers, dogs, and horses. No mountain bikes. No wheelchair facilities.

Permits: A free campfire permit is required for overnight stays and is available from the Hume Lake Ranger Station. There is a $20 entrance fee per vehicle at Sequoia and Kings Canyon National Parks, good for seven days in both the national forest and the national parks.

Maps: A Jennie Lakes Wilderness map is available from the U.S. Forest Service. A map of Sequoia and Kings Canyon is available from Tom Harrison Maps. For a topographic map, ask the USGS for Muir Grove.

Directions: From Fresno, drive east on Highway 180 for 55 miles to the Big Stump Entrance at Kings Canyon National Park. Continue 1.5 miles and turn right on the Generals Highway, heading for Sequoia National Park. Drive seven miles and turn left on Forest Road 14S11, at the sign for Big Meadows and Horse Corral. Drive three miles to the Big Meadows trailhead.

Contact: Giant Sequoia National Monument/ Sequoia National Forest, Hume Lake Ranger District, 35860 Kings Canyon Road, Dunlap, CA 93621, 559/338-2251, www.fs.fed.us/r5/ sequoia.

43 MITCHELL PEAK
5.2 mi / 3.0 hr

in the Jennie Lakes Wilderness

If you have the legs for a 2,000-foot climb over 2.6 miles, you can stand atop the summit of Mitchell Peak, the highest point in the Jennie Lakes Wilderness, at 10,365 feet in elevation. The peak used to have a fire lookout tower on top of it, but the Forest Service stopped using it and burned it down. What remains is the fabulous view, one of the best in this area. It's a one-mile climb from the trailhead to Marvin Pass and the boundary of the Jennie Lakes Wilderness. Bear left (east) and climb some more. At 1.6 miles, you reach the next junction, signed for Mitchell Peak. Head left (north), and in one more mile, you'll make the brief climb to Mitchell's summit, which straddles the border of Kings Canyon National Park. From your rocky perch, you can look out on the Great Western Divide and the Silliman Crest. It's an exemplary spot to catch your breath.

User Groups: Hikers, dogs, and horses. No mountain bikes. No wheelchair facilities.

Permits: A free campfire permit is required for overnight stays and is available from the Hume Lake Ranger Station. There is a $20 entrance fee per vehicle at Sequoia and Kings Canyon National Parks, good for seven days in both the national forest and the national parks.

Maps: A Jennie Lakes Wilderness map is available from the U.S. Forest Service. A map of Sequoia and Kings Canyon is available from Tom Harrison Maps. For a topographic map, ask the USGS for Muir Grove.

Directions: From Fresno, drive east on Highway 180 for 55 miles to the Big Stump Entrance at Kings Canyon National Park. Continue 1.5 miles and turn right on the Generals Highway, heading for Sequoia National Park. Drive seven miles and turn left on Forest Road 14S11, at the sign for Big Meadow and Horse Corral. Drive four miles to the Big Meadow Campground and continue six more miles to Horse Corral Meadow. Turn right on Forest Road 13S12 and drive 2.8 miles to the Marvin Pass trailhead.

Contact: Giant Sequoia National Monument/ Sequoia National Forest, Hume Lake Ranger District, 35860 Kings Canyon Road, Dunlap, CA 93621, 559/338-2251, www.fs.fed.us/r5/ sequoia.

44 BIG BALDY
4.6 mi / 2.5 hr

southeast of the Grant Grove area of Kings Canyon National Park

The trip to Big Baldy comes with a million views and a little workout besides. Views? We're talking Redwood Canyon, Redwood Mountain, Buena Vista Peak, Little Baldy, Buck Rock, and the Great Western Divide. A little workout? You've got to climb 1,000 feet, but it's nicely spread out over two miles. The trail alternates between thick forest cover and open granite areas as it winds along the rim of Redwood Canyon. In the forested stretches, we were amazed at how many birds were singing in the tall firs and cedars. The trail's initial vistas are to the west, but they keep changing and getting more interesting all the way to Big Baldy's 8,209-foot summit, where your view opens up to 360 degrees. Here you get your first wide-open views of the high Sierra peaks and the Great Western Divide to the east. This trail is so fun and rewarding, with so little suffering involved, that you may feel like you're getting away with something. A bonus: Because the first mile of trail faces to the west, this is a great area for watching the sunset. Big Baldy Trail is also ideal for snowshoeing in the winter.

User Groups: Hikers only. No dogs, horses, or mountain bikes. No wheelchair facilities.

Permits: No permits are required. There is a $20 entrance fee per vehicle at Sequoia and Kings Canyon National Parks, good for seven days.

Maps: A Sequoia and Kings Canyon map is available from Tom Harrison Maps. For a topographic map, ask the USGS for Muir Grove.

Directions: From Fresno, drive east on Highway 180 for 55 miles to the Big Stump Entrance at Kings Canyon National Park. Continue 1.5 miles and turn right on the Generals Highway, heading for Sequoia National Park. Drive approximately 6.5 miles on the Generals Highway to the Big Baldy trailhead, on the right, shortly before the turnoff for Big Meadows, on the left.

Contact: Sequoia and Kings Canyon National Parks, 47050 General Highway, Three Rivers, CA 93271-9651, 559/565-3341 or 559/565-4307, www.nps.gov/seki.

45 MUIR GROVE
4.0 mi / 2.0 hr

northwest of the Lodgepole area of Sequoia National Park

Few people hike this trail unless they are staying at Dorst Campground, so you have a lot better chance of seeing giant sequoias in solitude in the Muir Grove than at many places in the park. After crossing a wooden footbridge, the trail enters a mixed forest of red fir, white fir, sugar pines, and incense cedars. In early summer, you can count the many varieties of wildflowers along the trail, especially where you cross tiny streams. The trail heads west and curves around a deeply carved canyon at one mile out. Just off the trail to your right is a bare granite slab with an inspiring westward view. The trail undulates, never climbing or dropping much, making this an easy and pleasant stroll. At 1.9 miles, you reach the Muir Grove, a small, pristine grove of huge sequoias. The first one you come to on your left is a doozy. The grove is made even more enchanting by the thick undergrowth of blue and purple lupine blooming amid the trees in early summer.

HIKING

User Groups: Hikers only. No dogs, horses, or mountain bikes. No wheelchair facilities.

Permits: No permits are required. There is a $20 entrance fee per vehicle at Sequoia and Kings Canyon National Parks, good for seven days.

Maps: A Sequoia and Kings Canyon map is available from Tom Harrison Maps. For a topographic map, ask the USGS for Muir Grove.

Directions: From Fresno, drive east on Highway 180 for 55 miles to the Big Stump Entrance at Kings Canyon National Park. Continue 1.5 miles and turn right on the Generals Highway, heading for Sequoia National Park. Drive approximately 17 miles on the Generals Highway to the right turnoff for Dorst Campground. Turn right and drive through the campground to the amphitheater parking lot. Park there; the trail begins at a footbridge between the amphitheater parking lot and the group campground.

Contact: Sequoia and Kings Canyon National Parks, 47050 General Highway, Three Rivers, CA 93271-9651, 559/565-3341 or 559/565-4307, www.nps.gov/seki.

46 LITTLE BALDY
3.5 mi / 2.0 hr   👣2 ⛰9

northwest of the Lodgepole area of
Sequoia National Park

Little Baldy, Big Baldy, Buena Vista Peak.... Along this stretch of the Generals Highway, there are so many peak trails that offer far-reaching views, it's hard to choose where to start. Start here, on the Little Baldy Trail. It's a little more challenging than the Buena Vista Peak Trail, but it's shorter than Big Baldy Trail, and it offers eye-popping drama for remarkably little effort. Some claim that Little Baldy's view of the Silliman Crest, the Great Western Divide, Castle Rocks, Moro Rock, the Kaweah River Canyon, and the San Joaquin foothills is the best panorama in the park.

To see for yourself, set out from the trailhead, climbing through long, tree-shaded switchbacks,

heading first north, then south. Check out the unusual view of Big Baldy off to your left (far across the highway) as you climb. After 1.2 miles, the trail leaves the forest and its many wildflowers, and your views start to open up. Hike along Little Baldy's ridgeline and make the final steep summit ascent. The trail gets a little hard to discern as you near Little Baldy's wide, bare summit, but just wander around until you find the highest spot with the best view. Take a seat—you'll want to stay a while.

Special Note: Be sure to pick a clear day for this hike. In summer, your best bet is to hike the trail early in the morning, before the Central Valley haze rises to the mountains.

User Groups: Hikers only. No dogs, horses, or mountain bikes. No wheelchair facilities.

Permits: No permits are required. There is a $20 entrance fee per vehicle at Sequoia and Kings Canyon National Parks, good for seven days.

Maps: A Sequoia and Kings Canyon map is available from Tom Harrison Maps. For topographic maps, ask the USGS for Muir Grove and Giant Forest.

Directions: From Fresno, drive east on Highway 180 for 55 miles to the Big Stump Entrance at Kings Canyon National Park. Continue 1.5 miles and turn right on the Generals Highway, heading for Sequoia National Park. Drive approximately 18 miles on the Generals Highway to the Little Baldy trailhead, on the left, a mile beyond the turnoff for Dorst Campground.

Contact: Sequoia and Kings Canyon National Parks, 47050 General Highway, Three Rivers, CA 93271-9651, 559/565-3341 or 559/565-4307, www.nps.gov/seki.

47 THE LAKES TRAIL
13.0 mi / 2-3 days   👣3 ⛰10

off the Generals Highway in the Wolverton
area of Sequoia National Park

The Wolverton trailhead is at 7,200 feet, which gives you a boost at the start for this trip into the high country. The Lakes Trail is the most popular backpacking trip in Sequoia National Park, and it's easy to see why. Wide-open views and dramatic granite walls are standard fare as you hike. Part of the route is on a loop, with one side of the loop traveling to the Watchtower—a 1,600-foot-tall granite cliff that offers incredible vistas of Tokopah Valley and beyond. The trailside scenery begins in red fir forest, then enters polished granite country, and culminates in a rocky basin with three gemlike lakes—Heather, Emerald, and Pear—as well as many sparkling creeks. The total climb to Pear Lake is a mere 2,300 feet, spread out over 6.5 miles. Backpackers take note: You may camp only at Emerald and Pear Lakes, and no campfires are allowed.

Special Note: The Watchtower Trail usually isn't open until midsummer. When it is closed, you must take the alternate Hump Trail, which is not as scenic. If you're planning a trip for early in the year, check with the park to be sure Watchtower Trail is open.

User Groups: Hikers only. No dogs, horses, or mountain bikes. No wheelchair facilities.

Permits: There is a $20 entrance fee per vehicle at Sequoia and Kings Canyon National Parks, good for seven days. Wilderness permits are required for overnight stays. They are available on a first-come, first-served basis at the Lodgepole Visitors Center. For advanced wilderness permits or information on trail conditions, go to www.nps.gov/seki. Trailhead quotas are in effect from May to September.

Maps: A Sequoia and Kings Canyon map is available from Tom Harrison Maps. For a topographic map, ask the USGS for Lodgepole.

Directions: From Fresno, drive east on Highway 180 for 55 miles to the Big Stump Entrance at Kings Canyon National Park. Continue 1.5 miles and turn right on the Generals Highway, heading for Sequoia National Park. Drive approximately 27 miles on the Generals Highway, past the Lodgepole Village turnoff, to the Wolverton turnoff, on the left (east) side of the road. Turn left and drive to the parking area and trailhead.

Contact: Sequoia and Kings Canyon National Parks, 47050 General Highway, Three Rivers, CA 93271-9651, 559/565-3341 or 559/565-4307, www.nps.gov/seki.

48 HEATHER LAKE AND THE WATCHTOWER

9.0 mi / 5.0 hr   👣3 ⛰10

off the Generals Highway in the Wolverton area of Sequoia National Park

There's no reason that day hikers should be denied the incredible joys of hiking Lakes Trail from the Wolverton area of Sequoia National Park. You don't have to carry a backpack, get a wilderness permit, or have two or more free days to hike the first part of Lakes Trail, which ascends to the top of the 1,600-foot Watchtower (a big chunk of granite) and then continues to rocky Heather Lake. If you're hiking in spring or early summer, call the park first to make sure Watchtower Trail is open. Otherwise you'll have to take the alternate Hump Trail, which is steeper and nowhere near as scenic. The route to the Watchtower is a ledge trail, blasted into hard granite, which creeps along the high rim of Tokopah Valley. Your view is 1,500 feet straight down. You can even see tiny people walking on the path to Tokopah Falls. It's incredible, although perhaps not a good idea for people who are afraid of heights. Walking up to the Watchtower is plenty exciting, but it's even more so when you reach the other side, where you can look back and see what you were walking on. Just 0.75 mile farther and you're at Heather Lake, which is designated for day use only, so it has no campsites. It has a steep granite backdrop and a few rocky ledges to sit on. Too many people here when you arrive? No big deal. It's only another 0.5 mile to even prettier Emerald Lake, and the trail is nearly level. After a rest, you get to head back and hike the Watchtower route all over again.

User Groups: Hikers only. No dogs, horses, or mountain bikes. No wheelchair facilities.

HIKING

Permits: No permits are required. There is a $20 entrance fee per vehicle at Sequoia and Kings Canyon National Parks, good for seven days.

Maps: A Sequoia and Kings Canyon map is available from Tom Harrison Maps. For a topographic map, ask the USGS for Lodgepole.

Directions: From Fresno, drive east on Highway 180 for 55 miles to the Big Stump Entrance at Kings Canyon National Park. Continue 1.5 miles and turn right on the Generals Highway, heading for Sequoia National Park. Drive approximately 27 miles on the Generals Highway, past the Lodgepole Village turnoff, to the Wolverton turnoff on the left (east) side of the road. Turn left and drive to the parking area and trailhead.

Contact: Sequoia and Kings Canyon National Parks, 47050 General Highway, Three Rivers, CA 93271-9651, 559/565-3341 or 559/565-4307, www.nps.gov/seki.

49 ALTA PEAK

13.0 mi / 1-2 days   🏃5 ⛰10

off the Generals Highway in the Wolverton area of Sequoia National Park

BEST (

You say you like heights? You like vistas? Here's your trail, a 4,000-foot climb to the top of Alta Peak, an 11,204-foot summit in the Alta Country. Alta Peak and Mount Whitney are the only major summits in Sequoia National Park that have established trails, but both of them are still butt-kickers to reach. The trail to Alta Peak and Alta Meadow starts out the same as the Lakes Trail (from the Wolverton parking area), then it heads south (right) to Panther Gap, at 1.8 miles. After climbing through the forest to Panther Gap (at 8,450 feet), you get your first set of eye-popping views—of the Middle Fork Kaweah River and the Great Western Divide. Continue on the Alta Trail to Mehrten Meadow (at 3.9 miles), a popular camping spot, then reach a junction where you can go left for Alta Peak or right to Alta Meadow. You'll want to take both spurs

if you have the time and energy. If you're exhausted, just walk to Alta Meadow, with its flower-filled grasses and exquisite mountain views, a flat one mile away. Alta Peak is two miles away via the left fork, with a 2,000-foot climb. These two miles are considered one of the toughest stretches of trail in Sequoia National Park due to the brutal grade and the 10,000-plus foot elevation here above tree line. The summit is at 11,204 feet, and, of course, it offers a complete panorama. Even Mount Whitney and the Coast Range are visible on a clear day.

User Groups: Hikers only. No dogs, horses, or mountain bikes. No wheelchair facilities.

Permits: There is a $20 entrance fee per vehicle at Sequoia and Kings Canyon National Parks, good for seven days. Wilderness permits are required for overnight stays. They are available on a first-come, first-served basis at the Lodgepole Visitors Center. For advanced wilderness permits or information on trail conditions, go to www.nps.gov/seki. Trailhead quotas are in effect from May to September.

Maps: A Sequoia and Kings Canyon map is available from Tom Harrison Maps. For a topographic map, ask the USGS for Lodgepole.

Directions: From Fresno, drive east on Highway 180 for 55 miles to the Big Stump Entrance at Kings Canyon National Park. Continue 1.5 miles and turn right on the Generals Highway, heading for Sequoia National Park. Drive approximately 27 miles on the Generals Highway, past the Lodgepole Village turnoff, to the Wolverton turnoff, on the left (east) side of the road. Turn left and drive to the parking area and trailhead.

Contact: Sequoia and Kings Canyon National Parks, 47050 General Highway, Three Rivers, CA 93271-9651, 559/565-3341 or 559/565-4307, www.nps.gov/seki.

50 PANTHER GAP LOOP
6.0 mi / 3.5 hr   🏃3 ⛰8

off the Generals Highway in the Wolverton area of Sequoia National Park

If you're not up for the marathon trip to Alta Peak, you can still get a taste of the high country on this loop from the Wolverton trailhead. Start hiking on the Lakes Trail from the east end of the Wolverton parking lot, and at 1.8 miles, bear right on the Alta Trail to parallel Wolverton Creek, following it to Panther Gap. Here, at 8,450 feet, you get an inspiring vista of the Middle Fork Kaweah River and the Great Western Divide. Check out 9,081-foot Castle Rocks, an obvious landmark. From the gap, turn right (west) and follow the Alta Trail to Panther Peak and Panther Meadow, then on to Red Fir Meadow. Finally, at 4.6 miles, bear right and complete the loop by descending to Long Meadow and then edging along its east side to return to the parking lot. By the way, don't get any smart ideas about hiking this loop in the opposite direction—it's a much steeper climb.

User Groups: Hikers and horses. No dogs or mountain bikes. No wheelchair facilities.

Permits: No permits are required. There is a $20 entrance fee per vehicle at Sequoia and Kings Canyon National Parks, good for seven days.

Maps: A Sequoia and Kings Canyon map is available from Tom Harrison Maps. For a topographic map, ask the USGS for Lodgepole.

Directions: From Fresno, drive east on Highway 180 for 55 miles to the Big Stump Entrance at Kings Canyon National Park. Continue 1.5 miles and turn right on the Generals Highway, heading for Sequoia National Park. Drive approximately 27 miles on the Generals Highway, past the Lodgepole Village turnoff, to the Wolverton turnoff, on the left (east) side of the road. Turn left and drive to the parking area and trailhead.

Contact: Sequoia and Kings Canyon National Parks, 47050 General Highway, Three Rivers, CA 93271-9651, 559/565-3341 or 559/565-4307, www.nps.gov/seki.

51 TOKOPAH FALLS
3.6 mi / 2.0 hr   🏃1 ⛰10

off the Generals Highway in the Giant Forest area of Sequoia National Park

BEST (

This is unquestionably the best waterfall day hike in Sequoia and Kings Canyon National Parks, leading to 1,200-foot-high Tokopah Falls. It's also a perfect family hike, easy on the feet and even easier on the eyes. The scenery is spectacular the whole way, from the up-close looks at wildflowers and granite boulders to the more distant views of the Watchtower, a 1,600-foot glacially carved cliff on the south side of Tokopah Valley. Then there's the valley itself, with Tokopah Falls pouring down the smooth back curve of its U shape. Because the trail begins by the three huge Lodgepole Campgrounds, it sees a lot of foot traffic. Your best bet is to start early in the morning. Another unusual feature of the trail? Hikers see more yellow-bellied marmots on the Tokopah Falls route than anywhere else in the two parks. We saw at least 40 of the cute little blond guys sunning themselves on rocks. If you're lucky, one of them will whistle at you as you walk by.

User Groups: Hikers and horses. No dogs or mountain bikes. No wheelchair facilities.

Permits: No permits are required. There is a $20 entrance fee per vehicle at Sequoia and Kings Canyon National Parks, good for seven days.

Maps: A Sequoia and Kings Canyon map is available from Tom Harrison Maps. For a topographic map, ask the USGS for Lodgepole.

Directions: From Fresno, drive east on Highway 180 for 55 miles to the Big Stump Entrance at Kings Canyon National Park. Continue 1.5 miles and turn right on the Generals Highway, heading for Sequoia National Park. Drive approximately 25 miles

HIKING

on the Generals Highway to the Lodgepole Campground turnoff, then drive 0.75 mile to the Log Bridge area of Lodgepole Camp. Park in the large lot just before the bridge over the Marble Fork Kaweah River, and walk 150 yards to the trailhead, which is just after you cross the bridge.

Contact: Sequoia and Kings Canyon National Parks, 47050 General Highway, Three Rivers, CA 93271-9651, 559/565-3341 or 559/565-4307, www.nps.gov/seki.

52 TWIN LAKES
13.6 mi / 1-2 days

off the Generals Highway in the Giant Forest area of Sequoia National Park

From the Lodgepole Campground trailhead (at 6,740 feet), the Twin Lakes are a 2,800-foot elevation gain and 6.8 miles away, making this a moderate backpacking trip or a long, strenuous day hike. It's a classic Sequoia National Park trip; one that is heavily traveled each summer. The terrain is an interesting mix of dense conifer forests, glacial moraine, and open meadows. From the trailhead, you climb past Wolverton's Rock to Cahoon Meadow at three miles, 0.5 mile beyond a crossing of Silliman Creek. You then continue to Cahoon Gap at 4.2 miles, cross over Clover Creek at five miles (campsites are found along the creek), bear right at the J. O. Pass Trail junction at 5.5 miles, and reach the Twin Lakes at 6.8 miles. The trail leads you directly to the larger Twin Lake; the smaller one is reached by following a spur. Both are shallow and have forested banks; some hikers try their luck fishing in the larger lake. Backpackers spending the night at Twin Lakes can hike farther the next day—over rocky Silliman Pass (at 10,100 feet) to the less-visited Ranger Lakes, three miles farther. Note that campfires are not allowed at Twin Lakes.

User Groups: Hikers and horses. No dogs or mountain bikes. No wheelchair facilities.

Permits: There is a $20 entrance fee per vehicle at Sequoia and Kings Canyon National Parks, good for seven days. Wilderness permits are required for overnight stays. They are available on a first-come, first-served basis at the Lodgepole Visitors Center. For advanced wilderness permits or information on trail conditions, go to www.nps.gov/seki. Trailhead quotas are in effect from May to September.

Maps: A Sequoia and Kings Canyon map is available from Tom Harrison Maps. For a topographic map, ask the USGS for Lodgepole.

Directions: From Fresno, drive east on Highway 180 for 55 miles to the Big Stump Entrance at Kings Canyon National Park. Continue 1.5 miles and turn right on the Generals Highway, heading for Sequoia National Park. Drive approximately 25 miles on the Generals Highway to the Lodgepole Campground turnoff, and then drive 0.75 mile to the Log Bridge area of Lodgepole Camp. The Twin Lakes trailhead is just beyond the Tokopah Falls trailhead and the bridge over the Marble Fork Kaweah River.

Contact: Sequoia and Kings Canyon National Parks, 47050 General Highway, Three Rivers, CA 93271-9651, 559/565-3341 or 559/565-4307, www.nps.gov/seki.

53 CONGRESS TRAIL LOOP
2.9 mi / 1.5 hr

off the Generals Highway in the Giant Forest area of Sequoia National Park

BEST (

The Congress Trail, a two-mile loop that starts (and ends) at the General Sherman Tree, is a much-traveled route through the Giant Forest's prize grove of sequoias. The General Sherman sees the greatest number of visitors, because it is recognized as the largest living thing in the world (not by height, but by volume). After you leave its side and start on the Congress Trail, the crowds lessen substantially. You'll pass by many huge trees with placards displaying their very patriotic names, like the House and Senate clusters, the McKinley Tree, the Lincoln Tree, and... well, you get the idea. Every single giant sequoia is worth stopping to gape at. We rate the Congress Trail as the best level, easy trail for sequoia viewing in the park. Plus, the farther you walk, the more solitude you get. Make sure you pick up an interpretive brochure at the trailhead or at the Lodgepole Visitors Center.

The parking area for the Sherman Tree and the Congress Trail is 0.4 mile from the Sherman Tree for a total mileage of 2.9 miles—two miles for the loop plus the out-and-back to the parking area. (You can't park on the Generals Highway by the Sherman Tree as you could prior to 2005. This parking area is now reserved for the Giant Forest shuttle bus and wheelchair users only).

User Groups: Hikers only. No dogs, horses, or mountain bikes. Wheelchair users can access this trail; in some areas they may need assistance.

Permits: No permits are required. There is a $20 entrance fee per vehicle at Sequoia and Kings Canyon National Parks, good for seven days.

Maps: A Sequoia and Kings Canyon map is available from Tom Harrison Maps. For a topographic map, ask the USGS for Giant Forest.

Directions: From Fresno, drive east on Highway 180 for 55 miles to the Big Stump Entrance at Kings Canyon National Park. Continue 1.5 miles and turn right on the Generals Highway, heading for Sequoia National Park. Drive approximately 27 miles on the Generals Highway, past Lodgepole Village, to the Wolverton turnoff on the left (east) side of the road. Turn left and drive to the General Sherman Tree parking area. (If you are riding the free Giant Forest shuttle bus, you can disembark right at the Sherman Tree. For details see www.sequoiashuttle.com.)

Contact: Sequoia and Kings Canyon National Parks, 47050 General Highway, Three Rivers, CA 93271-9651, 559/565-3341 or 559/565-4307, www.nps.gov/seki.

54 HAZELWOOD AND HUCKLEBERRY LOOP

4.5 mi / 2.0 hr   🏃2 ⛰8

off the Generals Highway in the Giant Forest area of Sequoia National Park

This hike combines two loop trails in the Giant Forest area for an easy but excellent day hike, passing by many giant sequoias and peaceful grassy meadows. A bonus: These trails are generally less crowded than the other day hikes in the Giant Forest area.

From the Generals Highway, pick up the Hazelwood Nature Trail and take the right side of the loop to join Alta Trail and Huckleberry Meadow Trail Loop. Take Alta Trail for 0.25 mile and bear right on Huckleberry Meadow Trail, climbing a bit for 1 mile to the site of Squatter's Cabin, one of the oldest structures in Sequoia National Park, dating back to the 1880s. To stay on the loop, turn left by the cabin (don't take the trail signed for The Dead Giant). The trail skirts the edge of Huckleberry Meadow and heads north to Circle Meadow, where giant sequoias line the meadow's edges. There are several junctions, but stay on Huckleberry Meadow Trail. A half mile farther is a short spur trail on the left heading to the Washington Tree. Follow the spur to see the second-largest tree in the world (after General Sherman)—it's 30 feet in diameter and 246.1 feet tall. The trip finishes out on Alta Trail, where you return to Hazelwood Nature Trail and walk the opposite side of its short loop back to the Generals Highway.

User Groups: Hikers only. No dogs, horses, or mountain bikes. No wheelchair facilities.

Permits: No permits are required. There is a $20 entrance fee per vehicle at Sequoia and Kings Canyon National Parks, good for seven days.

Maps: A Sequoia and Kings Canyon map is available from Tom Harrison Maps. For topographic maps, ask the USGS for Giant Forest and Lodgepole.

Directions: From Fresno, drive east on Highway 180 for 55 miles to the Big Stump

HIKING

HIKING

Entrance at Kings Canyon National Park. Continue 1.5 miles and turn right on the Generals Highway, heading for Sequoia National Park. Drive approximately 30 miles on the Generals Highway, past Lodgepole and Wolverton, to the Giant Forest area of Sequoia National Park. The Hazelwood trailhead is on the south side of the highway, 0.25 mile before you reach the Giant Forest Museum.

Contact: Sequoia and Kings Canyon National Parks, 47050 General Highway, Three Rivers, CA 93271-9651, 559/565-3341 or 559/565-4307, www.nps.gov/seki.

55 HIGH SIERRA TRAIL TO HAMILTON LAKE
30.0 mi / 3 days   🏃3 ⛰10

off the Generals Highway in the Giant Forest area of Sequoia National Park

This is a classic, easy-to-moderate, three-day backpacking trip in the High Sierra, with a two-night stay at Bearpaw Meadow Camp, a shady campground that clings to the edge of a granite gorge. The route follows High Sierra Trail from Crescent Meadow to Eagle View, then continues for 10 nearly level miles along the north rim of the Middle Fork Kaweah River Canyon. It's views, views, views all the way.

After a good night's sleep at Bearpaw Meadow, elevation 7,700 feet (reservations for a wilderness permit are definitely necessary in the summer months), you start out on an eight-mile round-trip day hike to Upper and Lower Hamilton Lake (at 8,300 feet), set in a glacially carved basin at the base of the peaks of the Great Western Divide. On the final day, you hike 11 miles back to Crescent Meadow, once again witnessing 180-degree views from the sunny High Sierra Trail. By the time it's all over and you're back home, your mind is completely blown by all the high-country beauty, and you've shot about a million pictures, none of which can compare to the experience of actually being there.

User Groups: Hikers only. No dogs, horses, or mountain bikes. No wheelchair facilities.

Permits: There is a $20 entrance fee per vehicle at Sequoia and Kings Canyon National Parks, good for seven days. Wilderness permits are required for overnight stays. They are available on a first-come, first-served basis at the Lodgepole Visitors Center. For advanced wilderness permits or information on trail conditions, go to www.nps.gov/seki. Trailhead quotas are in effect from May to September.

Maps: A Sequoia and Kings Canyon map is available from Tom Harrison Maps. For topographic maps, ask the USGS for Giant Forest and Lodgepole.

Directions: From Fresno, drive east on Highway 180 for 55 miles to the Big Stump Entrance at Kings Canyon National Park. Continue 1.5 miles and turn right on the Generals Highway, heading for Sequoia National Park. Drive approximately 30 miles on the Generals Highway, past Lodgepole and Wolverton, to the Giant Forest area of Sequoia National Park. Just beyond the museum, turn left on Crescent Meadow Road and drive 3.5 miles to the Crescent Meadow parking area.

Contact: Sequoia and Kings Canyon National Parks, 47050 General Highway, Three Rivers, CA 93271-9651, 559/565-3341 or 559/565-4307, www.nps.gov/seki.

56 HIGH SIERRA TRAIL AND EAGLE VIEW
1.5 mi / 1.0 hr   🏃1 ⛰10

off the Generals Highway in the Giant Forest area of Sequoia National Park

Are you ready to be wowed? From the lower parking lot at Crescent Meadow, follow the trail that leads to the southern edge of Crescent Meadow, and at 0.1 mile, take the right fork that leads up the ridge on High Sierra Trail toward Eagle View. The High Sierra Trail is a popular trans-Sierra route that eventually leads to Mount Whitney, the highest peak in the contiguous United States. On this trip you won't go quite that far, but you will get a taste of the visual delights of this extraordinary trail. In less than 0.5 mile, you'll gain the ridge and start getting wondrous, edge-of-the-world views. Numerous wildflowers line the path, which hugs the edge of this high ridge. At 0.7 mile, you'll reach Eagle View, an unsigned but obvious lookout from which you get a fascinating look at Moro Rock to your right, Castle Rocks straight ahead, and dozens of peaks and ridges of the Western Divide far across the canyon. The vistas are so fine and the trail is so good that you might just want to keep walking all the way to Mount Whitney.

User Groups: Hikers only. No dogs, horses, or mountain bikes. No wheelchair facilities.

Permits: No permits are required. There is a $20 entrance fee per vehicle at Sequoia and Kings Canyon National Parks, good for seven days.

Maps: A Sequoia and Kings Canyon map is available from Tom Harrison Maps. For topographic maps, ask the USGS for Giant Forest and Lodgepole.

Directions: From Fresno, drive east on Highway 180 for 55 miles to the Big Stump Entrance at Kings Canyon National Park. Continue 1.5 miles and turn right on the Generals Highway, heading for Sequoia National Park. Drive approximately 30 miles on the Generals Highway, past Lodgepole and Wolverton, to the Giant Forest area of Sequoia National Park. Just beyond the museum, turn left on Crescent Meadow Road and drive 3.5 miles to the Crescent Meadow parking area.

Contact: Sequoia and Kings Canyon National Parks, 47050 General Highway, Three Rivers, CA 93271-9651, 559/565-3341 or 559/565-4307, www.nps.gov/seki.

57 CRESCENT MEADOW AND THARP'S LOG
1.6 mi / 1.0 hr   🏃1 ⛰8

off the Generals Highway in the Giant Forest area of Sequoia National Park

Crescent Meadow is more than 1.5 miles long and is surrounded by giant sequoias. John Muir called it "the gem of the Sierras." We don't know how Muir would feel about the pavement that lines the trail around this precious meadow, but we hope he'd like this loop hike anyhow. Follow the pavement for 200 yards from the eastern side of the parking lot, and just like that, you're at the southern edge of beautiful Crescent Meadow. Take the right fork and head for Log Meadow and Tharp's Log. Log Meadow is as large and beautiful as Crescent Meadow, and Tharp's Log was the homestead of Hale Tharp, the first white man to enter this forest. He grazed cattle and horses here, and built a modest home inside a fallen, fire-hollowed sequoia. You can look inside Tharp's Log and see his bed, fireplace, dining room table, and the door and windows he fashioned into the log. (Children find this incredibly thrilling.) From Tharp's Log, continue your loop back to Crescent Meadow and around its west side, where you return to the north edge of the parking lot.

User Groups: Hikers and wheelchairs (with assistance). No dogs, horses, or mountain bikes.

Permits: No permits are required. There is a $20 entrance fee per vehicle at Sequoia and Kings Canyon National Parks, good for seven days.

Maps: A Sequoia and Kings Canyon map is available from Tom Harrison Maps. For topographic maps, ask the USGS for Giant Forest and Lodgepole.

Directions: From Fresno, drive east on Highway 180 for 55 miles to the Big Stump Entrance at Kings Canyon National Park. Continue 1.5 miles and turn right on the Generals Highway, heading for Sequoia

HIKING

HIKING

National Park. Drive approximately 30 miles on the Generals Highway, past Lodgepole and Wolverton, to the Giant Forest area of Sequoia National Park. Just beyond the museum, turn left on Crescent Meadow Road and drive 3.5 miles to the Crescent Meadow parking area.

Contact: Sequoia and Kings Canyon National Parks, 47050 General Highway, Three Rivers, CA 93271-9651, 559/565-3341 or 559/565-4307, www.nps.gov/seki.

58 MORO ROCK

0.6 mi / 0.5 hr

off the Generals Highway in the Giant Forest area of Sequoia National Park

BEST (

Just about everybody has heard of Moro Rock, the prominent, pointy granite dome with the top-of-the-world sunset vistas, and if you're visiting the Giant Forest area of Sequoia National Park, well, you just have to hike to the top of it. When you climb those 380 stairs to the dome's summit and check out the view, you realize that unlike many famous attractions, Moro Rock is not overrated. It's as great as everybody says, and maybe even better. If you start your trip from the Moro Rock parking area, it's only 0.3 mile to the top, climbing switchbacks, ramps, and granite stairs the whole way. Railings line the rock-blasted trail to keep you from dropping off the 6,725-foot granite dome. What's the view like? Well, on a clear day, you can see all the way to the Coast Range, 100 miles away. In closer focus is the Middle Fork Kaweah River, the Great Western Divide, Castle Rocks (at 9,180 feet), Triple Divide Peak (at 12,634 feet), Mount Stewart (at 12,205 feet)… and on and on. In a word, it's awesome. And even better, you don't get this view just from the top of Moro Rock—you get it all the way up, at every turn in the trail.

If you want the absolute best visibility, show up early in the morning, before the afternoon haze from the Central Valley obscures

the view. On the other hand, that same haze creates amazingly colorful sunsets, so early evening is another fine time to be on top of Moro Rock.

User Groups: Hikers only. No dogs, horses, or mountain bikes. No wheelchair facilities.

Permits: No permits are required. There is a $20 entrance fee per vehicle at Sequoia and Kings Canyon National Parks, good for seven days.

Maps: A Sequoia and Kings Canyon map is available from Tom Harrison Maps. For a topographic map, ask the USGS for Giant Forest.

Directions: From Fresno, drive east on Highway 180 for 55 miles to the Big Stump Entrance at Kings Canyon National Park. Continue 1.5 miles and turn right on the Generals Highway, heading for Sequoia National Park. Drive approximately 30 miles on the Generals Highway, past Lodgepole and Wolverton, to the Giant Forest area of Sequoia National Park. Just beyond the museum, turn left on Crescent Meadow Road, drive 1.5 miles, and take the right fork to the Moro Rock parking area.

Contact: Sequoia and Kings Canyon National Parks, 47050 General Highway, Three Rivers, CA 93271-9651, 559/565-3341 or 559/565-4307, www.nps.gov/seki.

59 SUNSET ROCK

2.0 mi / 1.0 hr

off the Generals Highway in the Giant Forest area of Sequoia National Park

The trail to Sunset Rock is a first-rate easy hike, perfect at sunset or any time. It gets much less traffic than you might expect, considering its proximity to Giant Forest. Leave your car in the lot across from the Giant Forest museum (make sure you stop in before or after your trip), then pick up the trail on the west side of the lot. The level path leads through a mixed forest (with a handful of giant sequoias) and crosses Little Deer Creek on its way to Sunset Rock. The rock is a gargantuan, flat piece of granite—about the size of a football field—set at 6,412 feet in elevation. Standing on it, you get a terrific overlook of Little Baldy to your right and a sea of conifers below, in the Marble Fork Kaweah River Canyon.

User Groups: Hikers only. No dogs, horses, or mountain bikes. No wheelchair facilities.

Permits: No permits are required. There is a $20 entrance fee per vehicle at Sequoia and Kings Canyon National Parks, good for seven days.

Maps: A Sequoia and Kings Canyon map is available from Tom Harrison Maps. For a topographic map, ask the USGS for Giant Forest.

Directions: From Fresno, drive east on Highway 180 for 55 miles to the Big Stump Entrance at Kings Canyon National Park. Continue 1.5 miles and turn right on the Generals Highway, heading for Sequoia National Park. Drive approximately 30 miles on the Generals Highway, past Lodgepole and Wolverton, to the Giant Forest area of Sequoia National Park. Park in the lot across from the Giant Forest museum, then pick up the signed trail on the west side of the lot.

Contact: Sequoia and Kings Canyon National Parks, 47050 General Highway, Three Rivers, CA 93271-9651, 559/565-3341 or 559/565-4307, www.nps.gov/seki.

60 PARADISE CREEK TRAIL
1.2 mi / 0.75 hr   🥾1 ⛰8

off Highway 198 in the Foothills region of Sequoia National Park

BEST (

From Buckeye Flat Campground, Paradise Creek Trail meanders through oaks and buckeyes, and crosses a long, picturesque footbridge over the Middle Fork Kaweah River. An inviting, Olympic-sized pool is on the right side of the bridge, where campers often go swimming on summer afternoons. Save the pool for after

your hike; for now, take the signed Paradise Creek Trail, at the far side of the bridge. You'll briefly visit the creek and then leave it, climbing into oak and grassland terrain. There are some high views of Moro Rock and Hanging Rock, but most of the beauty is right at your feet, in the springtime flowers that grow in the grasses and in the leafy blue oaks that shade them. The maintained trail ends when it reaches Paradise Creek again, although a faint route continues along its banks.

User Groups: Hikers only. No dogs, horses, or mountain bikes. No wheelchair facilities.

Permits: No permits are required. There is a $20 entrance fee per vehicle at Sequoia and Kings Canyon National Parks, good for seven days.

Maps: A Sequoia and Kings Canyon map is available from Tom Harrison Maps. For a topographic map, ask the USGS for Giant Forest.

Directions: From Visalia, drive east on Highway 198 for 47 miles to the turnoff, on the right, for Buckeye Flat Campground, across from Hospital Rock. Turn right and drive 0.6 mile to the campground. Park in any of the dirt pullouts outside of the camp entrance; no day-use parking is allowed in the camp. You can also park at Hospital Rock and walk to the campground. The trailhead is near campsite No. 28.

Contact: Sequoia and Kings Canyon National Parks, 47050 General Highway, Three Rivers, CA 93271-9651, 559/565-3341 or 559/565-3135, www.nps.gov/seki.

61 MIDDLE FORK TRAIL TO PANTHER CREEK
6.0 mi / 3.0 hr   🥾2 ⛰8

off Highway 198 in the Foothills region of Sequoia National Park

You want to be alone? You don't want to see anybody else on the trail? Just sign up for this trip any time between June and September,

HIKING

when the foothills have warmed up to their summer extremes. Don't be fooled by this path's name: The Middle Fork Trail is no streamside meander. Rather, it's a shadeless, exposed trail that leads high along the canyon of the Middle Fork Kaweah River—always at least 250 feet above it. In summer, it's hot as Hades, but this trail is perfect in winter and spring. Whereas most other trails in Sequoia and Kings Canyon are still snowed under, you can take an early-season day hike or backpacking trip along Middle Fork Trail. The main destination is Panther Creek (at three miles), where the trail leads across the brink of Panther Creek's 100-foot dive into the Kaweah River. But you can hike farther if you wish. Although Middle Fork Trail is set in grasslands and chaparral, it offers some stunning views of the area's geology, including Moro Rock, Castle Rocks, and the Great Western Divide. We hiked this trail in August, and despite the fact that we were wilting from the heat, the expansive views kept our spirits up.

User Groups: Hikers only. No dogs, horses, or mountain bikes. No wheelchair facilities.

Permits: No permits are required. There is a $20 entrance fee per vehicle at Sequoia and Kings Canyon National Parks, good for seven days.

Maps: A Sequoia and Kings Canyon map is available from Tom Harrison Maps. For a topographic map, ask the USGS for Giant Forest.

Directions: From Visalia, drive east on Highway 198 for 47 miles to the turnoff, on the right, for Buckeye Flat Campground, across from Hospital Rock. Turn right and drive 0.5 mile to a left fork just before the campground. Bear left on the dirt road and drive 1.3 miles to the trailhead and parking area. In the winter, you must park at Hospital Rock and walk in to the trailhead, adding 3.6 miles to your round-trip.

Contact: Sequoia and Kings Canyon National Parks, 47050 General Highway, Three Rivers, CA 93271-9651, 559/565-3341 or 559/565-3135, www.nps.gov/seki.

62 POTWISHA TO HOSPITAL ROCK
5.0 mi / 2.5 hr

off Highway 198 in the Foothills region of Sequoia National Park

First, some advice: Don't hike this trail on a hot day. If it's summertime and you want to see the Monache Indian historical sites at Potwisha and Hospital Rock, drive to each of them and see them separately. In winter or spring, however, it's far more fun to take this five-mile hike through chaparral and oak woodlands, especially in March, when the wildflowers bloom. In the first 100 yards from the trailhead, you'll see Native American grinding holes and pictographs that look roughly like people and animals. You'll also pass many tempting pools in the Middle Fork Kaweah, which are frequented by swimmers and bathers in the summer. The trail climbs a gradual 2.5 miles from Potwisha to Hospital Rock, crossing the highway after the first mile. When you reach Hospital Rock, which is just a few feet off the road to Buckeye Flat Campground, you see a huge display of pictographs on its side. Across the campground road are more grinding holes in the boulders, and near them, a short paved path leads to deep pools and sandy beaches on the Middle Fork. Another path leads from the camp road to the underside of Hospital Rock, where there's a large, cavelike shelter. This is where a Native American medicine man healed the sick and injured, resulting in a white man naming this place Hospital Rock.

User Groups: Hikers only. No dogs, horses, or mountain bikes. No wheelchair facilities.

Permits: No permits are required. There is a $20 entrance fee per vehicle at Sequoia and Kings Canyon National Parks, good for seven days.

Maps: A Sequoia and Kings Canyon map is available from Tom Harrison Maps. For a topographic map, ask the USGS for Giant Forest.

Directions: From Visalia, drive east on Highway 198 for 44 miles to the turnoff, on the left, for Potwisha Campground, 3.8 miles east of the Ash Mountain entrance station to Sequoia National Park. Don't turn left into Potwisha campground; instead, turn right on the paved road opposite the campground. Drive past the RV dumping station to the signed trailhead and parking area.

Contact: Sequoia and Kings Canyon National Parks, 47050 General Highway, Three Rivers, CA 93271-9651, 559/565-3341 or 559/565-3135, www.nps.gov/seki.

63 MARBLE FALLS

7.0 mi / 4.0 hr

off Highway 198 in the Foothills region of Sequoia National Park

This is the waterfall to see in Sequoia National Park in late winter and spring. March and April are particularly good months to visit because of high flows in the Marble Fork Kaweah River and blooming wildflowers in the grasslands and chaparral that line the trail. From its rather banal start as a dirt road, this trail just keeps getting better as it follows the Marble Fork Kaweah River. There are no trail junctions to worry about; at 3.5 miles, the path simply dead-ends near the lower cascades of Marble Falls. Although much of the falls are hidden in the narrow, rocky river gorge, tucked out of sight, what is visible is an impressive billowing cascade of whitewater. Be very careful on the slippery granite near the river's edges; the current and the cold water are even more dangerous than they look. Aside from the waterfalls and the wildflowers, the other highlights on this trail are the colorful outcroppings of marble, particularly in the last mile as you near the falls. Remember, though, that in summer this area of the park can bake like an oven. If you make the trip to the falls from late May to September, get an early morning start.

User Groups: Hikers only. No dogs, horses, or mountain bikes. No wheelchair facilities.

Permits: No permits are required. There is a $20 entrance fee per vehicle at Sequoia and Kings Canyon National Parks, good for seven days.

Maps: A Sequoia and Kings Canyon map is available from Tom Harrison Maps. For a topographic map, ask the USGS for Giant Forest.

Directions: From Visalia, drive east on Highway 198 for 44 miles to the turnoff, on the left, for Potwisha Campground, 3.8 miles east of the Ash Mountain entrance station to Sequoia National Park. The trail begins across from campsite No. 15 in Potwisha Campground; park in the trailhead parking area in the camp.

Contact: Sequoia and Kings Canyon National Parks, 47050 General Highway, Three Rivers, CA 93271-9651, 559/565-3341 or 559/565-3135, www.nps.gov/seki.

64 PARADISE RIDGE

3.2 mi / 1.5 hr

off Highway 198 in the Mineral King region of Sequoia National Park

OK, you've just driven the 20 twisting miles into Mineral King from Three Rivers. You're tired, dusty, and itching to get out of the car and move your legs. What's the first trail you can reach in Mineral King? The Paradise Ridge Trail, and it climbs right away, getting you huffing and puffing and clearing out the road dust from your lungs. After the initial steepness of the trail, the grade becomes easier as it moves into switchbacks ascending the hill. Although much of this forest has been burned in recent years, the giant sequoia trees are thriving, some in clusters as large as 10 or more. At your feet are tons of ferns. As you climb, the views just keep improving—you see the East Fork Kaweah River Canyon below you, and far off, the Great Western

Divide. You can hike all the way to the top of the ridge at three miles, but the views aren't any better there than they are on the way up. Most people just cruise uphill a way, and turn around when they've had enough. Besides the big trees and the big views, our favorite thing about this trail was that we saw more bears than people.

User Groups: Hikers and horses. No dogs or mountain bikes. No wheelchair facilities.

Permits: No permits are required. There is a $20 entrance fee per vehicle at Sequoia and Kings Canyon National Parks, good for seven days.

Maps: A Mineral King map is available from Tom Harrison Maps. For a topographic map, ask the USGS for Silver City.

Directions: From Visalia, drive east on Highway 198 for 38 miles to Mineral King Road, 2.5 miles east of Three Rivers. If you reach the Ash Mountain entrance station, you've gone too far. Turn right on Mineral King Road and drive 20 miles to the Hockett Trail parking area, on the right, 0.25 mile past Atwell Mill Camp. Park there and walk back west on Mineral King Road about 0.3 mile to the trailhead for Paradise Ridge, on the north side of the road.

Contact: Sequoia and Kings Canyon National Parks, 47050 General Highway, Three Rivers, CA 93271-9651, 559/565-3341 or 559/565-3135, www.nps.gov/seki.

65 HOCKETT TRAIL TO EAST FORK BRIDGE

4.0 mi / 2.0 hr 🏃1 ⛰8

off Highway 198 in the Mineral King region of Sequoia National Park

The Hockett Trail makes a fine day-hiking path in Mineral King. It's suitable for all kinds of hikers. Families with small children can just walk a mile downhill to the footbridge over the East Fork Kaweah River, where there is a small waterfall and many sculptured granite pools, and then turn around and head back. People looking for a longer trip can continue another mile to the East Fork Grove of sequoias and Deer Creek. Although some of this forest has been burned in recent years, most of the big conifers were spared, and the area is still quite beautiful. The trail starts in an area of sequoia stumps, near where the Atwell Mill cut lumber in the 1880s. Live sequoias still flourish farther down the path, near the river's edge; apparently they were spared because of their distance from the mill. The trail is well graded, and even the uphill return is only a moderate climb.

User Groups: Hikers and horses. No dogs or mountain bikes. No wheelchair facilities.

Permits: No permits are required. There is a $20 entrance fee per vehicle at Sequoia and Kings Canyon National Parks, good for seven days.

Maps: A Mineral King map is available from Tom Harrison Maps. For a topographic map, ask the USGS for Mineral King.

Directions: From Visalia, drive east on Highway 198 for 38 miles to Mineral King Road, 2.5 miles east of Three Rivers. If you reach the Ash Mountain entrance station, you've gone too far. Turn right on Mineral King Road and drive 20 miles to the Hockett Trail parking area, on the right, 0.25 mile past Atwell Mill Camp. Park there and walk into the campground to campsite No. 16, where the trail begins.

Contact: Sequoia and Kings Canyon National Parks, 47050 General Highway, Three Rivers, CA 93271-9651, 559/565-3341 or 559/565-3135, www.nps.gov/seki.

66 COLD SPRINGS NATURE TRAIL
2.0 mi / 1.0 hr   🚶1 ⛰8

off Highway 198 in the Mineral King region of Sequoia National Park

You may not expect much from a campground nature trail, but Cold Springs Nature Trail is guaranteed to exceed your expectations. Not only is it lined with wildflowers along the East Fork Kaweah River and informative signposts that teach you to identify junipers, red and white firs, cottonwoods, and aspens, but the views of the Sawtooth Ridge are glorious. The loop is less than 0.5 mile, but from the far end of it, the trail continues along the East Fork Kaweah River, heading another mile into Mineral King Valley. Walk to the loop's far end, and then continue at least another 0.25 mile along the trail. It just gets prettier as it goes. You're in for a real treat if you take this walk right before sunset, when the valley's surrounding mountain peaks turn every imaginable shade of pink, orange, and coral, reflecting the sun setting in the west. The vistas are so beautiful that they can practically make you weep.

User Groups: Hikers and horses. No dogs or mountain bikes. No wheelchair facilities.

Permits: No permits are required. There is a $20 entrance fee per vehicle at Sequoia and Kings Canyon National Parks, good for seven days.

Maps: A Mineral King map is available from Tom Harrison Maps. For a topographic map, ask the USGS for Mineral King.

Directions: From Visalia, drive east on Highway 198 for 38 miles to Mineral King Road, 2.5 miles east of Three Rivers. If you reach the Ash Mountain entrance station, you've gone too far. Turn right on Mineral King Road and drive 23.5 miles to Cold Springs Campground on the right. The trail begins near site six. If you aren't staying in the camp, you can park by the Mineral King Ranger Station and walk into the campground.

Contact: Sequoia and Kings Canyon National Parks, 47050 General Highway, Three Rivers, CA 93271-9651, 559/565-3341 or 559/565-3135, www.nps.gov/seki.

67 FAREWELL GAP TRAIL TO ASPEN FLAT
2.0 mi / 1.0 hr   🚶1 ⛰9

off Highway 198 in the Mineral King region of Sequoia National Park

BEST (

If ever there was a perfect family hike, this would have to be it. Actually, if ever there was a perfect hike for every two-legged person on the planet, this would have to be it. The glacial-cut Mineral King Valley—a peaceful paradise of meadows, streams, and 100-year-old cabins—has to be one of the most scenic places in the West, and possibly in the world. An easy stroll along the canyon floor leads you past waterfalls and along the headwaters of the East Fork Kaweah River, in the awesome shelter of thousand-foot cliffs. After walking to the trailhead near the horse corral, you follow Farewell Gap Trail (an old dirt road) for a mile, then cross Crystal Creek and take the right fork off the main trail. This brings you closer to the river, where you follow a narrow use trail to Aspen Flat (a lovely grove of trees), or to Soda Springs, situated right along the river's edge. There you can see mineral springs bubbling up from the ground, turning the earth around them a bright orange color. Bring a fishing rod on this trail if you like, but be absolutely certain to bring your camera.

User Groups: Hikers and horses. No dogs or mountain bikes. No wheelchair facilities.

Permits: No permits are required. There is a $20 entrance fee per vehicle at Sequoia and Kings Canyon National Parks, good for seven days.

Maps: A Mineral King map is available from Tom Harrison Maps. For a topographic map, ask the USGS for Mineral King.

Directions: From Visalia, drive east on Highway 198 for 38 miles to Mineral King Road,

HIKING

HIKING

2.5 miles east of Three Rivers. If you reach the Ash Mountain entrance station, you've gone too far. Turn right on Mineral King Road and drive 25 miles to the end of the road and the Eagle/Mosquito trailhead. Take the right fork at the end of the road to reach the parking area. Walk back out of the parking lot and follow the road to the horse corral; the Farewell Gap Trail begins just beyond it.

Contact: Sequoia and Kings Canyon National Parks, 47050 General Highway, Three Rivers, CA 93271-9651, 559/565-3341 or 559/565-3135, www.nps.gov/seki.

68 MOSQUITO LAKES
8.0 mi / 4.0 hr or 2 days 3 9

off Highway 198 in the Mineral King region of Sequoia National Park

Ah, paradise. You know you're in it as soon as you park your car at the end of Mineral King Road. The Eagle/Mosquito trailhead is at 7,830 feet, and you set out from the parking lot near one of Mineral King's adorable cabins, left from the early 20th century and privately owned. Feel jealous? Keep walking; you'll get over it. In minutes you cross a footbridge over Spring Creek's cascade, called Tufa Falls because of the calcium carbonate in Spring Creek's water. Don't expect to see much of a waterfall—most of it is hidden by brush. At one mile, you reach the junction for Eagle Lake, the Mosquito Lakes, and White Chief Trails. Take the right fork, climbing steadily. At two miles, you reach the Mosquito Lakes junction and go right, leaving Eagle Lake Trail for another day. Climb up and then down the other side of Miner's Ridge, at 9,300 feet. The final descent covers 0.5 mile; you reach Mosquito Lake number one at 9,040 feet and 3.6 miles. It's considered to be the easiest lake to reach in Mineral King, with a mostly shaded trail and only a 1,500-foot gain on the way in, plus a 250-foot gain on the way out. Still, if you've visited any of the other spectacular

Mineral King lakes, this lake will look a little disappointing. It's small, shallow, and greenish. But fear not: This is the first of several Mosquito Lakes, all of which are linked by Mosquito Creek. Hikers with excess energy can follow the stream uphill to four more lakes. There is no maintained trail to the upper lakes, but if you follow the use trail near the stream, the going is easier. The use trail begins on the west side of the stream at the first lake, navigates around the rocky slope behind the lake, and then crosses the stream above it. The climb from lake number one to lake number two is steep, with a 600-foot elevation gain in 0.5 mile, but it's worth it. Lake number two is the usual destination for day hikers; it's a blue, deep, granite-bound beauty and makes for an eight-mile round-trip. Backpackers will find the first campsites at Mosquito Lake number two (no camping is allowed at the first lake). Mosquito Lake number five is five miles from the Eagle/Mosquito trailhead.

User Groups: Hikers and horses. No dogs or mountain bikes. No wheelchair facilities.

Permits: There is a $20 entrance fee per vehicle at Sequoia and Kings Canyon National Parks, good for seven days. Wilderness permits are required for overnight stays. They are available on a first-come, first-served basis at the Mineral King Ranger Station. For advanced wilderness permits or information on trail conditions, go to www.nps.gov/seki. Trailhead quotas are in effect from May to September.

Maps: A Mineral King map is available from Tom Harrison Maps. For a topographic map, ask the USGS for Mineral King.

Directions: From Visalia, drive east on Highway 198 for 38 miles to Mineral King Road, 2.5 miles east of Three Rivers. If you reach the Ash Mountain entrance station, you've gone too far. Turn right on Mineral King Road and drive 25 miles to the end of the road and the Eagle/ Mosquito trailhead. Take the right fork at the end of the road to reach the parking area. The trail begins at the far end of the parking lot.

Contact: Sequoia and Kings Canyon National Parks, 47050 General Highway, Three Rivers,

CA 93271-9651, 559/565-3341 or 559/565-3135, www.nps.gov/seki.

69 EAGLE LAKE TRAIL

6.8 mi / 4.0 hr 🥾3 ⛰10

off Highway 198 in the Mineral King region of Sequoia National Park

Eagle Lake has always been the glamour destination in Mineral King; the trail to hike if you can hike only one trail in the area. Why? The blue-green lake is drop-dead gorgeous, that's why, and the trail to reach it is challenging but manageable for most day hikers, with a 2,200-foot elevation gain spread out over 3.4 miles. Nonetheless, hikers who made the trek to Eagle Lake in the summer of 2003 were heartily disappointed when they arrived. The lake's historic dam had sprung a leak, and the water had dropped to a sadly diminished level. However, the Park Service got to work on fixing the dam, and soon the lake was restored to its formerly gorgeous self. The Eagle Lake Trail follows the same route as the Mosquito Lakes Trail (see listing in this chapter) until the two-mile point, near the Eagle Sink Holes. These geological oddities are small craters in the ground where Eagle Creek suddenly disappears underground. At the trail junction by the sink holes, go left for Eagle Lake. Enjoy the brief flat stretch here, because shortly, you'll gain another 1,000 feet over 1.4 miles. Much of the climb is in an exposed, rocky area—a large boulder field that gets baked by the sun on warm days. Well-graded switchbacks and beautiful scenery make it easier. Soon you arrive at Eagle Lake's dam, at 10,000 feet. The big lake is surrounded by glacially carved rock and has a few rocky islands. Brook trout swim in its clear waters. The trail continues along the lake's west side to many good picnicking spots and photo opportunities. Campsites are found near the lake; no camping is allowed between the trail and the lake.

User Groups: Hikers and horses. No dogs or mountain bikes. No wheelchair facilities.

Permits: There is a $20 entrance fee per vehicle at Sequoia and Kings Canyon National Parks, good for seven days. Wilderness permits are required for overnight stays. They are available on a first-come, first-served basis at the Mineral King Ranger Station. For advanced wilderness permits or information on trail conditions, go to www.nps.gov/seki. Trailhead quotas are in effect from May to September.

Maps: A Mineral King map is available from Tom Harrison Maps. For a topographic map, ask the USGS for Mineral King.

Directions: From Visalia, drive east on Highway 198 for 38 miles to Mineral King Road, 2.5 miles east of Three Rivers. If you reach the Ash Mountain entrance station, you've gone too far. Turn right on Mineral King Road and drive 25 miles to the end of the road and the Eagle/Mosquito trailhead. Take the right fork at the end of the road to reach the parking area. The trail begins at the far end of the parking lot.

Contact: Sequoia and Kings Canyon National Parks, 47050 General Highway, Three Rivers, CA 93271-9651, 559/565-3341 or 559/565-3135, www.nps.gov/seki.

70 FRANKLIN LAKES

10.8 mi / 6.0 hr or 2 days 🥾3 ⛰10

off Highway 198 in the Mineral King region of Sequoia National Park

Maybe the best thing about hiking to Franklin Lakes is the waterfalls you get to pass along the way—especially our favorite cascades, on Franklin Creek. Or maybe it's the prolific wildflowers along the trail, or the spectacular views over Mineral King Valley that you gain as you climb. Maybe it's the big lake itself, set below Tulare and Florence Peaks, or the fact that the trail to reach it is so well graded, with a 2,500-foot elevation gain spread out over 5.4 miles. What the heck—this trail is about as close to hiking perfection as you get.

HIKING

The first two miles are nearly flat; the route winds along the bottom of Mineral King's canyon, following Farewell Gap Trail alongside the East Fork Kaweah River. You'll pass Tufa Falls, across the canyon, at 0.25 mile and Crystal Creek's cascades, on your side of the canyon, at one mile. The trail leaves the valley floor and starts to climb moderately, reaching the bottom of Franklin Creek's cascades at 1.7 miles. After crossing Franklin Creek, you continue south along Farewell Canyon, negotiating some switchbacks as you gain elevation. The views get better and better. One mile farther, Franklin Lakes Trail forks left off Farewell Gap Trail and starts climbing in earnest up the Franklin Creek Valley. At nearly 10,000 feet, the trail crosses Franklin Creek again, then parallels the creek for another mile to the largest Franklin Lake. Note that when you see the lake's dam straight ahead and an obvious campsite about 150 yards below it to the right of the trail, you should cut off the main trail. Walk to the camp and follow its use trail to the dam and the lake. The main trail switchbacks up and above the lake but doesn't go directly to its shoreline. Franklin Lake is a dramatic sight, surrounded by steep, snow-covered slopes and a few pines and junipers. Rainbow Mountain is on its northeast side; Tulare Peak is to the southwest.

User Groups: Hikers and horses. No dogs or mountain bikes. No wheelchair facilities.

Permits: There is a $20 entrance fee per vehicle at Sequoia and Kings Canyon National Parks, good for seven days. Wilderness permits are required for overnight stays. They are available on a first-come, first-served basis at the Mineral King Ranger Station. For advanced wilderness permits or information on trail conditions, go to www.nps.gov/seki. Trailhead quotas are in effect from May to September.

Maps: A Mineral King map is available from Tom Harrison Maps. For a topographic map, ask the USGS for Mineral King.

Directions: From Visalia, drive east on Highway 198 for 38 miles to Mineral King Road, 2.5 miles east of Three Rivers. If you reach the Ash Mountain entrance station, you've gone too far. Turn right on Mineral King Road and drive 25 miles to the end of the road and the Eagle/Mosquito trailhead. Take the right fork at the end of the road to reach the parking area. Walk back out of the parking lot, and follow the road to the horse corral; Farewell Gap Trail begins just beyond it.

Contact: Sequoia and Kings Canyon National Parks, 47050 General Highway, Three Rivers, CA 93271-9651, 559/565-3341 or 559/565-3135, www.nps.gov/seki.

71 WHITE CHIEF MINE TRAIL
5.8 mi / 3.0 hr 🏃3 ⛰10

off Highway 198 in the Mineral King region of Sequoia National Park

If you're one of those liberated hikers who doesn't need to have an alpine lake in your itinerary to be happy, the trail to White Chief Bowl is a scenic route with much to offer, including an exploration of the White Chief Mine tunnel. Until the Park Service purchased it in 1998, the mine was private property within the national park and off-limits to hikers.

The first mile of the trail is the same as the route to Eagle and Mosquito Lakes, but you'll leave most everyone behind when you continue straight at the one-mile junction, while they bear right for Eagle Lake and the Mosquito Lakes. The White Chief Trail continues with a hefty grade—this second mile is the toughest part of the whole trip—until it tops out at the edge of a gorgeous meadow. Just after you cross a seasonal stream (often a dry ravine by late summer), look for the ruins of Crabtree Cabin, to the right of the trail. The cabin ruins are what is left of the oldest remaining structure in Mineral King. It was built by the discoverer of the White Chief Mine in the 1870s. Next comes White Chief Meadows, surrounded by high granite walls and filled with dozens of downed trees, evidence of harsh winter avalanches.

Beyond the meadow, the trail ascends slightly until it nears a waterfall on White Chief Creek. Shortly before the falls, the trail crosses the creek and heads uphill. Look for the opening to White Chief Mine in a layer of white rock just above the trail. Scramble off the trail a few yards to reach it. The mine tunnel is tall enough to walk into and dead-ends in about 150 feet. Beyond the mine the trail continues to Upper White Chief Bowl, passing dozens of limestone caverns along the way. Although tempting, these caverns should only be explored by those who are experienced and well equipped.

User Groups: Hikers and horses. No dogs or mountain bikes. No wheelchair facilities.

Permits: No permits are required. There is a $20 entrance fee per vehicle at Sequoia and Kings Canyon National Parks, good for seven days.

Maps: A Mineral King map is available from Tom Harrison Maps. For a topographic map, ask the USGS for Mineral King.

Directions: From Visalia, drive east on Highway 198 for 38 miles to Mineral King Road, 2.5 miles east of Three Rivers. If you reach the Ash Mountain entrance station, you've gone too far. Turn right on Mineral King Road and drive 25 miles to the end of the road and the Eagle/Mosquito trailhead. Take the right fork at the end of the road to reach the parking area. The trail begins from the far end of the parking lot.

Contact: Sequoia and Kings Canyon National Parks, 47050 General Highway, Three Rivers, CA 93271-9651, 559/565-3341 or 559/565-3135, www.nps.gov/seki.

7.2 TIMBER GAP TRAIL
4.0 mi / 2.0 hr

off Highway 198 in the Mineral King region of Sequoia National Park

On this short but steep trail, you'll stand witness to the mining history of Mineral King. The trail climbs abruptly from the Sawtooth

trailhead on an old mining path along Monarch Creek, and forks in 0.25 mile. Take the left fork for Timber Gap, which climbs through a dense fir forest and then opens out to switchbacks in a wide and treeless slope—the result of continual winter avalanches. The exposed slope is home to many mountain wildflowers. The climb ends in two miles at Timber Gap, elevation 9,450 feet, a forested pass. The stumps you see among the red firs remain from early miners who cut down the trees to fuel their fires and support their mining tunnels. A faint path heads east from the pass and leads to the remains of the Empire Mine and its buildings in just over one mile.

User Groups: Hikers and horses. No dogs or mountain bikes. No wheelchair facilities.

Permits: No permits are required. There is a $20 entrance fee per vehicle at Sequoia and Kings Canyon National Parks, good for seven days.

Maps: A Mineral King map is available from Tom Harrison Maps. For a topographic map, ask the USGS for Mineral King.

Directions: From Visalia, drive east on Highway 198 for 38 miles to Mineral King Road, 2.5 miles east of Three Rivers. If you reach the Ash Mountain entrance station, you've gone too far. Turn right on Mineral King Road and drive 24.5 miles to the Sawtooth parking area, 0.5 mile before the end of the road.

Contact: Sequoia and Kings Canyon National Parks, 47050 General Highway, Three Rivers, CA 93271-9651, 559/565-3341 or 559/565-3135, www.nps.gov/seki.

7.3 MONARCH LAKES
8.4 mi / 5.0 hr or 2 days

off Highway 198 in the Mineral King region of Sequoia National Park

The Monarch Lakes Trail leads from the Sawtooth trailhead at 8,000 feet in elevation and climbs 2,500 feet to the rocky, gemlike Monarch Lakes. The first lake is good, but the second lake is simply awesome, and the scenery along the trail is unforgettable. Walk 0.25 mile from the trailhead and take the right fork for Monarch and Crystal Lakes. After one steep mile, you'll reach Groundhog Meadow, named for the adorable yellow-bellied marmots that inhabit the area. (We like their blond coats and shrill whistles.) Beyond the meadow, the trail starts seriously switchbacking in and out of red fir forest, making a gut-thumping climb to the Crystal Lake trail junction. The trail forks sharply right for Crystal Lake, but you head left for one more mile—a relatively smooth mile, with the easiest grade of the whole route—to Lower Monarch Lake. (This section crosses an incredible talus slope.) Snow can often be found near the lake even in late summer, and the vista is dramatic, with Sawtooth Peak dominating the skyline. If you have a wilderness permit, you can find a campsite near the lake.

While the main trail continues north to Sawtooth Pass, a use trail leads southeast from the lower lake for 0.5 mile to Upper Monarch Lake. Basically you head directly up the cliff that forms the back wall of the lower lake. It's worth the climb. The upper lake is wide, deep blue, and dramatic, set at the base of barren, pointy Monarch Peak. The view from the upper lake's basin, looking back down at the lower lake and various Mineral King peaks, is breathtaking. A big surprise is that the upper lake has been dammed, like many of the high lakes in Mineral King, and is operated by Southern California Edison. Note: If you're backpacking and want to take a first-rate side trip, the trail to Sawtooth Pass is a 1.3-mile, 1,200-foot climb that's not easy, but Sawtooth Pass offers one of the best views in the Southern Sierra.

User Groups: Hikers and horses. No dogs or mountain bikes. No wheelchair facilities.

Permits: There is a $20 entrance fee per vehicle at Sequoia and Kings Canyon National Parks, good for seven days. Wilderness permits are required for overnight stays. They are available on a first-come, first-served basis

at the Mineral King Ranger Station. For advanced wilderness permits or information on trail conditions, go to www.nps.gov/seki. Trailhead quotas are in effect from May to September.

Maps: A Mineral King map is available from Tom Harrison Maps. For a topographic map, ask the USGS for Mineral King.

Directions: From Visalia, drive east on Highway 198 for 38 miles to Mineral King Road, 2.5 miles east of Three Rivers. If you reach the Ash Mountain entrance station, you've gone too far. Turn right on Mineral King Road and drive 24.5 miles to the Sawtooth parking area, 0.5 mile before the end of the road.

Contact: Sequoia and Kings Canyon National Parks, 47050 General Highway, Three Rivers, CA 93271-9651, 559/565-3341 or 559/565-3135, www.nps.gov/seki.

74 CRYSTAL LAKE TRAIL
9.8 mi / 6.0 hr or 2 days 🏃4 ⛰10

off Highway 198 in the Mineral King region of Sequoia National Park

The long and arduous path to Crystal Lake follows the same route as the trail to Monarch Lakes (see listing in this chapter) for the first 3.2 miles. In Chihuahua Bowl, a sharp right-hand turn puts you on the trail to Crystal Lake. In 0.5 mile, the trail leads past the ruins of the Chihuahua Mine (on the right), one of Mineral King's last hopes for silver riches. Like the other mines in the area, it never produced ore to equal the miners' dreams. The trail climbs abruptly over a rocky slope to a ridge of reddish foxtail pines, where your vista opens wide. Far off you can see the Farewell Gap peaks, and down below you see the Cobalt Lakes and Crystal Creek, pouring down to the Mineral King Valley and the East Fork Kaweah River. The trail continues, following more switchbacks, to upper Crystal Creek and Crystal Lake, which has been dammed. Off to the left (north), Mineral Peak stands out at 11,500 feet, and to the right (south), Rainbow Mountain shows off its colorful rock. Views are spectacular in every direction. If you scramble 0.25 mile off-trail toward Mineral Peak, you will reach Little Crystal Lake, where you have a near guarantee of solitude and a vista you won't forget.

User Groups: Hikers and horses. No dogs or mountain bikes. No wheelchair facilities.

Permits: There is a $20 entrance fee per vehicle at Sequoia and Kings Canyon National Parks, good for seven days. Wilderness permits are required for overnight stays. They are available on a first-come, first-served basis at the Mineral King Ranger Station. For advanced wilderness permits or information on trail conditions, go to www.nps.gov/seki. Trailhead quotas are in effect from May to September.

Maps: A Mineral King map is available from Tom Harrison Maps. For a topographic map, ask the USGS for Mineral King.

Directions: From Visalia, drive east on Highway 198 for 38 miles to Mineral King Road, 2.5 miles east of Three Rivers. If you reach the Ash Mountain entrance station, you've gone too far. Turn right on Mineral King Road and drive 24.5 miles to the Sawtooth parking area, 0.5 mile before the end of the road.

Contact: Sequoia and Kings Canyon National Parks, 47050 General Highway, Three Rivers, CA 93271-9651, 559/565-3341 or 559/565-3135, www.nps.gov/seki.

75 BLACK WOLF FALLS
0.5 mi / 0.5 hr

off Highway 198 in the Mineral King region of Sequoia National Park

This hike is really just a stroll, and the destination is readily apparent from the Sawtooth trailhead: Black Wolf Falls, tumbling down the canyon wall in Mineral King Valley. But aside from the chance to get close to a pretty waterfall, the hike is interesting because of its

historical significance. Black Wolf's name is actually an alteration of its original moniker, which was Black Wall Falls, named for the Black Wall copper mine that was located at the waterfall's base. Back in the 1870s, when miners believed that Mineral King was rich in more than just scenery, they mined the base of Monarch Creek with a modicum of success. Today you can walk right up to the falls and see the mine tunnel on its right side (it looks like a cave, but don't go inside; it's unstable). In summer, rangers lead group hikes to the waterfall and talk about Mineral King's mining history. Although the route to Black Wolf Falls isn't an official trail, the path is well used and clearly visible. If you can find its beginning across the road from the No Parking Any Time sign, the rest of the hike is easy.

User Groups: Hikers only. No dogs, horses, or mountain bikes. No wheelchair facilities.

Permits: No permits are required. There is a $20 entrance fee per vehicle at Sequoia and Kings Canyon National Parks, good for seven days.

Maps: A Mineral King map is available from Tom Harrison Maps. For a topographic map, ask the USGS for Mineral King.

Directions: From Visalia, drive east on Highway 198 for 38 miles to Mineral King Road, 2.5 miles east of Three Rivers. If you reach the Ash Mountain entrance station, you've gone too far. Turn right on Mineral King Road and drive 24.5 miles to the Sawtooth parking area, 0.5 mile before the end of the road. Walk up the road toward Black Wolf Falls, then look for a use trail across the road from the No Parking Any Time sign, just beyond where Monarch Creek flows under the road.

Contact: Sequoia and Kings Canyon National Parks, 47050 General Highway, Three Rivers, CA 93271-9651, 559/565-3341 or 559/565-3135, www.nps.gov/seki.

HIKING

76 LADYBUG TRAIL

3.8 mi / 2.0 hr

off Highway 198 in the South Fork region of
Sequoia National Park

BEST ☾

The South Fork area is the forgotten region
of Sequoia National Park. Accessible only by
a 13-mile dead-end road out of Three Rivers,
South Fork is the place to go when you just
want to get away from it all. Solitude in a
national park? You can find it here (mostly
because it takes about 40 minutes just to
drive from Highway 198 in Three Rivers to
the trailhead). The elevation is low (only 3,600
feet), so the area is accessible year-round, and
there may be no finer winter walk than a hike
on Ladybug Trail out of South Fork. The trail
leaves the far end of South Fork Campground
and heads through an oak and bay forest along
the South Fork Kaweah River. At 1.7 miles,
you reach Ladybug Camp, a primitive camping area along the river's edge, in the shade of
pines and firs. A short scramble downstream
of the camp gives you a look at Ladybug Falls,
a 25-foot waterfall set in a rocky grotto. If you
continue upstream, the trail leads another few
hundred yards and then switchbacks uphill,
heading for Whiskey Log Camp. A use trail
leaves the main trail and continues a short distance upriver, where there are many beautiful
rocky pools. And in case you haven't guessed,
the trail, camp, and falls are named for the
millions of ladybugs that winter near the river,
then take flight in the spring to head back to
the Central Valley to feed.

User Groups: Hikers and horses. No dogs or
mountain bikes. No wheelchair facilities.

Permits: No permits are required. There is a
$20 entrance fee per vehicle at Sequoia and
Kings Canyon National Parks, good for seven
days.

Maps: A Sequoia and Kings Canyon map is available from Tom Harrison Maps. For a topographic
map, ask the USGS for Dennison Peak.

Directions: From Visalia, drive east on Highway 198 for 35 miles to one mile west of Three

Rivers. Turn right on South Fork Drive and
drive 12.8 miles to South Fork Campground.
(Nine miles out, the road turns to dirt.) Park
at the Ladybug trailhead parking area.

Contact: Sequoia and Kings Canyon National
Parks, 47050 General Highway, Three Rivers,
CA 93271-9651, 559/565-3341 or 559/565-
3135, www.nps.gov/seki.

77 GARFIELD-HOCKETT TRAIL

5.8 mi / 3.0 hr

off Highway 198 in the South Fork region of
Sequoia National Park

The trip to the magnificent Garfield Grove
is only 2.9 miles from South Fork Campground, and if you don't mind a steep climb
and possibly sharing the trail with horse pack-
ers, you should be sure to take this hike. The
trail climbs immediately and keeps climbing,
but fortunately, it is shaded by oaks most of
the way. The ascent rewards you with a continual view of distant Homer's Nose, a granite
landmark that, although prominent, looks
little like anybody's nose. In just under three
miles of nonstop climbing, you reach the first
of many sequoias in the Garfield Grove, re-
ported to be one of the largest groves in the
national parks. By the time you reach it, you've
gained 2,000 feet in elevation, so pick a big
tree to lean against, pull out a snack, and take
a breather.

User Groups: Hikers and horses. No dogs or
mountain bikes. No wheelchair facilities.

Permits: No permits are required. There is a
$20 entrance fee per vehicle at Sequoia and
Kings Canyon National Parks, good for seven
days.

Maps: A Sequoia and Kings Canyon map
is available from Tom Harrison Maps. For
topographic maps, ask the USGS for Dennison Peak.

Directions: From Visalia, drive east on Highway 198 for 35 miles to one mile west of Three

Rivers. Turn right on South Fork Drive and drive 12.8 miles to South Fork Campground. (Nine miles out, the road turns to dirt.) Park at the trailhead at the far end of the campground loop, just before the parking lot for the Ladybug Trailhead.

Contact: Sequoia and Kings Canyon National Parks, 47050 General Highway, Three Rivers, CA 93271-9651, 559/565-3341 or 559/565-3135, www.nps.gov/seki.

78 BALCH PARK NATURE TRAIL

1.0 mi / 0.5 hr   🏃1 ⛰7

in Mountain Home Demonstration State Forest off Highway 190 near Springville

Balch Park is the small county-run park within the borders of Mountain Home Demonstration State Forest, and its easy, one-mile nature trail is a great place to take your kids for the afternoon. The trail begins next to the main entrance to Balch Park Camp, across from the museum, and your first stop is a visit to the Hollow Log, which was used as a dwelling by various pioneers, Indians, and prospectors. You also get to see the Lady Alice Tree, which was incorrectly billed in the early 20th century as the largest tree in the world. Nonetheless, it's no slacker in the size department. Continuing along the route, you'll see and learn all about dogwoods, bracken ferns, manzanita, and gooseberry. When you're finished hiking the nature trail, you can cross the road and throw a line into one of Balch Park's two small fishing ponds, which are stocked weekly.

User Groups: Hikers, dogs, and horses. No mountain bikes. No wheelchair facilities.

Permits: No permits are required. Parking and access are free.

Maps: A free brochure and map of Mountain Home Demonstration State Forest, which includes Balch Park, are available from park headquarters. For a topographic map, ask the USGS for Camp Wishon.

Directions: From Porterville, drive east on Highway 190 for 18 miles to Springville. At Springville, turn left (north) on Balch Park Road/Road 239, drive 3.5 miles, and turn right on Bear Creek Road/Road 220. Drive 14 miles to Mountain Home Demonstration State Forest Headquarters, pick up a free park map, and then continue 1.5 miles farther to the entrance to Balch Park and the nature trail.

Contact: Balch Park, 559/539-3896; Mountain Home Demonstration State Forest, P.O. Box 517, Springville, CA 93265, 559/539-2321 (summer) or 559/539-2855 (winter).

79 ADAM AND EVE LOOP TRAIL

2.0 mi / 1.0 hr   🏃2 ⛰9

in Mountain Home Demonstration State Forest off Highway 190 near Springville

On the Adam and Eve Loop Trail you can see the Adam Tree standing tall and proud, but its companion, the Eve Tree, is no longer thriving. It (she?) was axed during the infamous sequoia logging years, and it's strangely touching to see the gaping slash in her side. Begin your trip by taking the left side of the loop, heading uphill to the Adam Tree, the second-largest tree in this state forest, at 240 feet tall and 27 feet in diameter. The Eve Tree is shortly after. The big draw on the trail is visiting the "Indian bathtubs" at Tub Flat, halfway around the loop; these are basins, formed in solid granite, that were probably used by Native Americans. No one is sure whether they are natural or handmade. The basins are much larger than the traditional Indian grinding holes that are found elsewhere in the Sierra; they are truly large enough to take a bath in.

User Groups: Hikers, dogs, and horses. No mountain bikes. No wheelchair facilities.

Permits: No permits are required. Parking and access are free.

Maps: A free brochure and map of Mountain Home Demonstration State Forest are available from park headquarters. For a topographic map, ask the USGS for Camp Wishon.

Directions: From Porterville, drive east on Highway 190 for 18 miles to Springville. At Springville, turn left (north) on Balch Park Road/Road 239 and drive 3.5 miles; then turn right on Bear Creek Road/Road 220. Drive 14 miles to Mountain Home Demonstration State Forest Headquarters, pick up a free park map, and then continue one mile farther, turning right at the sign for Hidden Falls Recreation Area. Drive three miles to just past the pack station and before Shake Camp Campground, to the trailhead for Adam and Eve Loop Trail, on the left.

Contact: Mountain Home Demonstration State Forest, P.O. Box 517, Springville, CA 93265, 559/539-2321 (summer) or 559/539-2855 (winter).

80 REDWOOD CROSSING
4.0 mi / 2.0 hr

in Mountain Home Demonstration
State Forest off Highway 190 near Springville

An excellent easy hike for campers and day visitors at Mountain Home Demonstration State Forest is on Long Meadow Trail, from Shake Camp Campground to Redwood Crossing, on the Tule River. The trail starts by the public corral (elevation 6,800 feet) and leads through logged sequoia stumps to a thick mixed forest on the slopes high above the Wishon Fork Tule River. When the trail reaches clearings in the trees, the views of the Great Western Divide are excellent. At two miles out, you reach Redwood Crossing, a boulder-lined stretch of the river. Those willing to ford can cross to the other side and head into the Golden Trout Wilderness, but day hikers should pull out a picnic at the river's edge and make an afternoon of it. Backpackers heading for the wilderness need to secure a wilderness permit from the Tule River Ranger District office.

User Groups: Hikers, dogs, and horses. No mountain bikes. No wheelchair facilities.

Permits: No permits are required. Parking and access are free.

Maps: A free brochure and map of Mountain Home Demonstration State Forest are available from park headquarters. For a topographic map, ask the USGS for Camp Wishon.

Directions: From Porterville, drive east on Highway 190 for 18 miles to Springville. At Springville, turn left (north) on Balch Park Road/Road 239, drive 3.5 miles, and turn right on Bear Creek Road/Road 220. Drive 14 miles to Mountain Home Demonstration State Forest Headquarters, pick up a free park map, and then continue one mile farther. Turn right at the sign for Hidden Falls Recreation Area. Drive 3.5 miles to Shake Camp Campground. The Long Meadow trailhead is located by the public corral.

Contact: Mountain Home Demonstration State Forest, P.O. Box 517, Springville, CA 93265, 559/539-2321 (summer) or 559/539-2855 (winter); Tule River Ranger District, 32588 Highway 190, Springville, CA 93265, 559/539-2607, www.fs.fed.us/r5/sequoia.

81 MOSES GULCH TRAIL
4.0 mi / 2.0 hr

in Mountain Home Demonstration
State Forest off Highway 190 near Springville

For a less-crowded alternate to the popular Redwood Crossing (see listing in this chapter), you can take the other trail from the public corral at Shake Flat Campground and wind your way through stands of beautiful virgin sequoias to the Wishon Fork Tule River at Moses Gulch Campground. The Moses Gulch Trail crosses park roads twice—the only downer—but it's an easy walk for families, and it's peaceful besides. Once you reach the river (at two miles), you have the option of hiking alongside it to the north or south, adding some distance to your trip. The northern stretch leads to Hidden Falls Campground (the home of many small falls and pools), and the southern stretch crosses pretty Galena and Silver Creeks, leading past a mining cabin and an old copper mine.

User Groups: Hikers, dogs, and horses. No mountain bikes. No wheelchair facilities.

Permits: No permits are required. Parking and access are free.

Maps: A free brochure and map of Mountain Home Demonstration State Forest are available from park headquarters. For a topographic map, ask the USGS for Camp Wishon.

Directions: From Porterville, drive east on Highway 190 for 18 miles to Springville. At Springville, turn left (north) on Balch Park Road/Road 239, drive 3.5 miles, and then turn right on Bear Creek Road/Road 220. Drive 14 miles to Mountain Home Demonstration State Forest Headquarters and pick up a free park map, then continue one mile farther and turn right at the sign for Hidden Falls Recreation Area. Drive 3.5 miles to Shake Camp Campground. The Moses Gulch trailhead is by the public corral.

Contact: Mountain Home Demonstration State Forest, P.O. Box 517, Springville, CA 93265, 559/539-2321 (summer) or 559/539-2855 (winter).

82 DOYLE TRAIL
6.0 mi / 3.0 hr

in Giant Sequoia National Monument near Springville

The Doyle Trail is a great alternative to the heat of the Springville and Porterville Valleys. It's in the transition zone between foothills and conifers, with plenty of shade from tall manzanita, oaks, madrones, and pines. Squirrels and lizards are your primary companions on the trail, which laterals along the slopes above the Wishon fork of the Tule River. From the gated trailhead, hike up the paved road and bear left to bypass Doyle Springs, a community of private cabins. Follow the trail that is signed Trail to Upstream Fishing.

The route climbs gently through the forest for 2.5 miles and then suddenly descends to the same level as the river, where there are some primitive campsites available. Then the trail rises again, climbing for another 0.5 mile to a clearing on the right, where there is an outcrop of jagged green rock alongside the river. Leave the trail and cross over the rock, where you'll find a few picture-perfect swimming holes and small waterfalls.

User Groups: Hikers, dogs, horses, and mountain bikes. No wheelchair facilities.

Permits: No permits are required. Parking and access are free.

Maps: A Sequoia National Forest map is available from the U.S. Forest Service. For a topographic map, ask the USGS for Camp Wishon.

Directions: From Porterville, drive east on Highway 190 for 18 miles to Springville. From Springville, continue east on Highway 190 for 7.5 miles to Wishon Drive/Road 208, a left fork. Turn left and drive four miles on Wishon Drive, then take the left fork, which is signed for day-use parking (above the campground). Drive 0.25 mile and park off the road, near the gate.

Contact: Giant Sequoia National Monument/Sequoia National Forest, Tule River Ranger District, 32588 Highway 190, Springville, CA 93265, 559/539-2607, www.fs.fed.us/r5/sequoia.

83 JORDAN PEAK LOOKOUT
1.8 mi / 1.0 hr

in Giant Sequoia National Monument near Quaking Aspen

You'll see some logging activity out here by Jordan Peak, but if you can put up with it, you can climb a mere 600 feet over less than a mile to reach the summit of this 9,100-foot mountain. Few summits are so easily attained (it's a well-graded and well-maintained trail), and this one is not lacking in dramatic vistas.

HIKING

You can see the Wishon Fork Canyon of the Tule River, Camp Nelson, the Sequoia Crest, Slate Mountain, Maggie Mountain, and Moses Mountain close up, and the Tehachapis and the Coast Range far, far away. The peak is covered with microwave equipment, but it doesn't mar the stupendous view. Head west from the trailhead on Jordan Lookout Trail, switchbacking up until you reach the catwalked stairs to the lookout, which was built in 1934. All the materials to construct the lookout were hauled in by mules.

User Groups: Hikers, dogs, horses, and mountain bikes. No wheelchair facilities.

Permits: No permits are required. Parking and access are free.

Maps: A Sequoia National Forest map is available from the U.S. Forest Service. For a topographic map, ask the USGS for Sentinel Peak.

Directions: From Porterville, drive 45 miles east on Highway 190 to Forest Service Road 21S50, near Quaking Aspen Campground. Turn left on Road 21S50 and drive five miles. Bear left and continue on Road 21S50 for 2.8 miles, bearing left on Road 20S71, signed for Jordan Peak Lookout, and following it one mile to its end, at the trailhead.

Contact: Giant Sequoia National Monument/ Sequoia National Forest, Tule River Ranger District, 32588 Highway 190, Springville, CA 93265, 559/539-2607, www.fs.fed.us/r5/ sequoia.

84 CLICKS CREEK TRAIL
14.0 mi / 2 days

in the Golden Trout Wilderness near Quaking Aspen

If you like peace and quiet on your backpacking trips, Clicks Creek Trail, in the Golden Trout Wilderness, may suit you just fine. The trail leads northeast from Log Cabin Meadow (elevation 7,800 feet), heading steadily downhill along Clicks Creek to the

Little Kern River. The route crosses the creek several times. Shade lovers will thrill at the conifer forests that line the route, interspersed by large and grassy meadows, and anglers can bring along their gear to try their luck with the golden trout in the river. There are many possible campsites along the Little Kern, where the elevation is 6,200 feet.

User Groups: Hikers, dogs, and horses. No mountain bikes. No wheelchair facilities.

Permits: A free wilderness permit is required for overnight stays and is available from the Springville or Kernville Ranger Stations at the addresses below. Parking and access are free.

Maps: A Golden Trout Wilderness map is available from the U.S. Forest Service or Tom Harrison Maps. For a topographic map, ask the USGS for Sentinel Peak.

Directions: From Porterville, drive 45 miles east on Highway 190 to Forest Service Road 21S50 near Quaking Aspen Campground. Turn left on Road 21S50 and drive five miles; bear left and continue on Road 21S50 for 1.5 miles to the Clicks Creek trailhead, at Log Cabin Meadow.

Contact: Sequoia National Forest, Tule River Ranger District, 32588 Highway 190, Springville, CA 93265, 559/539-2607, www.fs.fed.us/ r5/sequoia; Sequoia National Forest, Kern River Ranger District, 105 Whitney Road, P.O. Box 9, Kernville, CA 93238, 760/376-3781, www.fs.fed.us/r5/sequoia.

85 JOHN JORDAN / HOSSACK MEADOW TRAIL
5.0-6.0 mi / 2.5-3.0 hr

in Giant Sequoia National Monument near Quaking Aspen

Your route on the John Jordan Trail begins with a crossing of McIntyre Creek, then traverses a level mile to an old fence, gate, and McIntyre Rock—a huge pile of granite boulders with an excellent view. Climb on top of the rock's well-graded, cracking-granite back side and peer over its startlingly steep front side. Surprise! It's straight down, about 600 feet. The trail heads downhill through a red fir forest to Nelson Creek, the site of some logging work. Although you can walk another 0.5 mile to the trail's end (at Hossack Meadow), most people turn around at the sight of logged trees, making for a five-mile round-trip with a 1,000-foot elevation gain on the return. So who was John Jordan, anyway? He was a trailblazer in the 1870s who unfortunately was most famous for drowning in the Kern River on his way back to the Central Valley to tell everybody he had completed this trail, a proposed toll road.

User Groups: Hikers, dogs, horses, and mountain bikes. No wheelchair facilities.

Permits: No permits are required. Parking and access are free.

Maps: A Sequoia National Forest map is available from the U.S. Forest Service. For a topographic map, ask the USGS for Sentinel Peak.

Directions: From Porterville, drive 45 miles east on Highway 190 to Forest Service Road 21S50, near Quaking Aspen Campground. Turn left on Road 21S50 and drive 6.6 miles, then bear left on Road 20S81. Follow Road 20S81 for 1.4 miles to the signed trailhead.

Contact: Giant Sequoia National Monument/ Sequoia National Forest, Tule River Ranger District, 32588 Highway 190, Springville, CA 93265, 559/539-2607, www.fs.fed.us/r5/ sequoia.

more than 1,000 years old. Among them is a tree named for former President George Bush Sr., who visited the grove in 1992. The trail is a pleasant downhill stroll along Freeman Creek, reaching the first sequoias in about one mile, after crossing the creek. In between the big trees are large meadow areas (many of which bloom with spring and summer wildflowers) and forests of red firs. Many campsites are found along the creek. The path finally ends at Lloyd Meadows, three miles from the trailhead, but most people don't travel that far, since it requires too much climbing on the way back. Two miles out and back is just about perfect.

User Groups: Hikers, dogs, horses, and mountain bikes. No wheelchair facilities.

Permits: No permits are required. Parking and access are free.

Maps: A Sequoia National Forest map is available from the U.S. Forest Service. For topographic maps, ask the USGS for Sentinel Peak.

Directions: From Porterville, drive 45 miles east on Highway 190 to Forest Service Road 21S50, near Quaking Aspen Campground. Turn left on Road 21S50 and drive 0.5 mile, then turn right at the sign for the Freeman Creek Grove.

Contact: Giant Sequoia National Monument/ Sequoia National Forest, Tule River Ranger District, 32588 Highway 190, Springville, CA 93265, 559/539-2607, www.fs.fed.us/r5/ sequoia.

HIKING

86 FREEMAN CREEK TRAIL
4.0 mi / 2.0 hr

in Giant Sequoia National Monument near Quaking Aspen

The easternmost grove of sequoias in the world is your destination on Freeman Creek Trail. Compared to most sequoia groves in the Sierra, the trees of the 1,700-acre Freeman Creek Grove are mere adolescents—probably not

87 SUMMIT TRAIL TO SLATE MOUNTAIN
8.0 mi / 4.0 hr

in Giant Sequoia National Monument near Quaking Aspen

If you're staying at Quaking Aspen Campground, you can set out on Summit National Recreation Trail from outside your tent door, but if you're not, drive to the trailhead just

HIKING

south of the camp off Road 21S78. Few people hike all 12 miles of the trail, but many take this four-mile jaunt to the summit of 9,302-foot Slate Mountain, the highest peak in the area. The first two miles of trail are easy, climbing gently through meadows and forest (some logging activity can be seen); then the route climbs more steeply, ascending first the east side and then the north side of Slate Mountain. Views of the granite spires of The Needles and Olancha Peak can be seen. At 3.8 miles you reach a junction with Bear Creek Trail, and from there, it's a short scramble to your left to the top of Slate Mountain, which is a big pile of rocks with a tremendous 360-degree view. There's no trail, but a couple well-worn routes are visible.

User Groups: Hikers, dogs, horses, and mountain bikes. No wheelchair facilities.

Permits: No permits are required. Parking and access are free.

Maps: A Sequoia National Forest map is available from the U.S. Forest Service. For a topographic map, ask the USGS for Sentinel Peak.

Directions: From Porterville, drive 46 miles east on Highway 190 to Forest Service Road 21S78, which is 0.5 mile south of Quaking Aspen Campground. Turn right on Road 21S78 and drive 0.5 mile to the Summit trailhead.

Contact: Giant Sequoia National Monument/ Sequoia National Forest, Tule River Ranger District, 32588 Highway 190, Springville, CA 93265, 559/539-2607, www.fs.fed.us/r5/ sequoia.

88 NEEDLES LOOKOUT
5.0 mi / 2.5 hr   🥾2 ▲10

In Giant Sequoia National Monument near Quaking Aspen

 BEST(

Here it is, the perfect easy day hike in Giant Sequoia National Monument. It's just long enough and undulating enough for beginning

and intermediate hikers, without being too demanding, and it's full of visual rewards. The trail starts with a placard bearing a great old black-and-white photo that shows what the fire lookout on top of The Needles looked like early in the 20th century. Five minutes down the trail, you leave the forest and come out to two wooden benches, good places to stare out at the magnificent view of the Kern River Basin before you. If you look ahead, you get a glimpse of the fire lookout, perched in what looks like a precarious fashion on top of The Needles' tall granite spires. As you continue along the trail, you lose your view of the lookout. The trail goes up, then down, then up again, through firs, ponderosa, sugar pines, granite, and sand. The only steep section is the final set of switchbacks up The Needles; they lead to a series of stairs and catwalks that ascend to the lookout tower. When you reach the first catwalk, the rest is a cakewalk. A sign tells you if the tower is open and you may come up and visit. If it's closed, just climb up on any boulder to admire the view—it's just as fine from the base of the tower as it is from above. You look out over Lloyd Meadow and the western half of the Golden Trout Wilderness. This is a perfect place to take someone who needs to get inspired.

User Groups: Hikers, dogs, horses, and mountain bikes. No wheelchair facilities.

Permits: No permits are required. Parking and access are free.

Maps: A Sequoia National Forest map is available from the U.S. Forest Service. For topographic maps, ask the USGS for Sentinel Peak and Durrwood Creek.

Directions: From Porterville, drive 46 miles east on Highway 190 to Forest Service Road 21S05, which is 0.5 mile south of Quaking Aspen Campground. Turn left (east) on Road 21S05 and drive 2.8 miles to the trailhead.

Contact: Giant Sequoia National Monument/ Sequoia National Forest, Tule River Ranger District, 32588 Highway 190, Springville, CA 93265, 559/539-2607, www.fs.fed.us/r5/ sequoia.

89 TRAIL OF 100 GIANTS
0.5 mi / 0.5 hr 👫1 ⛺10

in Giant Sequoia National Monument near Johnsondale

BEST (

The Trail of 100 Giants is as good as many of the giant sequoia trails in Sequoia and Kings Canyon National Parks. Trailhead elevation is 6,400 feet, and the trail is an easy and nearly flat loop that is paved and suitable for wheelchairs and baby strollers. Located within the Long Meadow Giant Sequoia Grove, the second-most southern grove where sequoias are found, the big trees on the Trail of 100 Giants are situated amid a mixed forest of cedars and pines. A dozen interpretive signs along the path unlock the secrets of this forest. As you walk in from the parking lot across the road, the first sequoia tree on your right is a doozy—probably the best one on the loop. Of all the sequoia groves we've seen and admired, the Trail of 100 Giants grove stands out because it has an unusual amount of twins—two sequoias growing tightly side by side in order to share resources. In fact, this grove even has one twin that rangers call a "sequedar," a sequoia and a cedar that have grown together. If you're staying at Redwood Meadow Campground, you have your own entrance to this loop, so you don't have to drive down the road to the main trailhead and parking lot.

User Groups: Hikers, wheelchairs, dogs, and horses. No mountain bikes.

Permits: No permits are required. A $5 parking fee is charged per vehicle.

Maps: A Sequoia National Forest map is available from the U.S. Forest Service. For a topographic map, ask the USGS for Johnsondale.

Directions: From Kernville on the north end of Isabella Lake, drive north on Sierra Way/ Road 99 for 27 miles to Johnsondale R-Ranch. Continue west (the road becomes Road 50) for 5.5 miles, turn right on the Western Divide Highway, and drive 2.4 miles to the trailhead parking area, on the right, just before Redwood Meadow Campground. Cross the road to begin the trail.

Contact: Giant Sequoia National Monument/ Sequoia National Forest, Tule River Ranger District, 32588 Highway 190, Springville, CA 93265, 559/539-2607, www.fs.fed.us/r5/ sequoia.

90 MULE PEAK LOOKOUT
1.2 mi / 1.0 hr 👫1 ⛺9

in Giant Sequoia National Monument near Johnsondale

While rock climbers come to Mule Peak to do their daring work, hikers can take a not-so-daring walk up the back side of Mule Peak; it's attainable for all ages and levels of hikers. The area around the peak has been logged, but much of the forest has grown back. The trail follows a series of easy switchbacks up the hillside, gaining 600 feet to the summit of Mule Peak (elevation 8,142 feet). A lookout tower is positioned there, built in 1936 and still in operation by Sequoia National Forest. The summit view includes Onion Meadow Peak, Table Mountain, the Tule River Valley, and the Tule River Indian Reservation to the west.

User Groups: Hikers, dogs, horses, and mountain bikes. No wheelchair facilities.

Permits: No permits are required. Parking and access are free.

Maps: A Sequoia National Forest map is available from the U.S. Forest Service. For a topographic map, ask the USGS for Sentinel Peak.

Directions: From Kernville on the north end of Isabella Lake, drive north on Sierra Way/ Road 99 for 27 miles to Johnsondale R-Ranch. Continue west (the road becomes Road 50), then in 5.5 miles, turn right on the Western Divide Highway. Drive five miles to the left turnoff signed for Mule Peak/Road 22S03. Turn left and follow Road 22S03 for five miles to the Mule Peak trailhead.

HIKING

Contact: Giant Sequoia National Monument/ Sequoia National Forest, Tule River Ranger District, 32588 Highway 190, Springville, CA 93265, 559/539-2607, www.fs.fed.us/r5/ sequoia.

91 DOME ROCK

0.25 mi / 0.5 hr

in Giant Sequoia National Monument near Quaking Aspen

Dome Rock wins the prize for "Granite Dome with the Most Pedestrian Name." But never mind. It also wins the prize for "Shortest Walk to an Incredible View." Trailhead elevation is 7,200 feet, and the trail is really just a route leading from the left side of the parking lot. Signs at the parking lot warn you not to drop or throw anything off the top of the dome, because there are rock climbers down below on the dome's steep side. It's a mere five-minute walk to the top of Dome Rock—a huge cap of bare granite—where the views are incredible of Slate Mountain, Isabella Lake, and The Needles. If you look very carefully, you can just make out the fire lookout tower on top of The Needles. You'll want to hang around here for a while to ooh and aah. If your scrambling skills are good, consider checking out another stunning destination just a few miles from here. Jump back in your car and drive back to the Western Divide Highway, then head south for four miles to an unmarked pullout on the east side of the road, 0.25 mile south of the Crawford Road turnoff. Start hiking on the dirt road that begins at the turnout; bear right where it forks. The path draws near to Nobe Young Creek, and soon you will hear a noisy waterfall. Take one of several spur trails on your left leading down to the base of the 125-foot fall, which drops over three granite ledges. The entire hike is only one mile round-trip, but because there is no formal trail, it's not for novices. Wear good boots and use caution on the steep and slippery slope.

User Groups: Hikers, dogs, horses, and mountain bikes. No wheelchair facilities.
Permits: No permits are required. Parking and access are free.
Maps: A Sequoia National Forest map is available from the U.S. Forest Service. For a topographic map ask the USGS for Sentinel Peak.
Directions: From Kernville on the north end of Isabella Lake, drive north on Sierra Way/ Road 99 for 27 miles to Johnsondale R-Ranch. Continue west (the road becomes Road 50) for 5.5 miles, and turn right on the Western Divide Highway. Drive 12 miles to the Dome Rock/Road 21S69 turnoff, on the right, across from Peppermint Work Center. Turn right and follow the dirt road for a few hundred yards; where it forks, bear left and continue to the trailhead, 0.5 mile from the Western Divide Highway. If you're traveling from the north, the turnoff is two miles south of Ponderosa Lodge.
Contact: Giant Sequoia National Monument/ Sequoia National Forest, Tule River Ranger District, 32588 Highway 190, Springville, CA 93265, 559/539-2607, www.fs.fed.us/r5/ sequoia.

92 ALDER CREEK TRAIL

1.8 mi / 1.0 hr

in Giant Sequoia National Monument near Johnsondale

BEST (

The granite slabs and pools on Alder Creek have gotten so popular with hikers, swimmers, and picnickers that the Forest Service has installed No Parking Any Time signs all over the road near the trailhead. But as long as you park where you're supposed to (off the road, in the day-use parking area), you can still pay a visit to the tons-of-fun pools and slides along Alder Creek. To reach them, walk up the gated dirt road (Road 22S83) and turn right on the single-track trail. The path descends to the confluence of Alder Creek and Dry Meadow

HIKING

Creek, where there is a long length of swimming holes and rocky slides that pour into them. Make sure you wear denim or some other heavy material on your backside so you can while away many happy hours pretending you are a river otter. It's exhilarating, but please use caution as you slip and slide. Slick granite can be very unforgiving.

User Groups: Hikers and dogs. No horses or mountain bikes. No wheelchair facilities.

Permits: No permits are required. Parking and access are free.

Maps: A Sequoia National Forest map is available from the U.S. Forest Service. For a topographic map, ask the USGS for Sentinel Peak.

Directions: From Kernville on the north end of Lake Isabella, drive north on Sierra Way/Road 99 for 27 miles to 0.5 mile north of Johnsondale R-Ranch. Turn right on Road 22S82 and drive 5.7 miles to the day-use parking area, on the right side of the road. Walk across Road 22S82 to the gated dirt road and the trailhead.

Contact: Giant Sequoia National Monument/Sequoia National Forest, Tule River Ranger District, 32588 Highway 190, Springville, CA 93265, 559/539-2607, www.fs.fed.us/r5/sequoia.

93 KEARSARGE PASS
10.0 mi / 6.0 hr or 2 days 3 ⛰10

in the John Muir Wilderness
in Inyo National Forest

The trailhead elevation for Kearsarge Pass Trail is 9,200 feet, and the elevation at Kearsarge Pass is 11,823 feet. Five miles and a good amount of climbing lie in between, but the route is well graded, and the scenery is spectacular. The trail, which was once an Indian trading route, leads to the backcountry of Kings Canyon National Park, but most day hikers just make the trip to the pass. Along the way, you are witness to several sparkling lakes and whitewater cascades, and a wealth of high-country wildflowers. Not surprisingly, this is a very popular trail. Remember to bring sunglasses, sunscreen, and a jacket for the summit, which is windy and exposed.

The trail climbs gradually from the trailhead, often nearing Independence Creek then veering away again as it winds through a multitude of switchbacks. You pass Little Pothole Lake at 1.5 miles, Gilbert Lake at 2.2 miles, and Flower Lake at 2.6 miles. Continue climbing high above tree line to Kearsarge Pass. You'll get a long-distance view of Heart Lake and pass the left spur trail leading to Big Pothole Lake along the way. Finally, just when you think you can climb no farther, you reach the pass, at five miles. A sign announces your arrival in Kings Canyon Park, and extraordinary Sierra views surround you. You'll gaze at Bullfrog and Kearsarge Lakes, University Peak, and Mount Gould.

Note that if you decide to turn this into an overnight trip, food storage regulations are in effect. Bear-resistant canisters are required for all backpackers, and no wood fires are permitted. Good camping and fishing is located 3.5 miles beyond the pass, at Charlotte Lake, but a one-night stay limit is in effect.

User Groups: Hikers, dogs, and horses. Dogs are allowed to Kearsarge Pass, but not beyond it. No mountain bikes. No wheelchair facilities.

Permits: A free wilderness permit is required year-round for overnight stays and is available from the Eastern Sierra Interagency Visitor Center, 1.5 miles south of Lone Pine. Quotas are in effect from May 1 to November 1; permits are available in advance for a $5 reservation fee per person.

Maps: A John Muir Wilderness map is available from the U.S. Forest Service. A Kearsarge Pass map is available from Tom Harrison Maps. For a topographic map, ask the USGS for Kearsarge Peak.

Directions: From Lone Pine, drive 15 miles north on U.S. 395 to Independence. Turn west on Market Street, which becomes Onion

Valley Road. Drive 14 miles to the end of the road and the trailhead parking area.

Contact: Inyo National Forest, Mount Whitney Ranger Station, P.O. Box 8, Lone Pine, CA 93545, 760/876-6200, www.fs.usda.gov/inyo; Eastern Sierra Interagency Visitor Center, 760/876-6222.

94 FLOWER AND MATLOCK LAKES
6.4 mi / 3.5 hr 🚶2 ⛰8

in the John Muir Wilderness
in Inyo National Forest

If you don't have the time or the energy for Kearsarge Pass (see listing in this chapter), the route to Flower Lake and Matlock Lake is a good second choice. Although it doesn't offer the astounding views that the pass has, it is still a stellar trip into dramatic granite country. Both lakes are deep blue waterways that draw in all the color of the Sierra sky. The trail climbs gradually from the trailhead, switchbacking along Independence Creek. You pass Little Pothole Lake at 1.5 miles and Gilbert Lake at 2.2 miles, reaching a junction for Matlock Lake at 2.5 miles. Continue straight for 0.1 mile to Flower Lake, then retrace your steps to the junction and head south for 0.7 mile to larger Matlock Lake. Pull out your camera and a picnic, and while away some time before returning to the trailhead.

User Groups: Hikers, dogs, and horses. No mountain bikes. No wheelchair facilities.

Permits: No day-hiking permits are required. Parking and access are free.

Maps: A John Muir Wilderness map is available from the U.S. Forest Service. A Kearsarge Pass map is available from Tom Harrison Maps. For a topographic map, ask the USGS for Kearsarge Peak.

Directions: From Lone Pine, drive 15 miles north on U.S. 395 to Independence. Turn west on Market Street, which becomes Onion Valley Road. Drive 14 miles to the end of the road and the trailhead parking area.

Contact: Inyo National Forest, Mount Whitney Ranger Station, P.O. Box 8, Lone Pine, CA 93545, 760/876-6200, www.fs.usda.gov/inyo; Eastern Sierra Interagency Visitor Center, 760/876-6222.

95 ROBINSON LAKE
3.0 mi / 2.0 hr 🚶4 ⛰9

in the John Muir Wilderness
in Inyo National Forest

The Robinson Lake Trail is best described as relentlessly steep but mercifully short. The hike is challenging in places due to the grade, loose surface, and relative obscurity of the trail, but the destination is superlative. In addition to beautiful Robinson Lake (at 10,500 feet), you get a close and personal view of 11,744-foot Independence Peak and an excellent wildflower display along Robinson Creek. Start at the trailhead by campsite No. 7 in Onion Valley Campground. Watch out for the overgrown vegetation that can sometimes hide the trail. Just climb, catch your breath, and climb some more. After a fairly punishing ascent, you'll reach the small, shallow lake in less than an hour. Campsites and picnicking sites are found in the sand on the lake's east side, or in the pine forest on the northwest side. Equally as pretty as the lake are the views from its shores of the valley below. Plan your trip for July to September; the trail is usually free of snow by midsummer. But whenever you go, watch your footing carefully. This trail is not maintained very often.

User Groups: Hikers, dogs, and horses. No mountain bikes. No wheelchair facilities.

Permits: No day-hiking permits are required. Parking and access are free.

Maps: A John Muir Wilderness map is available from the U.S. Forest Service. A Kearsarge Pass map is available from Tom Harrison Maps. For a topographic map, ask the USGS for Kearsarge Peak.

Directions: From Lone Pine, drive 15 miles north on U.S. 395 to Independence. Turn west on Market Street, which becomes Onion Valley Road. Drive 14 miles to the end of the road and the hikers' parking area. Walk into Onion Valley Campground to find the trailhead, by site No. 7.

Contact: Inyo National Forest, Mount Whitney Ranger Station, P.O. Box 8, Lone Pine, CA 93545, 760/876-6200, www.fs.usda.gov/inyo; Eastern Sierra Interagency Visitor Center, 760/876-6222.

96 MOUNT WHITNEY TRAIL
22.0 mi / 15.0 hr or 2-3 days
🥾5 ⛰10

in the John Muir Wilderness

BEST (

Mount Whitney, at 14,505 feet in elevation, is the highest peak in the contiguous United States and is also probably the most frequently climbed. It has become so well traveled that not only are quotas enforced for backpackers, but even day hikers must obtain a wilderness permit to hike the trail. And, yes, many people do hike the entire 22-mile round-trip trail in one single day, ascending and descending more than a vertical mile along the way (6,131 feet in all), but it means a predawn start and a grueling march. Many people who try this suffer from a variety of ailments, including dehydration, hypoglycemia, and even altitude sickness, and never make it to the top. Others make it but realize they would have had a lot more fun if they had divided the trip into two or even three days. So here's the smart way to hike Mount Whitney: Get your wilderness permit way in advance (see the permit information below), and plan your trip for a weekday, not a weekend. If possible, wait to make the climb until September or early October, when the crowds have thinned considerably; August sees the highest trail usage. Spend a couple days at high elevation before you set out on the Mount Whitney Trail, and come prepared with sunglasses, sunscreen, good boots, and warm clothes for the summit. And since all solid human waste must be packed out (not buried, as is permitted in other areas of the Sierra), it's a good idea to obtain a free "human waste pack-out kit" from the Eastern Sierra Interagency Visitor Center before leaving on your trip. Consider this: In the summer of 2010, visitors to Mount Whitney packed out more than 6,800 pounds of human waste. For more information on the Mount Whitney Trail, see the trail notes for the *Whitney Portal to Lake Thomas Edison (JMT/PCT)* hike in this chapter.

User Groups: Hikers only. No dogs, horses, or mountain bikes. (Dogs are allowed on the first 6.2 miles of trail, but not beyond.) No wheelchair facilities.

Permits: A wilderness permit is required year-round for both day hikers and backpackers and is available from the Eastern Sierra Interagency Visitor Center, 1.5 mile south of Lone Pine. Quotas are in effect from May 1 to November 1 for both day hikers and backpackers. Permit application forms are entered into a lottery during the month of February for all dates in the following season's quota period. Print out a permit application form online, or phone 760/873-2483 to have one mailed or faxed to you. All applications must be submitted by mail, with a February postmark, to be entered into the lottery. There is a $15 reservation fee per person. Bear canisters are required for overnight stays and no wood fires are permitted.

Special note: The reservation system for Mount Whitney hiking permits is expected to change significantly in 2012. Please contact the Eastern Sierra Interagency Visitor Center (760/876-6222) for the most updated information. The visitor center is located 1.5 miles south of Lone Pine at the junction of U.S. 396 and Hwy. 136.

Maps: A Mount Whitney Zone map is available from Tom Harrison Maps. For topographic maps, ask the USGS for Mount Whitney and Mount Langley.

Directions: From Lone Pine on U.S. 395, drive west on Whitney Portal Road for 13 miles to the end of the road and the trailhead.

Contact: Inyo National Forest, Mount Whitney

HIKING

Ranger Station, P.O. Box 8, Lone Pine, CA 93545, 760/876-6200, www.fs.usda.gov/inyo; Eastern Sierra Interagency Visitor Center, 760/876-6222.

97 WHITNEY PORTAL NATIONAL RECREATION TRAIL

4.0 mi one-way / 2.0 hr

in Inyo National Forest near Whitney Portal

Don't confuse this trail with the Mount Whitney Trail, because except for their nearby trailheads, they have zero in common. Although if you try to hike the Whitney Portal National Recreation Trail in both directions, instead of as a one-way downhill hike, you may find it feels darn near as demanding as the Mount Whitney Trail, which climbs nearly 6,000 feet to the top of Mount Whitney. (Okay, maybe not quite that demanding.) The recreation trail begins at Whitney Portal (elevation 8,360 feet) and heads downhill through conifers and granite to Lone Pine Campground (elevation 5,640). The best thing about the route is that no matter how crowded it is at Whitney Portal, this trail gets surprisingly few hikers, especially after the first 0.5 mile, which skirts Whitney Portal Campground. You get to leave the multitudes behind as you walk downhill along Lone Pine Creek, among the good company of granite formations and big pines. Vistas are excellent along the way, including Mount Whitney to the west and the Alabama Hills and White Mountains to the east.

User Groups: Hikers, dogs, and horses. No mountain bikes. No wheelchair facilities.

Permits: No permits are required. Parking and access are free.

Maps: A Mount Whitney High Country map is available from Tom Harrison Maps. For a topographic map, ask the USGS for Mount Langley.

Directions: From Lone Pine on U.S. 395, drive west on Whitney Portal Road for 13 miles to the end of the road and the trailhead, located across from the fishing pond. You will need to leave a shuttle car or arrange a pickup at Lone Pine Campground, four miles downhill on Whitney Portal Road.

Contact: Inyo National Forest, Mount Whitney Ranger Station, P.O. Box 8, Lone Pine, CA 93545, 760/876-6200, www.fs.usda.gov/inyo; Eastern Sierra Interagency Visitor Center, 760/876-6222.

98 MEYSAN LAKE

11.0 mi / 6.0 hr or 2 days

in the John Muir Wilderness near Mount Whitney

The Meysan Lake Trail is less popular than the neighboring trail to the top of Mount Whitney, but still, you should get your wilderness permit in advance or plan on day hiking. Better yet, plan your trip for late September and during the week. The trail to Meysan Lake is long, steep, hot, and dry—let's just say it's grueling—but it leads to a beautiful alpine lake basin and provides spectacular views of granite walls. It also gives climbers access to climbing routes on Mount Mallory and Lone Pine Peak. The trail is parallel to Meysan Creek and is not well maintained, which makes it even more demanding. You reach a left fork for Grass Lake at 4.5 miles, where the first water is available. The right fork continues to Camp Lake and its beautiful meadow (at five miles). The elevation here is 11,200 feet. The trail from Camp Lake to Meysan Lake is rather sketchy. Head to the right of Camp Lake, cross the inlet stream, and watch for rock cairns marking the way up the steep, rocky slope. Meysan Lake is often still frozen as late as June, even though the trail can be as hot as an oven. The trailhead elevation is 7,900 feet; Meysan Lake is at 11,460 feet.

User Groups: Hikers and dogs. No horses or mountain bikes. No wheelchair facilities.

Permits: A free wilderness permit is required year-round for overnight stays and is available from the Eastern Sierra Interagency Visitor Center, 1.5 miles south of Lone Pine. Quotas are in effect from May 1 to November 1; permits are available in advance for a $5 reservation fee per person.

Maps: A John Muir Wilderness map is available from the U.S. Forest Service. A Mount Whitney Zone map is available from Tom Harrison Maps. For topographic maps, ask the USGS for Mount Whitney and Mount Langley.

Directions: From Lone Pine on U.S. 395, drive west on Whitney Portal Road for 12 miles to Whitney Portal Campground and the Meysan Lake trailhead. Park on the side of Whitney Portal Road by the camp and walk through the camp to reach the trailhead.

Contact: Inyo National Forest, Mount Whitney Ranger Station, P.O. Box 8, Lone Pine, CA 93545, 760/876-6200, www.fs.usda.gov/inyo; Eastern Sierra Interagency Visitor Center, 760/876-6222.

99 LONE PINE LAKE
5.8 mi / 3.0 hr 👫2 ⛰8

in the John Muir Wilderness near Whitney Portal

The route to the top of Mount Whitney is so popular and so overcrowded that it has permits and quotas and regulations up the wazoo, but guess what? Sweet little Lone Pine Lake is just outside of the regulated Mount Whitney Zone, so you can hike to it anytime without dealing with any bureaucracy. However, you will have to deal with extremely limited parking at the trailhead during the summer months, so plan your trip for September or later if at all possible. Hiking to Lone Pine Lake is a fun trip for people who have always daydreamed of climbing Mount Whitney, because it follows the first three miles of the summit trail. While other hikers are trudging along carrying heavy

backpacks, you're stepping lightly, with only a sandwich and a bottle of water in your day pack. The trail leads through Jeffrey pines and manzanita to the John Muir Wilderness border at one mile, then switchbacks uphill and opens up to views of the Alabama Hills far below. You'll cross Lone Pine Creek at 2.8 miles, then bear left at a junction to leave the main Mount Whitney Trail and head a few hundred yards to Lone Pine Lake. It's a sweet spot, and although privacy is rare, you have a greater chance of it after Labor Day and on a weekday. Who knows, you might just get so inspired that next time you'll come back and hike all the way to the summit.

User Groups: Hikers and dogs. No horses or mountain bikes. No wheelchair facilities.

Permits: No day-hiking permits are required. Parking and access are free.

Maps: A John Muir Wilderness map is available from the U.S. Forest Service. A Mount Whitney Zone map is available from Tom Harrison Maps. For topographic maps, ask the USGS for Mount Whitney and Mount Langley.

Directions: From Lone Pine on U.S. 395, drive west on Whitney Portal Road for 13 miles to the end of the road and the Mount Whitney trailhead.

Contact: Inyo National Forest, Mount Whitney Ranger Station, P.O. Box 8, Lone Pine, CA 93545, 760/876-6200, www.fs.usda.gov/inyo; Eastern Sierra Interagency Visitor Center, 760/876-6222.

100 WHITNEY PORTAL TO LAKE THOMAS EDISON (JMT / PCT)
112.0 mi one-way / 11 days 👫5 ⛰10

from the trailhead parking area at Whitney Portal north to the trailhead parking area at Lake Thomas Edison

BEST (

You can have a foothold in the sky with every step on the John Muir Trail (JMT). This part of the trail is shared with the Pacific Crest Trail (PCT) and starts at practically the tip-top of North America—Mount Whitney—and takes you northward across a land of 12,000-foot passes and Ansel Adams–style panoramas.

From the trailhead at Whitney Portal, the hike climbs more than 6,100 feet over the course of 11 miles to reach Whitney's summit at 14,505 feet. That includes an ascent over 100 switchbacks, which are often snow covered even late in summer, to reach Trail Crest (13,560 feet). Here you turn right and take Summit Trail. In the final stretch to the top, the ridge is cut by huge notch windows in the rock; you look through, and the bottom drops out more than 10,000 feet to the town of Lone Pine below, at an elevation of 3,800 feet. Finally you make it to the top and notice how the surrounding giant blocks of rock look as if they were sculpted with a giant hammer and chisel. From here, the entire Western Divide is visible, and to the north, rows of mountain peaks are lined up for miles to the horizon. Be sure to sign your name in the register, kept in a lightning-proof metal box. You may feel a bit dizzy from the altitude, but you'll know you're someplace very special.

The journey farther north is just as captivating. The route drops into Sequoia National Park, then climbs above timberline for almost a day's worth of hiking as it nears Forester Pass (13,180 feet). It's not only the highest point on the PCT; it's the most dangerous section of trail on the entire route as well. The trail is narrow and steep, cut into a high vertical slab of rock, and is typically icy, with an iced-over snowfield near the top that's particularly treacherous. An ice ax is an absolute must. If you slip here, and you could fall thousands of feet.

Once through Forester, the trail heads onward into the John Muir Wilderness along Bubbs Creek, with great wildflowers at nearby Vidette Meadow. Then it's up and over Kearsarge Pass (10,710 feet), and after a short drop, you're back climbing again, this time over Glen Pass (11,978 feet)—a spectacular, boulder-strewn ridge with great views to the north looking into Kings Canyon National Park. Just two miles from Glen Pass is Rae Lakes, a fantasy spot for camping (one-night limit), with pristine meadows, shoreline campsites, and lots of eager brook trout.

The JMT then heads through Kings Canyon National Park by following sparkling streams much of the way, finally climbing up and over Pinchot Pass (12,130 feet), then back down along the upper Kings River for a long, steady ascent over Mather Pass (12,100 feet). The wonders continue as you hike along Palisade Lakes, then down into LeConte Canyon, followed by an endless climb up to Muir Pass (11,965 feet). In early summer, snowfields are common here, and this can be difficult and trying, especially if your boots keep postholing through the snow. The country near Muir Pass is extremely stark—nothing but sculpted granite, ice, and a few small turquoise lakes—crowned by the stone Muir Hut at the pass, where hikers can duck in and hide for safety from sudden afternoon thunderstorms and lightning bolts.

The views astound many visitors as the trail drops into Evolution Valley. It's like a trip back to the beginning of time, where all is pure and primary, yet incredibly lush and beautiful. You finally leave Kings Canyon National Park, following the headwaters of the San Joaquin River into Sierra National Forest. After bottoming out at 7,890 feet, the trail rises steeply in switchback after switchback as it enters the John Muir Wilderness. Finally you top Selden Pass (10,900 feet), take in an incredible view (where the rows of surrounding mountaintops look like the Great Pyramids), then make the easy one-mile descent to Marie Lakes, a pretty campsite with excellent trout fishing near the lake's outlet.

The final push on this section of the JMT is climbing up Bear Mountain, then down a terrible, toe-jamming stretch to Mono Creek. Here you make a left turn and continue for two more miles until you come to Edison

Lake, an excellent place to have a food stash waiting. (To continue north on the JMT/PCT, see the *Lake Thomas Edison to Agnew Meadows* hike in this chapter.)

Special Note: Crossing Mono Creek at the North Fork can be dangerous during high-runoff conditions.

User Groups: Hikers and horses. No dogs or mountain bikes. No wheelchair facilities.

Permits: A wilderness permit is required for traveling through various wilderness and special-use areas the trail traverses. Contact the Eastern Sierra Interagency Visitor Center for more information.

Maps: A John Muir Trail Map Pack is available from Tom Harrison Maps. For topographic maps, ask the USGS for Mount Whitney, Mount Williamson, Kearsarge Peak, Mount Clarence King, Mount Pinchot, North Palisade, Mount Goddard, Mount Darwin, Mount Henry, Ward Mountain, Florence Lake, and Graveyard Peak.

Directions: To reach the Mount Whitney trailhead from Lone Pine and U.S. 395, head west on Whitney Portal Road for approximately 13 miles to Whitney Portal and the trailhead for the Mount Whitney Trail. To reach the Lake Thomas Edison trailhead from the town of Shaver Lake, drive north on Highway 168 for approximately 21 miles to the town of Lakeshore. Turn northeast onto Kaiser Pass Road/Forest Service 4S01. Kaiser Pass Road becomes Edison Lake Road at Mono Hot Springs. Drive another five miles north past town to the Vermillion Campground and parking area for backcountry hikers. The PCT begins near the east end of the lake.

Contact: Inyo National Forest, Mount Whitney Ranger Station, P.O. Box 8, Lone Pine, CA 93545, 760/876-6200 or 760/873-2400, www.fs.usda.gov/inyo; Sierra National Forest, High Sierra Ranger District, P.O. Box 559, Prather, CA 93651, 559/855-5360, www.fs.fed.us/r5/sierra; Sequoia National Forest, Sequoia National Forest, Kern River Ranger District, 105 Whitney Road, P.O. Box 9, Kernville, CA 93238, 760/376-3781, www.fs.fed.us/r5/

sequoia; Eastern Sierra Interagency Visitor Center, 760/876-6222.

101 COTTONWOOD LAKES
**10.0-12.5 mi /
6.0 hr or 2 days** 🏃2 ⛰10

in the John Muir Wilderness south of Mount Whitney

The trailhead elevation is just over 10,000 feet here at Horseshoe Meadow, which makes this a wildly popular trailhead for climbing deeper into the backcountry. With the trailhead situated so high, you get a jump on the ascent; your four wheels do the work, instead of your two feet. An unusual feature of this hike is that it passes through two wilderness areas—first a small portion of the Golden Trout Wilderness and then the John Muir Wilderness. Cottonwood Creek accompanies you for much of the trip. The trail starts out in a sandy pine forest with a mellow grade. At 3.7 miles you reach a junction. Most hikers go left; the trail forms a loop around Cottonwood Lakes numbers one, two, and three. If you just want to see the closest lake and head back without making a loop, Cottonwood Lake number one is to the left, 1.5 miles from the junction. Your round-trip will be an even 10 miles. If you complete the whole loop, passing all three lakes, you'll travel 11.5 miles. But the most beautiful lakes by far are numbers four and five, worth an extra 0.5 mile of hiking beyond the far end of the loop. Total elevation gain is only 1,000 feet. Once at the lakes, remember two points: 1) Because the Cottonwood Lakes are home to golden trout, special fishing regulations are in effect, so get updated on the latest rules. 2) No wood fires are allowed, so bring your backpacking stove.

User Groups: Hikers, dogs, and horses. No mountain bikes. No wheelchair facilities.

Permits: A free wilderness permit is required year-round for overnight stays and is available from the Eastern Sierra Interagency Visitor

Center, 1.5 miles south of Lone Pine. Quotas are in effect from May 1 to November 1; permits are available in advance for a $5 reservation fee per person. Bear canisters are required.

Maps: A John Muir Wilderness map is available from the U.S. Forest Service. A Mount Whitney High Country map is available from Tom Harrison Maps. For a topographic map, ask the USGS for Cirque Peak.

Directions: From Lone Pine on U.S. 395, drive west on Whitney Portal Road for 3.3 miles and turn left (south) on Horseshoe Meadow Road. Continue 19.5 miles and bear right for the Cottonwood Lakes trailhead parking area, near the end of Horseshoe Meadow Road.

Contact: Inyo National Forest, Mount Whitney Ranger Station, P.O. Box 8, Lone Pine, CA 93545, 760/876-6200, www.fs.usda.gov/inyo; Eastern Sierra Interagency Visitor Center, 760/876-6222.

102 COTTONWOOD PASS

8.0 mi / 5.0 hr or 2 days 2 △9

in the Golden Trout Wilderness

The Cottonwood Pass Trail provides access to the Pacific Crest Trail and the Kern Plateau, a land of stark, sub-alpine meadows. You're entering the Golden Trout Wilderness, home of California's state fish and located at the very south end of the Sierra Nevada. This is where the steep, nearly perpendicular mountains start to mellow out into more gentle terrain—mostly in the form of rolling high-country hills and meadows. Start from wide Horseshoe Meadow and climb gently through forest for the first two miles of trail. Shortly, the switchbacks begin and the ascent becomes serious. After an 1,100-foot climb, you reach the pass (at four miles), where you can gaze out at the Great Western Divide, Big Whitney Meadows, and the Inyo Mountains. Bring a jacket with you for the windy, 11,250-foot summit. Ambitious hikers can continue beyond the pass and

take the right fork for Chicken Spring Lake, one mile away on the Pacific Crest Trail (no campfires allowed).

User Groups: Hikers, dogs, and horses. No mountain bikes. No wheelchair facilities.

Permits: A free wilderness permit is required year-round for overnight stays and is available from the Eastern Sierra Interagency Visitor Center, 1.5 miles south of Lone Pine. Quotas are in effect from May 1 to November 1; permits are available in advance for a $5 reservation fee per person.

Maps: A Golden Trout Wilderness map is available from the U.S. Forest Service or Tom Harrison Maps. For a topographic map, ask the USGS for Cirque Peak.

Directions: From Lone Pine on U.S. 395, drive west on Whitney Portal Road for 3.3 miles and turn left (south) on Horseshoe Meadow Road. Continue 19.5 miles to the Horseshoe Meadow trailhead, on the left, at the end of Horseshoe Meadow Road.

Contact: Inyo National Forest, Mount Whitney Ranger Station, P.O. Box 8, Lone Pine, CA 93545, 760/876-6200, www.fs.usda.gov/inyo; Eastern Sierra Interagency Visitor Center, 760/876-6222.

103 TRAIL PASS

5.0 mi / 3.0 hr 1 △7

in the Golden Trout Wilderness

Trail Pass may not be as spectacular as the other trails at Horseshoe Meadow, but it has two things going for it—far fewer people and an easier grade. It's only five miles round-trip from the trailhead to the pass, with a mere 500-foot elevation gain, unheard of in these parts. The main folks using the trail are backpackers accessing the Pacific Crest Trail and Golden Trout Wilderness, so a lot of the time, you can have this gently rolling, high-country terrain all to yourself. Follow the trail from the parking area to a junction 0.25 mile in, and bear left. In another 0.5 mile, the trail forks, and you bear right for Trail Pass. You'll hike past Horseshoe Meadow and Round Valley, where you'll have the company of many pack-horses. Views of Mount Langley and Cirque Peak are sure to inspire you. The pass is situated at 10,500 feet, just below Trail Peak (at 11,600 feet).

User Groups: Hikers, dogs, and horses. No mountain bikes. No wheelchair facilities.

Permits: No day-hiking permits are required. Parking and access are free. A free wilderness permit is required year-round for overnight stays and is available from the Eastern Sierra Interagency Visitor Center, 1.5 miles south of Lone Pine.

Maps: A Golden Trout Wilderness map is available from the U.S. Forest Service or Tom Harrison Maps. For a topographic map, ask the USGS for Cirque Peak.

Directions: From Lone Pine on U.S. 395, drive west on Whitney Portal Road for 3.3 miles and turn left (south) on Horseshoe Meadow Road. Continue 19.5 miles to the Horseshoe Meadow trailhead, on the right, at the end of Horseshoe Meadow Road.

Contact: Inyo National Forest, Mount Whitney Ranger Station, P.O. Box 8, Lone Pine, CA 93545, 760/876-6200, www.fs.usda.gov/inyo; Eastern Sierra Interagency Visitor Center, 760/876-6222.

104 CASA VIEJA MEADOW
4.0 mi / 2.0 hr   🏃2 ⛰9

in the Golden Trout Wilderness

BEST (

The Blackrock Mountain trailhead, at 8,800 feet, is the jump-off point for a variety of backpacking trips into the Golden Trout Wilderness. But day hikers can also sample the delights of this large, waterway-filled land, the home of California's state fish, the golden trout. From the end of Blackrock Road, walk for less than 0.25 mile to the wilderness boundary, then head gently downhill through a red fir forest to the western edge of Casa

Vieja Meadow. There you'll find a snow survey cabin and a wide expanse of grass and wild-flowers. Hope your day pack is full of picnic supplies. At the far end of the meadow, you must ford Ninemile Creek to continue hiking farther, so make this your turnaround point. Some people try their luck fishing here. You'll have a gradual 800-foot elevation gain on your return trip.

User Groups: Hikers, dogs, and horses. No mountain bikes. No wheelchair facilities.

Permits: No permits are required. Parking and access are free.

Maps: A Golden Trout Wilderness map is available from the U.S. Forest Service or Tom Harrison Maps. For a topographic map, ask the USGS for Casa Vieja Meadows.

Directions: From Kernville on the north end of Isabella Lake, drive north on Sierra Way/Road 99 for 22 miles to the turnoff for Sherman Pass Road/22S05. Turn right and drive approximately 35 miles on Sherman Pass Road to the Blackrock Information Station; continue straight on Road 21S03/Blackrock Road. Follow Road 21S03 north for eight miles to the end of the road and the Blackrock Mountain trailhead.

Contact: Sequoia National Forest, Kern River Ranger District, 105 Whitney Road, P.O. Box 9, Kernville, CA 93238, 760/376-3781, www.fs.fed.us/r5/sequoia; Inyo National Forest, Mount Whitney Ranger Station, P.O. Box 8, Lone Pine, CA 93545, 760/876-6200, www.fs.usda.gov/inyo.

105 JORDAN HOT SPRINGS
12.0 mi / 7.0 hr or 2 days   🏃4 ⛰9

in the Golden Trout Wilderness

You can do it in a day if you're ambitious, or you can take a more leisurely two-day trip to Jordan Hot Springs. But however you do it, it's critical to remember that almost all the work is on the way home. The trail is a descent (sometimes knee-jarring) to the grounds of an old hot springs resort, which was closed when this area became part of the Golden Trout Wilderness. The original buildings still stand, and the hot springs are still hot, which is the reason that this is one of the most popular trips in the wilderness. From the trailhead, take Blackrock Trail for two miles to Casa Vieja Meadow (see listing in this chapter), then cross Ninemile Creek and turn left (west) on Jordan Hot Springs Trail. Hike another three miles downhill along Ninemile Creek, crossing it a few more times. Once you reach the old resort, have a good soak and pull your energy together, because you've got a 2,600-foot gain on the return trip.

User Groups: Hikers, dogs, and horses. No mountain bikes. No wheelchair facilities.

Permits: A free wilderness permit is required year-round for overnight stays and is available from the Kern River Ranger Station. Parking and access are free.

Maps: A Golden Trout Wilderness map is available from the U.S. Forest Service or Tom Harrison Maps. For a topographic map, ask the USGS for Casa Vieja Meadows.

Directions: From Kernville on the north end of Isabella Lake, drive north on Sierra Way/Road 99 for 22 miles to the right turnoff for Sherman Pass Road/22S05. Turn right and drive approximately 35 miles on Sherman Pass Road to the Blackrock Information Station; continue straight on Road 21S03/Blackrock Road. Follow Road 21S03 north for eight miles to the end of the road and the Blackrock Mountain trailhead.

Contact: Sequoia National Forest, Kern River Ranger District, 105 Whitney Road, P.O. Box 9, Kernville, CA 93238, 760/376-3781, www.fs.fed.us/r5/sequoia.

106 NORTH FORK KERN RIVER TRAIL

10.4 mi / 5.0 hr or 2 days

in Sequoia National Forest north of Kernville

Sometimes you just want to walk alongside a beautiful river, and if that's what you're in the mood for, the Wild and Scenic North Fork Kern is a first-rate choice. From the giant parking lot, walk across the hikers' bridge (separate from but next to the highway bridge) to reach the far side of the river, and then descend on stairs to reach the trail. The North Fork Kern River Trail winds along gently, heading deep into the dramatic Kern Canyon, sometimes under the shade of digger pines, live oaks, and incense cedars, and sometimes out in the bright sunshine. Spring wildflowers are stunning, especially in March and April. Spring river rafters are also entertaining to watch. Most people who walk this trail bring a fishing rod with them, and if you do, make sure you're up-to-date on the special fishing regulations. They're in effect for the first four miles of river, which is a wild trout area. Backpackers will find many campsites along the trail, including some that are under the cavelike canopy of big boulders. This easy, mellow trail offers something for everyone. Note that if you venture out here at the height of spring runoff, parts of the trail may be submerged.

User Groups: Hikers and dogs. No mountain bikes or horses. No wheelchair facilities.

Permits: A free campfire permit is required for overnight stays and is available from the Springville or Kernville Ranger Stations at the addresses below. Parking and access are free.

Maps: A Sequoia National Forest map is available from the U.S. Forest Service. For a topographic map, ask the USGS for Fairview.

Directions: From Kernville on the north end of Lake Isabella, drive north on Sierra Way/Road 99 for 22 miles to the Johnsondale highway bridge over the Kern River. Turn right and park in the large paved parking lot by the signboard at the bridge.

Contact: Sequoia National Forest, Kern River Ranger District, 105 Whitney Road, P.O. Box 9, Kernville, CA 93238, 760/376-3781, www.fs.fed.us/r5/sequoia; Tule River Ranger District, 32588 Highway 190, Springville, CA 93265, 559/539-2607, www.fs.fed.us/r5/sequoia.

107 SHERMAN PEAK TRAIL
4.0 mi / 2.0 hr

in Sequoia National Forest near Sherman Pass

From the Sherman Pass Vista along the highway, you can look to the north to Mount Whitney and the Great Western Divide. After crossing the highway and hiking Sherman Peak Trail to the top of Sherman Peak (at 9,909 feet), you can pivot around and have a panoramic look at an even bigger chunk of the world. The trail is mostly forested with red firs and pines, and is gradual enough for children to climb. If you read the interpretive display at the vista, you'll be able to identify the myriad mountains you're looking at from the peak, including Split Rock and Dome Rock. It's only a 700-foot climb to the summit, mostly through a series of easy switchbacks. At one time, a fire lookout tower was positioned up here, but modern technology made it obsolete and it was taken down.

User Groups: Hikers, dogs, horses, and mountain bikes. No wheelchair facilities.

Permits: No permits are required. Parking and access are free.

Maps: A Sequoia National Forest map is available from the U.S. Forest Service. For topographic maps, ask the USGS for Durrwood Creek and Sirretta Peak.

Directions: From Kernville on the north end of Lake Isabella, drive north on Sierra Way/Road 99 for 22 miles to the right turnoff for Sherman Pass Road/22S05. Turn right and drive approximately 15 miles on Sherman Pass Road to the Sherman Pass Vista. The trailhead is across the road.

Contact: Sequoia National Forest, Kern River Ranger District, 105 Whitney Road, P.O. Box 9, Kernville, CA 93238, 760/376-3781, www.fs.fed.us/r5/sequoia.

108 BALD MOUNTAIN LOOKOUT
0.25 mi / 0.25 hr

in Sequoia National Forest on the north edge of the Dome Land Wilderness

This short hike to the summit of 9,430-foot Bald Mountain is the easiest possible introduction to the Dome Land Wilderness. It's a brief stroll to the lookout, which is perched on the very northern edge of the wilderness. This region is famous for its many granite domes and monolithic rocks, the happy hunting ground of rock climbers from all over Southern California. Of the many big hunks of rock, Church Dome is perhaps the most outstanding, and it can be seen from here directly to the south. White Dome and Black Mountain are also visible (east of Church Dome), as well as a sweeping vista of the Kern Plateau, the Whitney Range, and the Great Western Divide. Bald Mountain Lookout has the distinction of being the highest fire lookout tower in the southern Sierra Nevada.

User Groups: Hikers, dogs, horses, and mountain bikes. No wheelchair facilities.

Permits: No permits are required. Parking and access are free.

Maps: A Sequoia National Forest or Dome Land Wilderness map is available from the U.S. Forest Service. For a topographic map, ask the USGS for Crag Peak.

Directions: From Kernville on the north end of Lake Isabella, drive north on Sierra Way/Road 99 for 22 miles to the right turnoff for Sherman Pass Road/22S05. Turn right and drive approximately 25 miles on Sherman Pass Road to Forest Service Road 22S77, signed for Bald Mountain Lookout. Turn east (right) on Road 22S77 and follow it for one mile to its end.

HIKING

Contact: Sequoia National Forest, Kern River Ranger District, 105 Whitney Road, P.O. Box 9, Kernville, CA 93238, 760/376-3781, www.fs.fed.us/r5/sequoia.

109 JACKASS CREEK NATIONAL RECREATION TRAIL

5.0 mi / 2.5 hr   👥2 ⛰9

in Sequoia National Forest near the South Sierra Wilderness

The Jackass Creek Trail is way out there on the Kern Plateau, at a trailhead elevation of 8,000 feet. The trail climbs 5.5 miles to Jackass Peak (elevation 9,245 feet) on the border of the South Sierra Wilderness. Most people don't bother traveling that far; instead, they follow the trail along Jackass Creek for a couple of miles through red fir forest to the western edge of Jackass Meadow. In addition to the beautiful meadow, the trail offers a look at many handsome old-growth aspens. The trail is an old dirt road, wide enough for holding hands with your hiking partner. Unfortunately, it's also wide enough for motorcycles, which are allowed here. Our recommendation? Hike this trail in late September or early October for the best show of autumn colors, and for the best chance at having the trail to yourself. If you drive all the way out here and see a parking lot full of motorcycle trailers, try hiking the nearby Hooker Meadow Trail instead (the trailhead is at the end of Road 21S29, just east of Fish Creek Campground). The machines aren't allowed there, and this trail also leads to an outstanding grove of quaking aspens.

User Groups: Hikers, dogs, horses, and mountain bikes. No wheelchair facilities.

Permits: No permits are required. Parking and access are free.

Maps: A Sequoia National Forest map is available from the U.S. Forest Service. For a topographic map, ask the USGS for Crag Peak.

Directions: From Kernville on the north end

of Lake Isabella, drive north on Sierra Way/Road 99 for 22 miles to the right turnoff for Sherman Pass Road/22S05. Turn right and drive approximately 35 miles on Sherman Pass Road to the four-way intersection with Road 21S03, near Blackrock Information Station. Turn right to continue on Road 22S05, and drive five miles to Fish Creek Campground and Road 21S01, where the trail begins.

Contact: Sequoia National Forest, Kern River Ranger District, 105 Whitney Road, P.O. Box 9, Kernville, CA 93238, 760/376-3781, www.fs.fed.us/r5/sequoia.

110 WHISKEY FLAT TRAIL

5.0 mi / 2.5 hr   👥2 ⛰8

in Sequoia National Forest near Fairview

The Whiskey Flat Trail is a 14.5-mile trail that parallels the Kern River from Fairview Lodge all the way south to Burlando Road in Kernville. Primarily used by anglers working the Kern River, it's also a good springtime stroll for river lovers. If you walk out and back for a few miles on the northern end of the trail by Fairview, you can end the day with a meal at Fairview Lodge's restaurant, where you can brag about the fish you did or didn't catch, like everybody else there. The Whiskey Flat Trail can be somewhat difficult to follow, especially in springtime, when the numerous creeks you must cross are running full. Early in the year, the creeks can sometimes be impassable. The path begins on a suspension bridge, which is reminiscent of Huck Finn and his friends. You can hike as far as you please; a good distance is 2.5 miles out, or about an hour's walk each way. The terrain is grasslands and chaparral, with occasional digger pines, which means no shade but plenty of spring wildflowers. Although the route is basically level, there are numerous steep stretches where you climb in and out of stream drainages running into the Kern. The trailhead elevation is 2,800 feet.

User Groups: Hikers, dogs, horses, and mountain bikes. No wheelchair facilities.

Permits: No permits are required. Parking and access are free.

Maps: A Sequoia National Forest map is available from the U.S. Forest Service. For a topographic map, ask the USGS for Fairview.

Directions: From Kernville on the north end of Lake Isabella, drive north on Sierra Way/Road 99 for 17 miles to Fairview and the Fairview Lodge, on the left side of the road. A large parking area and a trailhead for the Whiskey Flat Trail are to the right of the lodge.

Contact: Sequoia National Forest, Kern River Ranger District, 105 Whitney Road, P.O. Box 9, Kernville, CA 93238, 760/376-3781, www.fs.fed.us/r5/sequoia.

111 PACKSADDLE CAVE TRAIL

4.6 mi / 2.3 hr   🚶2 ⛰8

in Sequoia National Forest near Fairview

Everybody enjoys the trip to Packsaddle Cave, even though the cave was long ago vandalized of its jewel-like stalactites and stalagmites. Nonetheless, the appeal of visiting the limestone cave keeps this trail well used and fairly well maintained. From the parking lot on Sierra Way, cross the highway and hike uphill on the path, huffing and puffing through some steep pitches. This is not a trail for summertime, because there is little shade among the manzanita, sagebrush, and deer brush, and the total climb is about 1,200 feet. At 1.8 miles, you cross Packsaddle Creek and see several campsites near it. Continue a short distance farther; the cave is off to the left, 0.25 mile before this trail's junction with Rincon Trail. Don't forget your flashlight so you can take a peek inside.

User Groups: Hikers, dogs, horses, and mountain bikes. No wheelchair facilities.

Permits: No permits are required. Parking and access are free.

Maps: A Sequoia National Forest map is available from the U.S. Forest Service. For a topographic map, ask the USGS for Fairview.

Directions: From Kernville on the north end of Lake Isabella, drive north on Sierra Way/Road 99 for 18 miles to the Packsaddle Cave trailhead, on the right, 0.25 mile beyond Fairview Campground. The parking area is across the road.

Contact: Sequoia National Forest, Kern River Ranger District, 105 Whitney Road, P.O. Box 9, Kernville, CA 93238, 760/376-3781, www.fs.fed.us/r5/sequoia.

112 RINCON TRAIL

4.0 mi / 2.0 hr   🚶2 ⛰7

in Sequoia National Forest near Fairview

Let's say right away that this Rincon has absolutely nothing in common with the other Rincon, the classic surfing break on the Ventura coast. For one, there's no water here, and two, there's no cool ocean breeze. That means you should plan your hike for winter or spring, before the Kern Valley heats up. The trail leads first east and then steadily north along the Rincon Fault, heading for Forks of the Kern. It undulates, following the drainages of Salmon and other creeks. The destination on this trail is the long-distance view of Salmon Creek Falls, about two miles in, and the good fishing and camping prospects on the way along Salmon Creek. The trail crosses Salmon Creek on a bridge 1.7 miles in, but the waterfall view is about 0.25 mile farther. You might want to bring your binoculars to get a good look. If you wish to hike farther on Rincon Trail, it intersects the route to Packsaddle Cave in another two miles, then crosses Sherman Pass Road in another 2.5 miles, and keeps going straight north all the way to Forks of the Kern. The total one-way trail length is a whopping 19.5 miles. Be forewarned that the Rincon Trail is popular with motorcycle enthusiasts, so your peaceful nature experience may be shattered by their noise.

User Groups: Hikers, dogs, and mountain bikes. No horses. No wheelchair facilities.

Permits: No permits are required. Parking and access are free.

Maps: A Sequoia National Forest map is available from the U.S. Forest Service. For a topographic map, ask the USGS for Kernville.

Directions: From Kernville on the north end of Isabella Lake, drive north on Sierra Way/Road 99 for 13 miles to the Rincon trailhead, on the right, across from the Ant Canyon dispersed camping area.

Contact: Sequoia National Forest, Kern River Ranger District, 105 Whitney Road, P.O. Box 9, Kernville, CA 93238, 760/376-3781, www.fs.fed.us/r5/sequoia.

113 SUNDAY PEAK TRAIL
3.4 mi / 2.0 hr   🏃2 ⛰9

in Sequoia National Forest near
Wofford Heights

From the Sunday Peak trailhead, at 7,200 feet in the Greenhorn Mountains, it's a 1,000-foot climb to the top of Sunday Peak, an excellent day hike for families. The grade is moderate and shaded by big conifers, and the destination is perfect on a day when the heat is sweltering down near Isabella Lake. From the top, you can look down at the Kern River Valley and feel sorry for all those people sweating it out down there. The peak's fire lookout tower was abandoned and then destroyed by the Forest Service in the 1950s when it was determined that nearby Tobias Peak was a better spot to have a lookout. However, the wide-angle views of the Kern Valley, Kern Plateau, and far-off high Sierra peaks are still here for the taking. There are many good picnicking spots on the summit.

User Groups: Hikers, dogs, horses, and mountain bikes. No wheelchair facilities.

Permits: No permits are required. Parking and access are free.

Maps: A Sequoia National Forest map is available from the U.S. Forest Service. For a topographic map, ask the USGS for Posey.

Directions: From Wofford Heights on the west side of Isabella Lake, turn west on Highway 155 and drive eight miles to Greenhorn Summit. Turn right on Road 24S15/Forest Highway 90, signed for Portuguese Pass, and drive 6.5 miles north to the parking area for Sunday Peak Trail, near the Girl Scout Camp.

Contact: Sequoia National Forest, Kern River Ranger District, 105 Whitney Road, P.O. Box 9, Kernville, CA 93238, 760/376-3781, www.fs.fed.us/r5/sequoia.

114 UNAL TRAIL
3.0 mi / 1.5 hr   🏃1 ⛰8

in Sequoia National Forest near
Wofford Heights

This is a first-rate trail for families or for anybody who wants a good leg-stretching walk or run around a beautiful mountain. The Unal Trail is a three-mile loop that climbs gently for two miles to Unal Peak, and then descends in one mile of switchbacks back to the trailhead. (After the first 100 yards, where the trail forks, be sure you take the left fork and hike the trail clockwise.) The trail passes a Native American cultural site on the return of the loop, the homestead of the Tubatulabal Indians. With only a 700-foot climb and an excellent grade, even mountain bikers can manage this trail, although few bother with it. You'll likely see some deer on the hillsides, and the view from the top of Unal Peak makes the whole world seem peaceful and serene. Although most of the trail is lined with conifers, the top of the loop is a little exposed and catches a strong breeze.

User Groups: Hikers, dogs, horses, and mountain bikes. No wheelchair facilities.

Permits: No permits are required. Parking and access are free.

Maps: A Sequoia National Forest map is available from the U.S. Forest Service. For a topographic map, ask the USGS for Posey.

Directions: From Wofford Heights on the west side of Lake Isabella, turn west on Highway 155 and drive eight miles to Greenhorn Summit. Turn left at the sign for Shirley Ski Meadows and drive 100 yards to the Greenhorn Fire Station and Unal trailhead, on the right side of the road.

Contact: Sequoia National Forest, Kern River Ranger District, 105 Whitney Road, P.O. Box 9, Kernville, CA 93238, 760/376-3781, www.fs.fed.us/r5/sequoia.

115 CANNELL MEADOW NATIONAL RECREATION TRAIL

24.0 mi / 3 days   🚶4 ⛰8

in Sequoia National Forest north of Kernville

The Cannell Meadow National Recreation Trail is the first trailhead you reach out of Kernville, and if it's summertime, you should start at the other end of this 12-mile trail. That's because the Kernville end is at 2,800 feet, set in rocky chaparral and digger pine country, and, baby, it's hot out here. Still, if you can time your trip for late winter or spring, hiking this end of Cannell Trail is a great adventure, watching the terrain and environment change as the elevation rises. The shadeless trail climbs right away, through sage and occasional live oaks, affording views of the Kern River Valley. The trail gets more and more steep as you near conifer country at Pine Flat, but then you also get some blessed shade. It crosses Cannell Creek twice and reaches the Cannell Meadow Forest Service Cabin, a log cabin that was built in 1904. Cannell Meadow is a beautiful spot on the western edge of the Kern Plateau, edged by Jeffrey and lodgepole pines. Elevation is 7,500 feet, which means a total climb of 4,700 feet. Spread it out over a few days.

User Groups: Hikers, dogs, horses, and mountain bikes. No wheelchair facilities.

Permits: A free campfire permit is required for overnight stays and is available from the Kernville Ranger Station. Parking and access are free.

Maps: A Sequoia National Forest map is available from the U.S. Forest Service. For a topographic map, ask the USGS for Kernville.

Directions: From Kernville on the north end of Isabella Lake, drive north on Sierra Way/Road 99 for 1.4 miles to the Cannell Meadow trailhead, on the right. Parking is available near the horse corrals.

Contact: Sequoia National Forest, Kern River Ranger District, 105 Whitney Road, P.O. Box 9, Kernville, CA 93238, 760/376-3781, www.fs.fed.us/r5/sequoia.

116 SALMON CREEK FALLS

8.0 mi / 4.0 hr or 2 days   🚶2 ⛰9

in Sequoia National Forest near Big Meadow

The eight-mile round-trip to the brink of Salmon Creek Falls is a stellar walk through lodgepole pines and white fir, with a chance for fishing, skinny-dipping, and admiring a lot of beautiful scenery at 7,600 feet in elevation. Since there are campsites located along the trail, it's easy enough to turn the trip into an overnight excursion, but the trail also makes a good long day hike. The trail is downhill all the way, dropping 600 feet over 0.5 mile, and follows granite-lined Salmon Creek. After skirting the edge of Horse Meadow, you simply follow the creek's meander. Trails run on both sides of the stream for the first two miles, so you can walk either side, but then they join as one. The path comes to an end above Salmon Creek Falls, where you can swim, fish, and camp, but don't expect to gaze out at the big waterfall. There's no way to get a good look at it from here, since you're perched on top of it.

User Groups: Hikers, dogs, horses, and mountain bikes. No wheelchair facilities.

Permits: A free campfire permit is required for overnight stays and is available from the Springville or Kernville Ranger Stations at the addresses below. Parking and access are free.

Maps: A Sequoia National Forest map is available from the U.S. Forest Service. For topographic maps, ask the USGS for Sirretta Peak and Fairview.

Directions: From Kernville on the north end of Isabella Lake, drive north on Sierra Way/Road 99 for 22 miles to the right turnoff for Sherman Pass Road/22S05. Turn right and drive 6.1 miles on Sherman Pass Road, then turn right on Road 22S12, signed for Horse Meadow Campground. Drive 6.3 miles on Road 22S12 until you reach a fork. Stay straight. At eight miles, bear left. At 9.3 miles, turn right at the Horse Meadow Campground sign (Road 23S10). You'll reach the camp at 10.7 miles, but take the right turnoff just before the camp to reach the trailhead.

Contact: Sequoia National Forest, Kern River Ranger District, 105 Whitney Road, P.O. Box 9, Kernville, CA 93238, 760/376-3781, www.fs.fed.us/r5/sequoia; Tule River Ranger District, 32588 Highway 190, Springville, CA 93265, 559/539-2607, www.fs.fed.us/r5/sequoia.

117 SIRRETTA PEAK
8.0 mi / 5.0 hr

near the Dome Land Wilderness

Hey, what's that big meadow down there? It's Big Meadow, of course, that huge expanse of green you see from the top of Sirretta Peak. From Sirretta's summit, you get an eyeful of it, as well as long, lingering glances at the many granite domes of the Dome Land Wilderness Area, Sirretta and Deadwood Meadows, and the peaks of the High Sierra. The route to the peak starts at Big Meadow's northern edge, then travels north on Cannell Trail for 0.5 mile. Bear right (northeast) at the fork with Sirretta Peak Trail and climb 2.5 miles to a spur trail that leads to the summit. There are many switchbacks and plenty of fine views along the way. Take the left spur (it's obvious) for 0.5 mile to the rocky summit, and congratulate

yourself on your fine mountaineering skills. The trail has an elevation gain of 1,200 feet, and if you decide to make the final summit climb, you'll add on another 700 feet. Sirretta Peak is just shy of 10,000 feet in elevation.

User Groups: Hikers and dogs. No horses or mountain bikes. No wheelchair facilities.

Permits: No day-hiking permits are required. Parking and access are free.

Maps: A Sequoia National Forest map is available from the U.S. Forest Service. For a topographic map, ask the USGS for Sirretta Peak.

Directions: From Kernville on the north end of Isabella Lake, drive north on Sierra Way/Road 99 for 22 miles to the right turnoff for Sherman Pass Road/22S05. Turn right and drive 6.1 miles on Sherman Pass Road. Turn right on Road 22S12, signed for Horse Meadow Campground, and drive 6.3 miles on Road 22S12 until you reach a fork. Stay straight. At eight miles, bear left, staying on Road 22S12. Continue four more miles, passing the Horse Meadow Campground turnoff, to Road 23S07, at the northern edge of Big Meadow. Turn left on Road 23S07 and drive 0.5 mile to the Cannell trailhead.

Contact: Sequoia National Forest, Kern River Ranger District, 105 Whitney Road, P.O. Box 9, Kernville, CA 93238, 760/376-3781, www.fs.fed.us/r5/sequoia.

118 MANTER MEADOW LOOP
10.0 mi / 6.0 hr   🏃2 ⛰9

in the Dome Land Wilderness

BEST

For people who love meadows, granite, and solitude, this loop trip is just about perfect. From the South Manter trailhead at 7,800 feet, the trail goes uphill for four miles to Manter Meadow, so bring your wildflower identification book and a map to identify surrounding peaks and domes. Along the way, several side trails branch off the main trail, leading to some of the granite domes of the Dome Land Wilderness, including spectacular Taylor Dome and Church Dome. A two-mile loop trail encircles the entire perimeter of the meadow, which you can add on to your trip if you wish. At the meadow's western edge, South Manter Trail meets North Manter Trail, and you follow the latter back to Forest Service Road 23S07 (the road you drove in on). Then it's a 1.5-mile walk on the dirt road back to your car. If you want to avoid the road, hike South Manter Trail both ways, and take the loop walk around the meadow. The mileage is about equal to the other trip.

User Groups: Hikers, dogs, and horses. No mountain bikes. No wheelchair facilities.

Permits: No permits are required. Parking and access are free.

Maps: A Sequoia National Forest or Dome Land Wilderness map is available from the U.S. Forest Service. For a topographic map, ask the USGS for Sirretta Peak.

Directions: From Kernville on the north end of Isabella Lake, drive north on Sierra Way/Road 99 for 22 miles to the right turnoff for Sherman Pass Road/22S05. Turn right and drive 6.1 miles on Sherman Pass Road. Turn right on Road 22S12, signed for Horse Meadow Campground, and drive 6.3 miles on Road 22S12 until you reach a fork. Stay straight. At eight miles, bear left, staying on Road 22S12. Continue four more miles, passing the Horse Meadow Campground turnoff, to Road 23S07 at the northern edge of Big Meadow. Turn left on Road 23S07 and drive three miles to the southeast edge of Big Meadow and the South Manter trailhead.

Contact: Sequoia National Forest, Kern River Ranger District, 105 Whitney Road, P.O. Box 9, Kernville, CA 93238, 760/376-3781, www.fs.fed.us/r5/sequoia.

119 ROCKHOUSE BASIN
8.6 mi / 4.0 hr

on the eastern side of the
Dome Land Wilderness

You're driving along in no-man's-land on Highway 178 between U.S. 395 and Lake Isabella, staring at thousands of those odd-looking piñon pines. This is the transition zone between the Mojave Desert to the east and the Sierra Nevada to the west, and it doesn't look quite like either one of them. Want to see this strange land up close? This hike to Rockhouse Basin can take you there, and since it requires a long drive on dirt roads to reach the trailhead, you're likely to be free of the Eastern Sierra's hiking masses. The trail heads downhill through a burned area, losing about 1,500 feet in elevation on its way to the Kern River and Rockhouse Basin. A half mile from the trailhead, turn right and head north to Rockhouse Basin, where the noise of cicadas serenades you almost as loudly as the river. Explore the rocks and cool off in the river. It can be as hot as Hades out here, so plan your trip for early in the year, when you can hike along the Kern River in relative comfort.

User Groups: Hikers, dogs, and horses. No mountain bikes. No wheelchair facilities.

Permits: No permits are required. Parking and access are free.

Maps: A Sequoia National Forest or Dome Land Wilderness map is available from the U.S. Forest Service. For a topographic map, ask the USGS for Rockhouse Basin.

Directions: From the junction of Highway 14 and Highway 178 north of Mojave, drive west on Highway 178 for 18 miles to the right turnoff for Chimney Peak National Backcountry Byway, or Canebrake Road. Turn right and drive approximately nine miles. Turn left (west) on Long Valley Loop Road and drive 13 miles to the gate at the start of Rockhouse Basin Trail.

Contact: Bureau of Land Management, Ridgecrest Field Office, 300 South Richmond Road, Ridgecrest, CA 93555, 760/384-5400, www.ca.blm.gov/ridgecrest; Sequoia National Forest, Kern River Ranger District, 105 Whitney Road, P.O. Box 9, Kernville, CA 93238, 760/376-3781, www.fs.fed.us/r5/sequoia.

Index

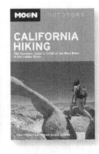

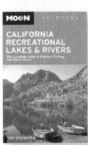
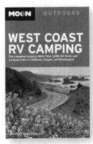

www.moon.com

DESTINATIONS | ACTIVITIES | BLOGS | MAPS | BOOKS

MOON.COM is ready to help plan your next trip! Filled with fresh trip ideas and strategies, author interviews, informative travel blogs, a detailed map library, and descriptions of all the Moon guidebooks, Moon.com is all you need to get out and explore the world—or even places in your own backyard. While at Moon.com, sign up for our monthly e-newsletter for updates on new releases, travel tips, and expert advice from our on-the-go Moon authors. As always, when you travel with Moon, expect an experience that is uncommon and truly unique.

KEEP UP WITH MOON ON FACEBOOK AND TWITTER
JOIN THE MOON PHOTO GROUP ON FLICKR

MOON SEQUOIA & KINGS CANYON CAMPING & HIKING

Avalon Travel
a member of the Perseus Books Group
1700 Fourth Street
Berkeley, CA 94710, USA
www.moon.com

Editor and Series Manager: Sabrina Young
Production and Graphics Coordinators:
    Elizabeth Jang and Domini Dragoone
Cover Designer: Kathryn Osgood
Interior Designer: Darren Alessi
Map Editor: Mike Morgenfeld
Cartographers: Mike Morgenfeld and Kaitlin Jaffe
Proofreaders: Annie Blakely and Deana Shields

ISBN-13: 978-1-61238-176-3

Front cover photo: © Dgrilla | Dreamstime. com, Sequoia National Forest
Title page photo: © boyenigma/123rf.com

Printed in the United States

ABOUT THE AUTHORS

Tom Stienstra

For 30 years, Tom Stienstra's full-time job has been to capture and communicate the outdoor experience. This has led him across California – fishing, hiking, camping, boating, biking, and flying – searching for the best of the outdoors and then writing about it.

Tom is the nation's top-selling author of outdoors guidebooks. He has been inducted into the California Outdoor Hall of Fame and has twice been awarded National Outdoor Writer of the Year, newspaper division, by the Outdoor Writers Association of America. He has also been named California Outdoor Writer of the Year five times, most recently in 2007. Tom is the outdoors columnist for the *San Francisco Chronicle*; his articles appear on www.sfgate.com and in newspapers around the country. He broadcasts a weekly radio show on KCBS-San Francisco and hosts an outdoor television show on CBS/CW San Francisco.

Tom lives with his wife and sons in Northern California. You can contact him directly via the website www.tomstienstra.com. His guidebooks include:

Moon California Camping
Moon California Fishing
Moon California Recreational Lakes & Rivers
California Wildlife
Moon Northern California Cabins & Cottages
Moon Northern California Camping
Moon Oregon Camping
Moon Pacific Northwest Camping
Moon Washington Camping
Moon West Coast RV Camping
Tom Stienstra's Bay Area Recreation

Ann Marie Brown

The author of 13 outdoor guidebooks, Ann Marie Brown is a dedicated California outdoorswoman. She hikes, bikes, and camps more than 150 days each year in an effort to avoid routine, complacency, and getting a real job.

Ann Marie's work has appeared in *Sunset, VIA, Backpacker,* and *California* magazines. As a way of giving back a little of what she gets from her experiences in nature, she writes and edits for several environmental groups, including the Sierra Club and National Resources Defense Council.

In addition to *California Hiking*, Ann Marie's guidebooks include:

Moon 101 Great Hikes of the San Francisco Bay Area
250 Great Hikes in California's National Parks
Moon California Waterfalls
Easy Biking in Northern California
Easy Camping in Southern California
Easy Hiking in Northern California
Easy Hiking in Southern California
Moon Bay Area Biking
Moon Monterey & Carmel
Moon Northern California Biking
Moon Northern California Waterfalls
Moon Tahoe
Moon Take a Hike Los Angeles
Moon Yosemite
Southern California Cabins and Cottages

For more information on these titles, visit Ann Marie's website at www.annmariebrown.com.